Fritz Schultze

Fetichism:

A contribution to anthropology and the history of religion

Fritz Schultze

Fetichism:
A contribution to anthropology and the history of religion

ISBN/EAN: 9783337716509

Printed in Europe, USA, Canada, Australia, Japan

Cover: Foto ©Lupo / pixelio.de

More available books at **www.hansebooks.com**

FETICHISM,

A CONTRIBUTION TO ANTHROPOLOGY AND THE HISTORY OF RELIGION.

BY

FRITZ SCHULTZE, Ph. D.

TRANSLATED FROM THE GERMAN,
By J. FITZGERALD, M.A.

New York:
THE HUMBOLDT PUBLISHING CO.,
64 FIFTH AVENUE.

CONTENTS.

CHAPTER	PAGE
I. INTRODUCTORY..	1
II. THE MIND OF THE SAVAGE IN ITS INTELLECTUAL AND MORAL ASPECTS........	3
1. The Intellect of the Savage.................................	4
2. The Morality of the Savage.................................	9
3. Conclusion...	14
III. THE RELATION BETWEEN THE SAVAGE MIND AND ITS OBJECT...............	15
1. The Value of Objects.......................................	15
2. The Anthropopathic Apprehension of Objects.................	18
3. The Causal Connection of Objects...........................	22
IV. FETICHISM AS A RELIGION....................................	26
1. The Belief in Fetiches.....................................	26
2. The Range of Fetich Influence..............................	31
3. The Religiosity of Fetich Worshipers.......................	37
4. Worship and Sacrifice......................................	42
5. Fetich Priesthoods...	45
6. Fetichism among Non-Savages...............................	61
V. THE VARIOUS OBJECTS OF FETICH WORSHIP......................	64
1. Stones as Fetiches...	64
2. Mountains as Fetiches......................................	65
3. Water as Fetich...	66
4. Wind and Fire as Fetiches.................................	67
5. Plants as Fetiches...	69
6. Animals as Fetiches..	71
7. Men as Fetiches...	82
VI. THE HIGHEST GRADE OF FETICHISM............................	83
1. The New Object..	83
2. The Gradual Acquisition of Knowledge.......................	87
3. The Worship of the Moon....................................	91
4. The Worship of the Stars...................................	94
5. Transition to Sun Worship..................................	94
6. The Worship of the Sun.....................................	95
7. The Worship of the Heavens.................................	100
VII. THE AIM OF FETICHISM.....................................	109
1. Retrospect..	109
2. The New Problem...	110

FETICHISM:

A CONTRIBUTION TO ANTHROPOLOGY AND THE HISTORY OF RELIGION.

By FRITZ SCHULTZE, Dr. Phil.

TRANSLATED FROM THE GERMAN BY J. FITZGERALD, M.A.

[COPYRIGHT, 1885, BY J. FITZGERALD.]

CHAPTER I.

INTRODUCTORY.

DAVID HUME was the first in modern times to reject the transcendental theories of Religion and to seek an explanation for it in the empiric world of man, on psychological principles. "No passions," says he, "can be supposed to work upon such barbarians, but the ordinary affections of human life ; the anxious concern for happiness, the dread of future misery, the terror of death, the thirst of revenge, the appetite for food and other necessaries. These are their only motives." *

To these motives of fear and hope Hume now adds, on the one hand, man's ignorance of Nature and of its phenomena ; and on the other the faculty of imagination, as factors going to make up the notion of God. "We hang in perpetual suspense between life and death, health and sickness, plenty and want, which are distributed among the human species by secret and unknown causes,

* David Hume, *Works*, Vol. IV.

whose operation is oft unexpected and always unaccountable. These *unknown causes*, then, become the constant object of our hope and fear ; and while the passions are kept in perpetual alarm by an anxious expectation of the events, the imagination is equally employed in forming ideas of those powers, on which we have so entire a dependence. Could men anatomize nature, according to the most probable, at least the most intelligible philosophy, they would find that these causes are nothing but the particular fabric and structure of the minute parts of their own bodies and of external objects ; and that, by a regular and constant machinery, all the events are produced, about which they are so much concerned. But this philosophy exceeds the comprehension of the ignorant multitude, who can only conceive the *unknown causes*, in a general and confused manner ; though their imagination, perpetually employed on the same subject, must labor to form some particular and distinct idea of them. The more they consider these causes themselves, and the uncertainty of their operation, the less satisfaction do they meet with in their researches ; and, however unwilling, they must at last have abandoned so arduous an attempt, were it not for a propensity in human nature, which leads into a system that gives them satisfaction. There is a universal tendency among mankind to conceive all beings like themselves, and to transfer to every object those qualities with which they are familiarly acquainted, and of which they are intimately conscious. We find human faces in the moon, armies in the clouds, and by a natural propensity, if not corrected by experience and reflection, ascribe malice or good-will to everything that hurts or pleases us. Hence the frequency and beauty of the *prosopopœia* in poetry, where trees, mountains and streams are personified, and the inanimate parts of nature acquire sentiment and passion." "No wonder, then, that mankind, being placed in such an absolute ignorance of causes, and being at the same time so anxious concerning their future fortune, should immediately acknowledge a dependence on invisible powers, possessed of sentiment and intelligence." Such is the account which Hume gives of Polytheism. He does not, it is true, make an application of his theory to Fetichism directly, though much of what he says about the rise of Polytheism will serve equally well to account for fetichism.

Benjamin Constant, inasmuch as he looks for the origin of religion in man himself, agrees with Hume ; but inasmuch as he postulates a special faculty, "the religious sentiment," which is not demonstrable, he again quits the empirical standpoint. Meiners, in his History of Religions, agrees fully with Hume, whose theory he states, and then makes this application of it to the subject of fetichism : "Fetichism," says he, "is not only the most ancient, but it is also the most universal form of religion. It furnishes incontrovertible proof that the lack of correct knowledge was the true and only cause of poly-

theism ; and that for the uncultured savage everything is God, or may be God." [*] Kaiser, in his ": Biblical Theology," places the origin of religion, not in this or that sentiment, but "subjectively in the entire character of man," and "objectively in Nature, to which man is related." [†] He holds that primitive man was without the impress of Spirit, that he was developed out of inferior organisms and that his first attempt at a religious belief took the form of fetichism. "The first, or the best piece of wood, or stone he meets,— some animal, some star will be esteemed a god." "While the intellectual faculties are still dormant, and in the absence of knowledge and experience, of invention and culture, whether mental or moral, we are not to be surprised if man regards proximate causes as ultimate, and pays worship to material objects, especially those which arrest his attention by their brightness, their velocity, their great size, etc." "The necessities of the case, and history itself prove that fetichism is the primitive religion of man. The base of human culture rests upon the earth, but its summit penetrates the invisible spaces of heaven, and reaches into infinity."

This theory of Kaiser's, in so far as it differs from Hume's and agrees with that of Meiners in asserting that fetichism is the primitive religion, is rejected by Theodor Waitz in his "Anthropology of Savage Tribes." He holds with Hume, that "a rude systemless Polytheism" was the primitive religion ; and his arguments are identical with those of Hume as already set forth.[‡] According to him,

---

[*] C. Meiners, Allg. Krit. Gesch. d. Religionen. Hannover, 1806, Vol. I. S. 143.

[†] Gottl. Phil. Christ. Kaiser, Die biblische Theologie oder Judaismus u. Christianismus nach der grammatisch-historischen Interpretationsmethode u. nach einer freimüthigen Stellung in die Kritisch-vergleichende Universalgeschichte der Religionen und in die universale Religion. Erlangen, 1813. Theil, I. S. 2.

[‡] Th. Waitz, Anthropologie der Naturvölker.

fetichism springs from polytheism, and here he agrees with Pfleiderer. But whereas according to Pfleiderer external causes bring about its development, Waitz assigns for it causes purely internal and psychological. "The negro," says he, "carries the belief in an animated Nature to its uttermost limits; but as his mind is too rude to conceive of *one* universal animated nature, his imagination leads him to regard every trifling object around him as endowed with life. In every material thing he sees a spirit, often of great power, and quite disproportionate to the object itself." This object and this spirit make up a whole, the *fetich*. Waitz, however, does not explain to us the reason why the savage takes this view of material and inanimate things, and yet this is a question of high importance.

And precisely this point do I find treated with great clearness by Reinhard in his valuable "Historical Sketch of the Rise and Progress of Religious Ideas." * From the fact that religion is to be found among men, whatever their condition, he concludes that it must have its basis in the human mind itself, and he holds that if we would study the origin of religious ideas we must go back to the ages of barbarism, that is, to primitive times. That religion then was monotheistic cannot be shown : but on the other hand fetichism always characterizes the lowest stage of intellectual development. [The account given by Reinhard of the rise of fetichism, being substantially that which is set forth in the present work, need not be given here, as it will be found in full detail in the subsequent ·chapters ; and as Feuerbach agrees in essentials with Reinhard it will be enough to make a general reference to his work upon this subject.†]

The true way of arriving at an understanding of fetichism is by observing savage life; and here, books of travel are of great importance. Among these there is none more instructive than A. Bastian's "Visit to San Salvador, Capital of the Kingdom of Congo : a Contribution to Mythology and Psychology." * As the author never transfers to the savage his own thoughts and motives, but views him as he is, from the psychological point of view, his work is properly called a contribution to psychology, and with equal justice a contribution to mythology, since fetichism is the first step in religion.

CHAPTER II.

THE MIND OF THE SAVAGE IN ITS INTELLECTUAL AND MORAL ASPECTS.

By fetichism we understand the religious veneration of material objects. If such objects are to be worshiped, they must first of all appear to be worthy of veneration, or, in other words, the worshiper must so consider them. The fetich, however, *e.g.* a piece of metal, still continues to be, in external form and in essential constitution, the self-same thing, whether observed by a European or by an African. Hence that which renders it a fetich is nothing intrinsic to the thing itself, but the view which the fetichist takes of it. If therefore we would understand fetichism in its true nature, we must investigate the savage's mode of apprehending objects, or in other words, we must study the intellectual status of the fetichist. Fetichism has an historical position in all nations which stand lowest in intellectual development, that is, among savages, so-called. Our first

----

* Phil. Christ. Reinhard, Abriss einer Geschichte der Entstehung der religiösen Ideen. Jena, 1794.

† Ludwig Feuerbach, Das Wesen der Religion. Vorlesungen über das Wesen der Religion. Nebst Zusätzen u. Aumerkungen. Leipzig, 1851.

* Afrikanische Reisen von Dr. A. Bastian. Ein Besuch in San Salvador, der Hauptstadt der Königreichs Congo. · Bremen, 1859.

task, accordingly, will be to ascertain the savage's intellectual status. We propose therefore to sketch the savage mind first in its logical, and then in its ethical aspects.

1. *The Intellect of the Savage.*

The understanding has cognition only of those objects which are given to it in experience, and its range is consequently restricted by the limits of its experience. But what are the objects of experience? Those which are to be found in the man's *world:* and hence a man's cognitions can never go beyond *his world.* We say *his* world, meaning the universe, as far as he knows it. If therefore we would fix the intellectual status of any individual, we must first ascertain the number and the nature of his cognitions or objects.

As the understanding, then, has no cognitions save those which come to it out of its world, it follows that the number and the nature of one man's cognitions, or objects—in other words, the empiric contents of his mind—will differ from those of another, just as their respective *worlds* differ. Thus the sum-total of cognitions held by a mountaineer is different from that held by a seafaring man; and an Eskimo's cognitions are different from those of a Hindu, in proportion as their respective worlds differ; and they mutually resemble each other, in proportion as their worlds are alike. The *number* of objects (cognitions) differs in the same way. Thus the savage has but few, while the civilized European has many. From the paucity or the multiplicity of these flow consequences of the highest importance for a just estimate of the respective individuals. The greater the number of objects which a man has, the better equipped and the more cultivated will be his understanding, the more alert his thinking faculty, and the higher his development as a human being. On the other hand, the fewer his objects, the lower is his grade of development. It is univers-

ally true that man grows only as he apprehends objects.

The most fully developed intellect, therefore, is that which possesses the greatest number of objects. But if I would have many objects, I must discriminate and distinguish between them sharply; for unless they be thus defined, they tend to amalgamate, and so the number of objects would be diminished. Hence it is only in proportion as the understanding draws distinctions, that its objects are manifold and varied, and *vice versa*, it can make sharp distinctions only where its objects are varied. From this it follows that the faculty of accurate thinking or of sharply defining depends immediately and necessarily upon the number of the objects; so that, given the number of a man's objects, we might determine the strength or the feebleness of his thinking powers, or of his intellectual faculty. But since the objects are distinct only in so far as the understanding discriminates between them, the number of the objects must depend upon the sharpness with which these distinctions are drawn.

The status of a people as regards civilization might be determined by the greater or less accuracy with which they discriminate between objects, and the lowest grade of culture will accordingly be characterized by a lack of the power of discrimination. In the domain of *thought* that man only will attain eminence who can make distinctions where others do not. All erroneous and illogical thinking owes its rise to a weakness of the intellect, which fails to perceive really existent distinctions. The critic is a critic only in so far as he perceives distinctions, and consequently disparity, between objects which another takes to be identical. We call a man well-bred, or refined, in the social sense, who in every circumstance of life knows how to adapt his demeanor to the various individuals he meets with: but this he cannot do unless he can appreciate differences of character and of circumstance. The rude and unobservant treat all alike, under all circumstances, as though no differences existed. A man of refined *moral* sense is he who, in judging of what is due to each individual, makes the nicest distinctions : and, on the other hand, the less accurate the distinctions a man makes in moral questions, the more one-sided, prejudiced, and vicious he will be.

Accordingly, the lowest stage of intellect is characterized by a lack of many distinctions which are found in higher stages : or in other words by the absence of many objects possessed by the higher stages.

As compared then with a well developed intelligence, one which is undeveloped has a very contracted sphere of objects. The world it inhabits, its object-world, must be very narrow and restricted. Consider only the grade of intelligence which animals attain, and the number of objects which they have : both stand equally low. The intellect of the child is less developed, logically and ethically, than that of the adult ; and the reason is, that the objects of the former are inferior to those of the latter, whether as regards their number or their value. The child is yet ignorant of those things which are the objects of the adult. Abstract conceptions, such as virtue and vice, are strange and incomprehensible to him. His conceptions are all of a concrete nature, such as are given him in his *world;* and this world is restricted to the nursery, to his home, or to the town in which he lives, all regarded as objects of sense. His world widens by degrees, but it is only by becoming engrossed with still new objects, that he reaches the stage of culture attained by his times or by his nation. If these objects had not been presented to him, he would have remained a child all his life, as far as intellectual growth is concerned. The child's world is contracted, and so is his intellect : but this world of his lies immediately within the compass of a larger world. Betwixt the two there exist most intimate relations, and an uninterrupted commerce, and hence the child's world and intellect are ever expanding.

But in the case of the savage there is no such commerce between his little world and the great world around, and hence he fails to advance beyond a certain degree of sensuous apprehension. When our child has made some progress in the formation of sensuous conceptions, he comes in contact with a whole world of abstract and scientific notions, which are instilled into his mind at school. He learns reading and writing, and hears of heaven and earth, and of foreign countries and nations. The results of centuries of laborious study are set before him on the blackboard, as it were. His will also is disciplined and his passions controlled ; he is taught how best to shape his conduct, and hence he is not under the necessity of making a long series of painful experiments. But these intellectual notions and objects are utterly wanting in the world which surrounds the savage. His whole life long he continues in the stage of mere sensuous apprehension ; and even this will fail to furnish him with as many objects as the child possesses : for we can contemplate only that which is within our world. What then does a savage see, an Eskimo for instance ? Ice and snow, bears and fishes, and—Eskimos. Nothing more ; for "the whole expanse of Greenland is in great part covered with ice from 2000 to 3000 feet in thickness, as we judge from the height of the fragments of glaciers dropping into the sea." Nature therefore presents to the contemplation of the Eskimo no objects, save ice : there is no change, but everlasting sameness ; and man too remains unchanged and undeveloped. With regard to the Eskimos, Captain Parry says that they are not aware that there is any world different from their own, or that Nature may wear an aspect other than that with which they are familiar. The savage's world is narrow, the number of his objects contracted, and therefore is his intellect undeveloped.

Hence the broader the world in

which a man lives, and the more his various conceptions are multiplied, the better equipped is his brain for the exercise of thinking : and *vice versa*, the narrower his world, and the fewer his conceptions, the less practiced is his brain in making distinctions, and the less able is he to *think*. It is a truth confirmed by every one's experience that the thinking faculty, like every other, needs practice to give it dexterity ; and that unless it is rigorously and continuously exercised, it will still lack expertness, no matter what may be the natural advantages. If a man begins to be a student at forty, without any previous acquaintance with books, he sets a task for his intractable brain which it is still as ill-fitted to perform, as a Chinese lady with compressed feet would be to dance like Pepita. For "passé cet âge, les opinions sont faites ; quant aux fondements, ils sont bâtis, maçonnés, inébranlables ; autour d'eux l'habitude, la paresse d'esprit, les occupations pratiques sont comme un ciment que rien ne peut dissoudre." *

Bearing these principles in mind, let us consider the state of some wretched savage, some native of Tierra del Fuego, for instance. He has never come in contact with civilization, has never heard of abstract terms, nor knows anything of the outer world, which for him is undiscovered land, as was the New World for Europeans before Columbus's times. He knows only the barren deserts of his native home, where there are neither towns nor houses. He has never entered a school ; and his only desire is the gratification of his hunger, his lust and his indolence. His conceptions are all sensuous, nor are these numerous, being such only as come to him from the few miles of territory around him—from arid wastes and bare rocks, from birds and fellow-savages. Hence the number of his concrete notions is very small ;

nor can it increase, for he never quits his native place and never sees new objects. The necessary consequence, on psychological grounds, is that he is unable to apprehend or to think like a civilized European. It is for this reason that the instruction conveyed to savages by the missionaries is received by them "as meaningless words, and quickly absorbed into their fetichism, without producing any lasting effect." * Their power of apprehending must be exceedingly feeble, and they "will not trouble their brains with nice distinctions." † Now we can understand why it is that "thinking is a very laborious exercise for the savage ;" and also why it is that "when he is questioned as to intellectual things, he quickly complains of weariness and headache." ‡ The thinking faculty of the Bushman is unable to seize the simplest ideas and is characterized by extreme stupidity.§ The Abipones, who are more advanced in culture than the Bushmen, have numbers only as high as *three*. *Four* they express by three-and-one ; *five*, by the fingers of one hand ; *ten*, by those of both hands ; *twenty*, by the hands and feet : but when the number exceeds twenty, they express it by taking up in the hand an indefinite quantity of sand.‖ The Corannas experience difficulty in counting beyond *three;* ¶ a nation in Guinea has numbers as high as *five*,** and some Brazilian aborigines, as high as *four :* whatever exceeds that number is

---

* Taine, Les Philosophes Classiques du XIX. Siècle en France.

* Bastian, S. 102, *Aumerkung.*
† *Ibid.* 143. This does not imply the incapacity of a savage's child, when instructed, to attain a higher degree of intellectual culture. "The negro is tolerably apt to learn, but his whole development depends on the first instruction he receives. When taken into the factories, his brain is a tabula rasa, but ready to receive new impressions." (Bastian, 140.)
‡ Burchell, Travels in the Interior of S. Africa, II. p. 307.
§ *Ibid.* I. 338.
‖ M. Dobrizhofer, Historia de Abiponibus. Vienna, 1784.
¶ Campbell, Travels in South Africa, 71, 281.
** Bowdich, Mission to Ashantee, 542.

many.[*] It is difficult for us to imagine ourselves in so lowly an intellectual status as this : but that such status is possible, we may see in the analogous case of young children, who are unable to appreciate a number when it exceeds four or five. But the American Indian, whose world possesses a greater number of objects, and who is continually engaged in the struggle with wild beasts and other foes, leads a more active life. As he has more objects, so he has a greater number of conceptions, and hence his intellectual power is greater. Still his conceptions are little better than mere sensuous impressions. Now these impressions he is receiving daily as long as he lives, and it is no wonder if in distinguishing between them he acquires a degree of acuteness which we lack, owing to our being more taken up with abstract notions. Hence the Indian's nice discernment of scarcely perceptible tracks on the prairie, and of scarcely visible signs in the primeval forest. Hence, too, his power of taking in notions that are somewhat abstract : though this power of his must not be exaggerated. " In North America many Indians can count up to a thousand by scoring ; "[†] but only up to a thousand, and that only by scoring. Some African nations use the numbers *five* or *six* as the basis of their numeration, instead of *ten*, so that *five-and-two* or *six-and-one* will express seven.[‡] It is plain that these tribes must lack all the advantage derived from numeration. They cannot reckon : and yet without reckoning according to the four simple rules of arithmetic, commerce is impossible. It is impossible *suum cuique reddere* without some system of measurement, and this requires numeration and reckoning.[§] Hence simply for the reason that their nu-meration is defective, apart from all other reasons, savages fail duly to appreciate the difference between *meum* and *tuum*. It needs no words to show that they totally lack all such scientific knowledge as is based on measurement.

" They are wont to make an inexact division of time into moons and days, and many of them are ignorant of any division save the diurnal. The day they divide according to the sun's course into three or four parts of indefinite length."[*] Chronology they have none, nor indeed is such a thing possible among a people whose memory scarce goes back of yesterday.[†] The mere narration of historical facts were therefore an impossibility for them, even if they had a history. But as their lives are uneventful, they furnish no material for history. Let us consider what events transpire among them that might be deemed worthy of remembrance. The day opens ; they feel hungry ; they take some game ; they sleep : then they repeat *da capo*. " Though the American Indians resemble the natives of Africa and of the Polar Regions in their distaste for work, they differ from them in this that they love repose above all things ; while the others rather love to give themselves up to sport and enjoyment. The Indian never exerts himself, except where exertion is unavoidable , and when the hunt is over he enjoys undisturbed repose in his hammock."[‡] Hence the life of the savage is uneventful, monotonous, stagnant. The individual may be developed to a certain degree ; but not so the tribe. " The total development of all the successive generations of a Bushman stock is little more than the development of the first Bushman." [§] " Some tribes have legends and ballads recounting sundry warlike exploits of their forefathers, but these records do not refer to

---

[*] Eschwege, Journal von Brasilien, I. 168.
[†] Wuttke, Bd. I. S. 156.
[‡] Th. Winterbottom, Acct. of the Native Africans in the Neighborhood of Sierra Leone. Lond. 1803, p. 230.
[§] *Cf.* Kuno Fischer, Logik, 2, Aufl. § 94, ff.

[*] Wuttke, I. S. 156.
[†] Bastian, S. 100.
[‡] Wuttke, I. S. 164.
[§] *Cf.* the Author's work " Die Thierseele." Leipzig, 1868, Cap. I. § 2.

events of any antiquity. Most savages are as destitute of historic records as though they were the primitive stock of mankind, and just sprung into existence. The Greenlanders, who stand considerably above the lowest grade of savagery, have, instead of history, only genealogies, oftentimes of ten generations." * Similar genealogical lists, but not so long, are found among Negroes, Indians and South Sea Islanders: but never actual history. In fact, they regard the past as very unimportant; and even those among them whose intellect is somewhat developed prefer legend to history.

As the world of such savages is extremely narrow and circumscribed, the number of conceptions formed by them is necessarily very scanty. Their notions are merely of the things of sense, and they *think* not at all—if by *thinking* is meant the elaboration of conceptions not immediately referable to sensible objects. He who entertains no thoughts is unable to give expression to thoughts. Hence, from the conditions of life amid which savages are placed it flows as a necessary consequence, that their language will be as undeveloped and as scanty as their circle of conceptions.† They can have words only for those objects of which they are cognizant. But as these objects are but few, it follows that their vocabulary must be scant. Then, inasmuch as they have no abstract notions, they cannot have any words to express objects not directly perceived by the senses. In the next place their language will be very deficient in those formulas which simply indicate the mutual relations of objects, as recognized by the human mind, and hence will lack inflexions, conjunctions and prepositions. Accordingly the Negro languages are generally very defective : the language spoken in Acra and in Fanti has

neither adverbs nor prepositions: neither a comparative degree, nor a passive voice.* From this we may conclude that the people who speak these languages are still ignorant of some of the most elementary distinctions between conceptions, and that they remain through life in the same low stage of intellectual development in which children among us are found when they are learning to speak. It is stated that the Bushmen of South Africa are not distinguished from one another by separate names,† and Herodotus makes the same statement as to a tribe dwelling in the Sahara, the Atarantes : " They alone of men, so far as I can learn, are without names." ‡

Inasmuch as the circle of their conceptions embraces only sensible objects, it is to be expected that on the whole they will discriminate more nicely between such objects than we can, provided a considerable number of them come under their cognizance. The reason of this is that their senses are constantly exercised, and that they have no abstract notions to divert their attention. Hence the North American Indians perceive distinctions, and mark these distinctions with special names, where we use one general term. Thus, for instance, in place of our one verb "to go" they have many words, one signifying " to go in the morning," another " in the evening," another " to go in moccasins," etc. Everything is viewed as unique and individual, and as though it had no connection, no relation with other things. This is owing to the fact that the savage does not compare his conceptions with one another, a process performed not by the senses but by the intellect. Hence it is that the languages of the Indians abound in sesquipedalian word-combinations to express purely concrete notions. But these combinations

---

* D. Cranzen's Historie von Grönland. Barby, 1762, I. 261.
† *Cf.* Steinthal, Die Mande-Neger-Sprachen, psychologisch und phonetisch betrachtet. Berlin, 1867.

* Bowdich, p. 470.
† Lichtenstein, R. um südl. Afrika (1803-6), I. 192, II. 82.
‡ Herodot. IV. 181. *Cf.* Plin. Hist. Nat. V. 8.

are as void of intellectual suggestion as they are minute in describing every outward aspect and every minor particular of the object; and this very minuteness so fatigues and distracts the attention, that the main object is often obscured and hid from view. Awkward story-tellers have the like habit. Instead of going direct to the kernel of the story, they ramble away from it, and go into such long and minute explanations, that at length they do not themselves know what they had intended to communicate.

This redundancy of words is really a sign of a weak and uncritical understanding, unable to handle all its material by the principle of unity. Each phenomenon as it appears is taken to be *sui generis*, and is designated by a special name. Hence such languages, dependent as they are on the slightest external changes of objects, must be themselves ever changing, and the more so, as they are not fixed in writing. "In South African villages, where the children are left by themselves for months at a time, they often are found, when their parents return, to speak a language unintelligible to the latter, and the missionaries have observed that this language of the children is different for almost every generation of them. Among the Australian tribes, who taboo every word whose sound could remind them of a dead relative, and substitute a new term, this change of language must be of still more frequent occurrence. The savage coins new words as he needs them; and when the laws of grammar will not bend to his purpose, or when he is ignorant of them, he makes laws to suit himself. So long as languages are not consolidated and fixed in writing, they are ever in process of construction: and the elaborate grammars written by the old missionaries with the assistance of their ingenious penitents would be as unintelligible to the latter as the systems of religion attributed to them." * "The American languages,

* Bastian, S. 38, 39, 40.

generally rich in grammatical forms and in compound words, but poor in expression, because the Indians do not think, are such incoherent conglomerates that when families or tribes break up, a notable divergence of language among the sundered fragments is the immediate consequence." * The reason of this is that each of the fragments finds itself amid conditions differing, if only slightly, from those surrounding the others. As the objects differ, so will the conceptions, and the languages in the same proportion; for *mind* and *world* are dependent on one another. Whenever a savage tribe is not tied down to its native soil by its possessions or by some law of necessity, and wherever its migrations are not checked by the previous occupation of the surrounding country, it readily breaks up into smaller clans, and each one of these will soon have its peculiar dialect. This is the case in America; and Prince Max von Neuwied gives specimens of thirty-three different North American languages which he himself had met with.† In what was once Spanish North America there are over twenty, and in all America about 500 languages entirely different from one another.‡

2. *The Morality of the Savage.*

We have seen how narrow and contracted is the intellectual sphere, the mental horizon of savage tribes, owing to the circumstances by which they are surrounded. Their mental power is not greater than that of the child. But besides mind, man is also possessed of will, and it is will that constitutes his moral character. Our present task therefore is to study the operations of the savage's will, his moral character.

* Max von Neuwied, Reise in Brasilien, II. S. 213.
† *Ib.* II. 445–645.
‡ Humboldt, Essai polit. I. 352; Adelung und Vater, Mithrid. III. 2, 370; V. Neuwied, II. 302; Beechey, Voy. to Pacific, II. 139. For Negro languages *cf.* Bowdich, 454.

Man's will cannot aim at an abstraction, or at the indefinite, but must always have its determinate object. In this it resembles the understanding, which must also have a definite object. But if the understanding has no conceptions, the will can have no objects; for only that which is the object of the understanding can be an object of the will. Hence the savage can desire only those things which are found in the world of which he has cognizance. But this world is different for different races: for one, it will contain many objects; for another, but few. As for the savage, his world is very contracted. Let us now consider what must be the effect upon the savage's will of a greater or a less number of objects.

That can be an object of will which is perceived by the understanding. The first object which a man is conscious of, and the one which, as being inseparable from himself, he must always have, is himself,* his own organism, and whatever necessarily has its rise in it. Man is an organism: whatever originates in this organism and becomes an object of consciousness—*e. g.*, the natural instincts and appetites (hunger, lust, desire of repose)—must necessarily be also an object for the will; and these objects of the will must exist in all men, whatever their culture, simply because man is an organism. But to these objects which are common to the whole race, others are appended which vary according to the conditions of life in which a man is placed; and in proportion as the world around him is rich or scant in objects, diversified or uniform, his consciousness will take in more or fewer objects.

Hence the objects of will may be divided into two classes: first, those which are inseparable from the organism, and which we may call the Instincts; second, those which are found in the world without. Man

wills both of these; still it is clear that, all things else being equal, a man will expend less will-force upon individual objects, in proportion as their number is greater. Further, it is clear that in proportion as he exerts his will in one direction, he relaxes it in another. Hence the greater the number of objects found without the organism, and the stronger the energy of will with which they are desired, the more is the will withdrawn from those immediately connected with the organism, that is, from the natural instincts. Conversely, too, the fewer objects a man has, derived from the outer world, and the less his will is attracted by these, the more will he be controlled by his instincts, and the more time and attention will he devote to the gratification of these. Hence it is no wonder if the so-called civilized man controls his instincts more easily than the savage, seeing that his will is directed toward so many objects outside his organism. But on the other hand, we need not, be surprised at finding savages, who are controlled by these instincts, committing excesses in the gratification of them, which to us appear to be brutal and shameless.

The savage has no intellectual objects, and consequently no intellectual occupations. He can occupy himself only with such objects as are given to him in consciousness; hence only with such as remain after we shut out all intellectual objects, viz.: hunger, lust, indolence. As objects in the external world he has none, or but few, he cannot occupy himself with them.

When he has appeased his hunger, there is nothing more for him to do, so he will play, or sleep, or engage in debauch; and as this is the only course open to him, he will go to excess. He must needs act thus, nor can he do otherwise; and surely that is not to be accounted a crime in him, which is the necessary product of his natural condition. The unrestrained gratification of natural instincts is as clearly right in the savage (taking his

---

* *Cf.* Schopenhauer, Vierfache Wurzel, 3 Aufl. § 22.

world into account) as it would be wrong in us, whose world is very different from his. Hence morality, as interpreted by us, has no application to the savage. Our refined distinctions in question of morals do not exist for him: his obtuseness of understanding is such that he cannot grasp them. Our definition of *good* and *evil* applies to him as little as to beasts, and it were unjust to measure him by such a standard, or to require him to conform to it. He can recognize no law save that of instinct, so long as his world remains contracted. Whatever his instincts require, that he seeks; what they reject, that he avoids. As his will is attached to trifling objects, they being the only objects he possesses, he must needs esteem as highly things of no value to us, as we esteem things of high importance to us, though of no account to him. Hence matters perfectly indifferent to us will have for him moral importance (if we may so speak); and conversely, what we take to be highly important will be indifferent to him, because his will is not directed toward it. By the aid of these principles we can explain such traits as the following: Certain Bushmen, being asked by a European what they meant by good and what by bad, could not give any reply: but they held fratricide to be perfectly harmless.* The Kamtchatdales hold that an act is sinful which is unlucky: for instance, to visit hot springs; to brush snow off the shoes out of doors; to seize a red-hot coal otherwise than with the fingers, when you would light your pipe; to bring home the first fox you have taken; to tread in the tracks of a bear, etc.† The Orangoo Negroes hold it sinful to spit on the earth,‡ while the natives of Labrador regard nothing as sinful save only the murder of an innocent man.§

In the gratification of his indolence, hunger and lust the savage can acknowledge no restraint, as he has no outward objects to counterbalance them. But here another point is to be considered, namely, that this unrestraint tends to grow from day to day. Egoism prompts each individual savage to assert his mastery over all others. Hence the quarrels and competitions of man against man, each striving to surpass the other. But since this competition must regard only those activities which occupy the savage, and as these three instincts furnish his chief occupation, it follows that the natural condition of unrestraint will be carried by competition to a truly bestial degree of perfection in indolence, gluttony and lust. The Missouri Indians used to practice promiscuous intercourse as a point of honor.* In like manner, in Tahiti and the adjacent islands, there was the association of the Arreoi, who made it a point of honor to practice unchastity in all its degrees.

The Indian never exerts himself except so far as strict necessity requires. After the hunt, unbroken repose. The women do all the work, as is the universal rule among savages. "An Indian chief once said to a white man, 'Oh, brother, you will never learn what happiness it is to think of nothing and to do nothing: this is, next after sleep, the most delightful thing on earth. That was our condition before we were born, and will be our condition after we die.' Then, after expressing his contempt for the restless life of the white man, he went on: 'But we live for the present moment. The past is but smoke driven by the wind. As for the future, where is it? As it has not yet come, we shall never see it perhaps. Let us then enjoy the day that is, for to-morrow it will be gone far from us!'" † It is plain that among such people, to whom the past has bequeathed no problems to be

* Burchell, I. 338, 340.
† G. W. Steller, Beschreibung von Kamtschatka. Frankfurt und Leipzig, 1774, S. 274.
‡ Bastian, 261.
§ Nachrichten aus der Brüdergemeinde, 835, No. 5.

* M. v. Neuwied, Nordamerika, II. 131.
† Crevecœur, Voy. dans la haute Pensylvanie et dans l'état de New-York. Par. 1801, Vol. I. p. 362.

solved, no tasks to be performed, and who will themselves bequeath none to futurity, there can be no advance in knowledge or in morals. "The boy accompanies his father: if the latter follows any pursuit—fishing, for instance—the son too learns the craft. But inasmuch as the Negroes pass the greater part of their time in doing nothing, the education thus obtained is of no importance." * In the South Sea Islands the grandees have the food put in their mouths bit by bit.† In Tahiti the missionaries, having endeavored to introduce the art of weaving, all the girls who had come to learn quit work after a few days, saying, "Why should we work? Have we not as much bread-fruit and cocoa-nuts as we can eat? You who need ships and fine clothes must work: but we are content with what we have." ‡

Lust and gluttony are regarded by all savages as the acme of earthly felicity. · The inhabitants of Northern Asia perform wonderful feats of gormandizing. Three Yakuts will devour a reindeer at one meal, including the contents of the intestines, and a single Yakut once devoured 28 lbs. of porridge with 3 lbs. of butter.§ The baptized Kamtchatdales often say, as they recall the past when they were still heathen: "When do we ever have jovial days now? Time was when we used to bespew the whole floor of the hut three or four times a day, but now we can do it but rarely even once a day. Formerly we could wade ankle-deep in spew, now the soles of our feet even are not wetted."‖ "In all Negro languages the word *belly* is one of great import."¶ Politeness re-

quires that one inquire if all is well with his neighbor's belly. The South Sea Islanders call thoughts, *words in the belly*. The stomach of one who dies is kept as a relic; and the Kroo Negroes hold that the stomach ascends into heaven after death.*

As regards the passion of lust, the absolute shamelessness of the savage almost surpasses belief. The Bushmen have only one word to signify girl, maiden and wife; they consort together like cattle, have no real marriage, and the men exchange their women freely.† "Woman is a chattel, to be bought and sold, having no rights of choice or of refusal. Being a mere possession, not the object of love, when by reason of age or for any other cause she can no longer minister to lust, she becomes a despised thing, without any rights, often contemned even by her own children, shut out from the ceremonies of religion, oftentimes even forbid to come near the sanctuary as being unclean, and in death she is esteemed unworthy of being lamented."‡ "In Nucahiva the bride is the property of all the male guests for the space of three days."§ Bushmen and California Indians make no account of blood-relationship, and incest is common among many Indian tribes.‖ Among the Aleutian Islanders brothers and sisters, children and parents, have sexual commerce with one another, alleging the example of the seal.¶ South American savages, the Puris, Botokuds and others, and most of the New Holland tribes, go entirely naked, while among the South Sea Islanders, at least the men, if not both sexes, wear no bodily covering. Some Indian tribes use clothing to protect them against the weather, but disregard the claims of modesty.** Sodo-

---

* Halleur, das Leben der Neger West-Afrikais; Ein Vortrag. Berlin, 1850, S. 31. *Cf.* Bosmaun, R. nach Guinea, 1708, S. 148.
† Forster, S. 206.
‡ Beechey, I. 337.
§ Cochrane, Travels on Foot through Siberia, 155; J. Sarytschew, Achtjährige Reise im nordöstlichen Sibirien, auf dem Eismeere u. dem nordöstlichen Ocean. Aus d. Russischen übers. Leipz. 1805, I. S. 129.
‖ Steller, Kamtschatka, S. 286.
¶ Bastian, S. 35.

* *Ib.*, S. 207.
† Lichtenstein, R. in Afrika, II. 376; Campbell, 13.
‡ *Cf.* Wuttke, I. 177.
§ Langsdorff, Reise, I. 132.
‖ Eschwege, Journ. v. Brasilien, I. 121; Mackenzie, Travels through N. America, 108.
¶ Langsdorff, II. 5843.
** Mackenzie, 5471. *Cf.* Wuttke, I. 182.

my is wide-spread in certain tribes.* The South Sea Islanders abandon themselves at a very early age to the most unbridled licentiousness; and their songs, dances and shows are instinct with sensuality.† The Tungoos have wanton dances which conclude with the stripping off of all clothing and indulgence in unlimited debauchery;‡ and immoral dances prevail throughout all Northern Asia.§ The Greenlanders and Eskimos are notorious, but the life led by the Kamtchatdales in former times was bestial. All their thoughts and imaginations were concerned with unchastity, and even little children delighted their parents by licentious indulgence. Adultery was universal, and the women used to boast of it. Strangers were required to make return for any service they received, by ministering to the ruling passion; and men and women engaged in unnatural and sodomitic commerce. They were acquainted with syphilis, as they themselves admit, long before the advent of Europeans.‖

Where there in no moral family life there can be no family, in our sense of the word, that is, with the members united together in love and friendship. Here the rule of the stronger prevails, and the man is everything. "The idea of the State is nowhere ¶ developed, and the individual, instead of gaining strength from union with others, imagines himself to be safe from danger only when he oppresses all around him. The father makes slaves of his children, and the husband enslaves the wife, in order that he himself may be free: and he is free so long as he does not meet some one mightier than he, for then the domestic tyrant falls himself under the control of an inexorable master. His neighbor he regards as his foe. In short, nothing can be more foreign to the savage mind and the state of savagery than the dogma of Universal Equality."* "The child has no rights, being simply the chattel of his parents, who can do with him as they please, without being bound to him by any obligations. Rarely do they exhibit any true parental love for their children, beyond the fondness of animals for their young; and when a child is born to them inopportunely, or when they take a dislike to it, it is put to death; and the fearful crimes of infanticide, fœticide, abortion, abandonment and sale, and even slaughter and eating of children, are so common as to explode all the sentimental idyllic tirades that have ever been sung about the innocent life of man in the state of nature."†

When such are the relations between parent and child, education is out of the question.` The American Indians are pleased when they see the child strike its mother and refuse to obey her. "He will one day be a brave warrior," say they. Among them obedience and respect for parents are very rare.‡ Among the Kamtchatdales children never ask their parents for anything, but take it without more ado: and they never manifest joy on seeing their parents after a protracted separation from them.§ Among the Tungoos duels between father and son are frequent, and not seldom terminate fatally.‖ The Arekuna, as in Guiana, bring up children and monkeys together. The monkeys are members of the family, eat with the other members, are suckled by the women, and have great affection for their human nurses.

---

* Eschwege, I. 132; Franklin's First Voyage, 7273.
† Mackenzie, 108.
‡ Ermann, Reise um die Erde II. 36.
§ Cochrane, 298.
‖ Steller, Kamtschatka, 287, 350, 357.
¶ Among savages.

---

* Bastian, S. 67, 68.
† Wuttke, Gesch. der Heidenthums, I. S. 185.
‡ M. v. Neuwied, Nordamerika, II. 129; Mackenzie, 106; Franklin, First Voy. 73; Eschwege, I. 121; Spix u. Martius, Reise, I. S. 380.
§ Steller, Kamtschatka, S. 353. Cf. Wuttke, I. 187, ff.
‖ Georgi, Beschr. einer Reise durch das Russische Reich im J. 1772, S. 242. Cf. M. v. Neuwied, R. in Brasilien, I. 141, 146.

Oftentimes a woman is to be seen with a child and a monkey at the breast, the two nurselings quarreling.*

As the parents care little for the children, so in turn the children care little for the parents. When the American Indians go out on their hunting expeditions they often leave behind in a state of utter destitution the aged and the infirm who are unable to make the tramp:† and in most of the tribes it is customary for relatives to dispatch the old and the feeble without remonstrance from the victims.‡ The Bechuanas have less regard for the aged than for cattle, and abandon them to their fate without compunction.§ Their neighbors, the Corannas, expose the old people to wild beasts, they being, as they say, of no account, and only serving to use up the provisions.‖ Among the Bushmen the daughter often turns her old mother out of the hut, and leaves her to be devoured by wild beasts. Sons put their fathers to death with impunity.¶ The Kamtchatdales often eject the sick from their house and cast them to the dogs;** and the Eskimo often bury alive old sickly widows, and not unfrequently suffer old men to perish of hunger.††

3. *Conclusion.*

We have now set forth the intellectual and moral condition of the savage so far as was needful for our present purpose. Our criticism, aided by experimental investigation, unfolds before our eyes a picture very different from what certain enthusiasts would paint, who hold the present condition of civilized man to be a corruption, a degeneration from the primitive innocence and purity of man in his natural state. An indolent savage, who has neither objects nor aims nor ambitions to occupy his mind, can never be *moral*.

Of course the picture we have painted does not represent with equal fidelity all savages, for there are degrees of higher and lower even in savagery. We are not called upon here to ascertain the specific differences of these various degrees; it is sufficient if we have an idea of the average condition of the savage intellectually and morally considered.

The savage's world is narrow and contracted, presenting but few objects, and hence he has but few conceptions. But the fewer his conceptions the less does he distinguish between them; *i.e.*, the less he thinks, the less is his faculty of thought exercised, and the greater is his stupidity. Then, his will can be directed only upon the objects given him through his understanding. But since external objects there are none to engage it, of course all its energies must be expended upon internal objects, of which he is conscious through his organism. Hence he is as free from restraint as a beast in the gratification of his instincts. Such is the savage, and such he must be; for intellect, world and will are inseparable; one never stands without the others; they stand ever together, or they exist not at all. It is needless to inquire which has precedence, for they all three make up the essence of man. His intellect extends as far as his world, and his will extends only so far as his intellect, or his world. Conversely, too, his world extends only so far as his intellect and his will.

* R. Schomburgk in the "Ausland," No. 288.
† Mackenzie, 431; Franklin, First Voyage, 192; Second, 91.
‡ Robertson, History of America, I. 466; Mackenzie, ib.
§ Campbell, Trav. in S. Africa, 49, 245.
‖ *Ib.*, Second Journey, 258.
¶ *Ib.* 272.
** Steller, S. 271.
†† Cranz, Grönland, 201; Beechey, II. 394. Bastian makes a similar statement as to Negroes, S. 320.

CHAPTER III.

THE RELATION BETWEEN THE SAVAGE MIND AND ITS OBJECT.

In the preceding chapters we have been laying the foundation for a correct understanding of fetichism, and have ascertained the range of the savage intellect. As fetichism is really a mode of intellectual apprehension, we had first to study that particular phase of the understanding wherein a sensible object obtains significance as a fetich. It remains for us now in the present chapter to show what is the necessary relation of the savage mind to its object; for it is this relation which gives rise to the fetichistic apprehension of objects, and which accounts for it.

1. *The Value of Objects.*

As things are for us what we apprehend them to be, so their value for us will be in accordance with our apprehension of them. Now the mind has a clearer and more exact apprehension of objects in proportion as it distinguishes between them more clearly. Therefore the sharper the distinctions we can make with regard to the minutest details of an object, the more exactly can we determine its value. An object is distinctly apprehended, only when we can discriminate between it and other objects. If therefore I would form a clear understanding and an accurate estimate of a thing, I must also clearly understand all other objects related to it ; and so I cannot rightly estimate anything without an acquaintance with a number of other things. My estimate of things will thus vary according to the number of objects of which I take cognizance. But since all things stand to each other in a causal relation, it follows that a *perfectly* exact estimate of any single object can only be had when the entire series is known. For the greater the number of the objects apprehended, the better do we understand the interrelations of them all,

and so the causal value of each. On the contrary, the smaller the number of objects, the less accurate will be our estimate of each.

The mind, then, whose object-world is very contracted must of necessity form a very different estimate of things from that formed by a mind which has many objects, nor will its estimate be as exact as that of the latter. From all this it follows that the estimate formed of things by children as well as by savages must be very different from our estimate, as their world is very contracted and the number of their objects very limited.

The untutored intellect which, as having but few objects, is defective in the power of distinction, cannot estimate the true value of things. It is liable either to overestimate objects or to undervalue them. It can estimate only the objects which it has. As it knows only these and is ignorant of all others, it cannot compare the known with the unknown, and the known must of necessity be esteemed the best and the most precious. The peasant who has never left his native soil, regards his home as the most desirable place on earth, though the soil be half bog. Be the objects which the untutored mind contemplates never so lowly, and worthy only of contempt as viewed by a mind which has a wider range, still it will set an exorbitant value on them inasmuch as they are the only objects it contemplates. On the other hand, as there are many objects which do not occur to the undeveloped mind (*v.g.* objects of a purely intellectual value) these it will not estimate aright, or in other words, not according to their true worth. It will undervalue them. The peasant values his field of rye , not so the rare varieties of flower: growing in the neighborhood; he knows nothing about these. If his mind were stored with as many plant-objects as is that of the botanist ; if he were acquainted with their different classes and their mutual relations, he would value these rare flowers : as it is, he plucks them up as weeds and casts them away. His undeveloped understanding does not apprehend distinctions between things, and as he cannot distinguish between them, they are all alike to him. For him leaves are leaves, and he knows no such distinctions as heart-shaped, lancet-shaped leaves, etc. Objects with which he is unacquainted he undervalues in proportion to his ignorance of them.

The fewer and less important the objects which a man possesses, the more excessive will be his overestimate. He will discern valuable treasures in trifles which, to a mind of greater range, will appear as very nothings. If a man is worth a million of dollars, a few pence will be a trifle in his eyes; but if a man has only a few pence, then one penny will have a considerable value for him. If then we would determine what are the objects which a man will regard as valuable, we must take account of how many objects he has. What then are the objects that a child will prize? Those which he has. What are these? Let us consider those which he *has not*. He has none of those which lie within the domain of science or of art. He has none of those things which the adult values, steady occupation, its products, its remuneration, etc. He values only those things which he knows and has, and these are the merest trifles, his playthings.

Children must of necessity prize these trifles, for they have no knowledge of the more important objects known and prized by adults. It is worth while to observe how the understanding is enlarged in proportion to the number of objects to which it addresses itself. As it becomes acquainted with new and more important objects, its standard of values changes; yet so long as these new objects are unknown, it esteems as most important those objects which it already has. In youth we have a very different estimate of things from that which we have in old age, for youth does not value those things which are most prized by age. In like manner the child does not value the objects which are of importance to youth. The child values only the objects with which he is acquainted. But these must be of but little importance, for it is only by slow degrees that the mind comes to value objects of real importance. Inasmuch as every object is a novelty to the child, it is a necessity for him to take the same interest in trifling objects which we take in more important ones. The child is receiving an education, and has enough to occupy his mind in the contemplation of familiar household things. For these alone he has eyes, ears, attention. After a man is grown up and no longer admires, for instance, his watch, merely glancing at the dial to ascertain the time of the day, he forgets the time in the past when things now the most familiar were to him new and strange, and wonders that the child should want to look at the watch again and again, and to listen to its ticking. Yet nothing is more natural or more inevitable for as yet everything is a novelty to the child. We say that children *play* with things. If by *play* we mean simply pastime, amusement, we do not correctly describe the occupation of the child, who is as seriously employed with his toys as an adult might be in the management of state affairs. The child's play is work, study, acquisition of knowledge, and occupation of the mind suited to the measure of his faculties.

We have been somewhat prolix in describing the relation of the infantile intelligence to its objects, for the reason that it throws light upon the matter in hand, viz., the relations between the mind of the savage and its objects. The savage's mind is in the same embryonic state as that of the infant. It has but a limited range of objects, and therefore will value these, however inconsiderable they may be, as we value objects of greater moment. Let us take an inventory of the possessions of a naked savage, a Bushman, for instance. He has none of the products of industry or art; he weaves not, neither does he spin; he neither plants nor gathers in a harvest; he has not even a knife beyond some sharp-edged stone he chances to find. He knows nothing of such objects. Previous to his coming in contact with Europeans he has no idea of such a trifling thing even as a brass button, or a nail. What then does he possess? A few articles that he has chanced to find, that he has picked up off the ground, or found growing on trees, or taken from wild beasts. His possessions consist of stones, shells, a club, fruits, peltries, a dead carcass, skulls and bones, teeth, horns, gaudy feathers, fishbones—such is the sum total of his property. "The Bushmen have scarcely any possessions. If they steal a few head of cattle, they devour as much as they can, and leave the remainder on the ground."* The negroes of West Africa are more favored. "Simpler even than his house is the furniture—a bed made of leaves and rushes, a block of wood for a pillow, a few pots and bowls, a gun and a long knife, with a few large and small calabashes, the large ones used as wardrobes (his clothing being a few yards of cloth to wrap around the body), and as receptacles for ball, lead, powder, etc.; the small ones serving as flagons. And that is about all the furniture to be seen in a negro's hut."†

Beyond this inventory the savage neither has nor knows of any possessions. He must therefore overestimate these objects. Accordingly a fishbone will serve him for an ornament.‡ "They trick themselves out with feathers, shells and the like, which they consider things of beauty."§ If now they meet with some strange object, a nail, for instance, or a glass bead, or a bit of tinsel ornament, it excites their wonder, and they long to possess it. "The sister of a South Sea Island king whose subjects thought themselves highly civilized,

stole a couple of iron nails from Cook's vessel, and her brother connived at the theft."* "A negro who wears European clothing at once ranks with Europeans, though he be as black as coal. There are gradations of rank, however: a fellow that wears only one article of European costume, the vest, for instance, or the hat, ranks as a mulatto. To hold rank as an out and out European, he must wear the full costume, his head being crowned with the hat."† "Oftentimes as I stood in the presence of ebon Majesty, the king would be possessed by the god of poesy, and my interpreter would inform me that he was singing my praise and great renown. This was extremely gratifying and of course flattered my vanity in no small degree. Unfortunately, however, my attention was on one occasion specially directed to the noble strains wherein the Greots, or bards, committed my fame to posterity; and it was suggested that the least I might do was to give them a kronthaler: so I had the curiosity to request of my interpreter a more minute analysis of the pæan. The Greots were lauding in transcendental metaphors, my hat, which just then was not according to the latest *mode de Paris;* and in its last days that hat cost me double the price I had paid for it new. The Lord of Shemba-Shemba I suppose sung the praises of my shoes, as shoes in that land are the prerogative of the Blood Royal. Princes alone are there permitted to wear shoes, to travel in mat hammocks, or to carry umbrellas."‡ The inhabitants of the Pelew Islands used to append to their ears all the valuables they cribbed from Europeans, scraps of leather, bits of paper, etc.

This fact, which has a psychological basis in the intellect of the savage, must be taken into account in the study of fetichism; and this for two reasons, viz.: First, it will, in connec-

* Lichtenstein, Reise im Südl. Afrika, 1803–6. Berlin, 1811, II. 321, 83.
† Halleur, 23, 18. .
‡ Bastian, 317.
§ Halleur, 19.

* Forster, Bemerkungen, S. 338.
† Halleur, 19.
‡ Bastian, S. Salv. 56.

tion with other facts, enable us to see how an object comes to be regarded as a fetich. Then it will guard us against the error of thinking that every object that the savage prizes is for him a fetich. It is true, any object may become a fetich; still, every object is not necessarily a fetich. We might here recall what Azara says about the savages of the Rio de la Plata: "When the ecclesiastics saw certain figures engraved or pictured on the pipes, bows, clubs and pottery of the Indians, they at once concluded these were idols, and burnt them up. The Indians still employ the same figures, but only to please the fancy, for they are without religion."*

2. *The Anthropopathic Apprehension of Objects.*

It is plain that in the view of the savage, objects will have a very different value from what they have for us. But furthermore, owing to the contracted range of the savage's mind and his consequent deficiency of mental power, or, which is the same thing, his defective faculty of distinction, an object, whether living or inanimate, will have for him a very different meaning from what it has for us.

The savage differs but little from the mere animal, nor does he himself draw the same line of distinction between the two which we draw. Inasmuch as his consciousness, which extends only as far as the objects which enter it, is extremely contracted, he is on this ground also less distinguished than we from the unconscious nature which surrounds him. He has but few objects, and so distinguishes but few; and thus his power of ascertaining substantial differences between things lies all unemployed, uninstructed and feeble. Consequently, he does not see things with the same distinctness as we do, and hence it is clear that in his view nature must appear more homogeneous than it does to us. But

we must consider this point more closely.

We too regard all nature as one and homogeneous, and view all beings as essentially homogeneous, but yet on characteristic grounds very different from those of the savage. After having traveled in many devious paths, and so far even exaggerated the distinction between Man and Nature, as almost to dissolve the tie which binds them together, and thus established the characteristic differences between the two, we came to recognize the truth that in the last analysis man is not essentially distinct from nature, and we regard nature as homogeneous in all its parts, though for reasons very different from those of the savage. The difference lies in this, that we consider nature in its several parts: that we arrive at the knowledge of its homogeneity through the consideration of its distinctions and differences, and that nature lies before us as a very complex object, which has been investigated in many of its parts. The savage knows nothing of these distinctions and definitions: to him nature is all unknown; yet he too regards it as homogeneous, but on these grounds:

He is unacquainted with the peculiar nature of those things he comes in contact with, having never investigated them: he knows nothing of their inner specific properties and constitution. He recognizes a distinction only between their external phenomena, as regards their form, color, smell or taste. Then, he has never made his own being a subject of contemplation either from a psychological or from a physiological point of view. He is therefore ignorant of the distinction between himself and other beings. Accordingly his apprehensions of outward objects will picture them not according to their real nature, which he has never investigated, but in quite different shapes. It is impossible for him to attribute to objects properties he never yet has apprehended. He has no conception of the true, specific nature of things, and

* Azara, Voyage dans l'Amerique Meridionelle. Paris, 1809, T. II p. 3.

consequently his apprehension of them is defective. Whatever object he perceives he invests with those properties of which he has already a notion, and then for him the two things are inseparable and identical. This process is inevitable, and the savage never doubts but that his perception is entirely correct, for he has no suspicion of having transferred to the object the incongruous impressions of his own mind. And indeed why should he doubt? In order to entertain a doubt whether or no his apprehension corresponds with the reality, the thought must first have arisen in his mind that perhaps the object might be apprehended differently: but this presupposes a mind furnished with a great variety of conceptions, and that has investigated much, so as to be possessed of a number of different actual and possible notions. Precisely because the cultured mind possesses such an abundance of varied notions, any one of which may appear to represent some new object which attracts its attention, it will not accept its first impression as absolutely correct and final, but will be skeptical for a time, while it sifts and weighs, in order to choose among many conceptions that which exactly fits the matter in hand. Now the savage has no such store of conceptions. He possesses but few himself, nor has he the slightest suspicion of any others. As the savage of Tierra del Fuego has no notion of Europe, Asia, Africa, etc., and just as he has not the remotest idea of what a magnifying glass is, so he is utterly unable to conceive of any other mode of apprehension but his own, and therefore he can entertain no doubt as to the correctness of his notions. Having no suspicion of the existence of any notions beyond those he himself possesses, he necessarily thinks his are the only ones possible. The adversaries of Columbus saw, according to the ideas they entertained, that his undertaking was chimerical: they regarded their own notions as the only correct and conceivable ones, and were free from all doubt.

Who could have imagined the possibility of traveling by land without the employment of draught animals, before the invention of the steam-engine. It is impossible for the savage to doubt the correctness of his notions, as there are no others by means of which he might set them right. Having no suspicion of any others he is obliged to see all things in the light of his own understanding alone, and to transfer to everything he meets the impressions already existing in his mind.

Hence it is plain that the savage must regard all objects, as far as concerns their inner nature, as being endowed with those inner properties only, of which he has formed to himself some notion. Now what are these? Not the inner properties of the objects themselves, for of these he knows nothing. The only properties of this kind with which he is acquainted are those of his own mind. But how far does his knowledge of his own mind extend? He knows nothing of its psychological laws, nothing of its essential character, so to speak: he is acquainted only with accidental properties: his transient impressions and emotions, his momentary humors, and his aimless pursuits. These notions he necessarily transfers to exterior things, as their inner properties; for on the one hand he has no idea of the real inner nature of the objects, and on the other he is acquainted with no inner properties whatever, save those of his own mind. He must necessarily consider all nature, and not alone animals but even inanimate things, as living, thinking and willing, even as he himself lives and thinks and wills: that is to say, he takes an *anthropopathic* view of nature. We shall in the sequel find abundant proofs of this position, for it is a fact that has been time and again recognized, admitted and proclaimed. We have attempted only to assign its psychological grounds. It is the utter ignorance of the savage that directly leads him to view nature in this light, for we must bear in mind that for a man in the earliest stage of development, viz., a savage, everything, however trifling, is as novel, as unknown and as wonderful as a rattle is for the infant. As the man gradually advances toward civilization, this mode of viewing nature is given up, yet far more slowly and more grudgingly than we might be disposed to expect. For it is with this habit as with every system of ideas. If those who went before have adopted it, and their whole life long cherished it, and held it for true, it becomes implanted in their children into whom it was inculcated during their early years, and in them becomes a truth, resting on the authority of their ancestors. The belief grows stronger day by day, and finally becomes indisputable dogma which is not to be set aside even though it be in conflict with facts. Thus the anthropopathic view of objects endures even where men's acquaintance with nature is no longer in the lowest grade.

If we transfer ourselves into the narrow field within which the savage observes nature we shall find this result so inevitable, that any other result will appear to be impossible. Though I have said that we ourselves, no less than the savage, must regard man and nature as homogeneous, still we must admit this difference between our point of view and his: by investigating nature we have come to recognize man as a product of nature. We say, man is as the rest of the universe. But the savage knows neither the nature of other things, nor yet his own; as regards the latter, he is acquainted merely with his varying impressions and desires. Therefore he can only say: Nature is like Man, i.e., has the same petty, individual and altogether subjective impressions and desires. When Schopenhauer says, The Universe is Will, for man in the last analysis is Will, and at the same time merely a part of the Universe, he asserts that the common being of all men is also the being of the Universe. On the contrary, the savage says: The individual being which pertains

to one man, to me alone, to this particular savage creature, with all its petty, personal propensities, is the being of the universe. The distinction is broad. Schopenhauer says: The Substance of man is the being of the Universe. The savage says: Accidental properties (which differ for different individuals) are the being of the Universe.

Thus the intellectual status of the undeveloped man, the savage, necessitates a mode of contemplating nature very different from ours. He ascribes to all things essentially the same properties he possesses himself: he cannot avoid considering all things as being endowed with the same inner properties he discerns in himself, for he has no critical power of discriminating. For him, therefore, every object lives, wills, is kindly or unfriendly disposed; and thus everything inspires him with fear and awe, "so that he scarce ventures to touch any object: even the very plant which affords him nourishment he plucks from the ground with propitiatory rites."[*] In America and in Northern Asia all things are supposed to be possessed of souls—works of nature and of human art alike. These souls they consider as something dwelling in the object and inseparable from it, which can benefit or harm mankind."[†] The more these objects resemble man in their general appearance the more readily will they be regarded as actually human. First, therefore, would come the anthropopathic apprehension of animals, then of all the phenomena of motion—the sea, rivers, clouds, the wind, lightning, fire (which some savages regard as an animal,[‡] as did the ancient Egyptians, according to Herodotus);[§] plants would follow next, and then finally rocks and mountains. This subject we will consider in detail farther on. "Natural objects pass for mighty spirits. Thus, for instance,

* A. Bastian, Beiträge zur vergleichenden Psychol. S. 10.
† Meiners, Hennepin, Lafiteau, Steller, etc.
‡ Wuttke, I. 59.
§ Herod. III. 16.

among the Australians the rock-crystal is esteemed sacred; the savage attributes special good qualities to stones of bright colors. The bloodstone is supposed by the Indians of South America to be possessed of beneficent qualities. Even the products of human skill, such as watches, telescopes and the like, are inhabited by spirits. An intelligent Bechuana said, on first seeing the sea and a ship, 'This surely is no created thing, it has sprung into existence of itself, and was not made by man.'"* This anthropopathic view of nature is the very essence of poetry: and hence it is that the view which the savage takes of nature appears to us so poetical, though he himself is so accustomed to this mode of apprehension that he is utterly unconscious of the poetry.

As man can ascribe to objects only those notions and passions which he has himself, the savage attributes to his fetich precisely his own wild, unbridled desires in all their natural unconstraint, and magnified to the highest degree, his hunger and thirst, his love and hate, his anger and his rage. Still the object continues to be, in the mind of the savage, that which it is in its external form. It is not as if the savage in his anthropopathic apprehension represented to himself a self-existent superior Power, a self-existent soul, which merely assumed for a time the external shape of the fetich. No: the stone remains a stone, the river a river. The water itself, in its proper form and with its native properties is invested with anthropopathic characteristics. This is very different from a symbolic conception. Here the object as it presents itself in all its external manifestations, is identical with the anthropopathic conception. When a thing comes to be regarded as in some way the symbol of another and a different thing, then the mind has made a very considerable step in advance.

The object has therefore a greater value for the savage than for us, both as a commodity and as something anthropopathically regarded as possessing life. "One of the followers of the envoy Isbrand exhibited before a crowd of Ostiaks who wanted to sell fish to the embassy, a Nürnberg watch, fashioned in the shape of a bear. The Ostiaks viewed the article with great interest. But their joy and astonishment were increased when the watch began to go, and the bear began to strike the hours, and his head and eyes to be in motion. The Ostiaks bestowed on the watch the same honor they paid to their principal Saitan, and even gave it precedence over all their gods. They wanted to purchase it. 'If we had such a Saitan,' said they, 'we would clothe him with ermine and black sable.'"* "Father Hennepin, during his stay among the savages, had in his possession a compass and a large kettle in the form of a lion. Whenever he made the needle vibrate, the chief with whom he lodged assured all that were present that the white men are spirits and capable of doing extraordinary things. The savages had such fear of the kettle that they never would touch it, without having first wrapped it up in beaver pelts. If women happened to be present, the kettle had to be made fast to a tree. Hennepin offered the kettle to several chiefs as a present; but none of them would accept the gift, for it was thought that an evil spirit dwelt within it, who would slay the new owner."†

The same anthropopathic apprehension of things is to be observed in children. The little girl who in perfect seriousness regards her doll as a playmate, who strips and clothes it, feeds and chastises it, puts it to bed and hushes it to sleep, calls it by a personal name, etc., never imagines that all her care is expended on a

---

* Waitz, I. 457.

* Isbrand, Voyage de Moscou a la Chine, in Vol. VIII. of Voyages au Nord, p. 38.
† Hennepin, in the Voyages au Nord, IX. 332, 333. Cf. Constant, La Religion, I. p. 254

lifeless thing, she does not make any such reflections as these: This is all merely an illusion that I indulge on purpose; a play that I engage in, but with the distinct understanding that it is only play. She has no thought that the doll is a lifeless thing: for her it is possessed of a human life, which is bestowed upon it by the child herself. The boy's hobby-horse is for him no mere symbol. This anthropopathic view of lifeless objects is to be seen among people everywhere. Especially do we observe it in the way people vent their rage in blows and abuse bestowed on inanimate things that have occasioned them some hurt. In the heat of passion, reflection and judgment are silenced, and then momentarily the mental range is contracted as it is in the savage permanently. An Indian who in his cups had received a burn expressed his indignation against the fire in the most abusive language, and then *mingens eum extinxit.**

3. *The Causal Connection of Objects.*

We now proceed to study the operations of the mind in its profoundest depths. The act of consciousness implies the perception of the principle of causality. We *perceive* objects by referring to outward phenomena, as to a *cause*, certain modifications produced in our nerves of sense, and we connect objects themselves with one another by the same causal nexus. In the latter process the mind arranges the objects in a certain orderly series, so that one shall appear as accounting for another, or explaining it. Thus one object would be cause, and another, effect. The mind invariably perceives this relation in all the objects which come under its cognizance; and even in the most trivial conversation the several conceptions are explanatory, illustrative, confirmatory of one another, and

so inter-related causally. It is a law of the mind therefore that it shall regard its objects as standing to one another in the relation of cause and effect.

Now it is clear that the mind can discern this relation only between those objects of which it has consciousness. But the more restricted its range, the fewer will be its objects. A mind which possesses but few objects will be liable, owing to this very paucity of objects, to assume immediate causal relations where they do not exist: in the absence of the true cause, it will take for cause some object within its own range. This is the real ground of all error, and any erroneous apprehension whatsoever might serve as an example of what we here assert. In the course of this chapter we shall fall in with many examples, but we cite only the following in this place: The true cause of the so-called rain of blood in Southwestern Europe was long unknown. People accordingly connected this unknown and unexplained phenomenon with a conception which they already had, and said, "It rains blood," and so believed, until it was discovered that the color of the rain was owing to the presence in it of particles of sand from the Sahara.* "When the keel of Portuguese ships first furrowed the waters of the Atlantic, the savages viewed with consternation the white-winged ships driven along their coasts by a power to them incomprehensible." They had never seen a ship. What could this apparition be which was borne along as it were on wings? One only conception had they which could aid them in accounting for the motion, and they said, "They are cloud-birds come down on earth." † It is just because the mind can assign only those objects as causes, which it already possesses, that you hear men uttering so much nonsense when they discourse about things quite

---

* Adair, Hist. Amer. Indians. Lond. 1775, p. 117.

* M. Perty, Die Natur, p. 283.
† Bastian, S. Salvador, S. 269.

without their sphere, but which they try to explain by conceptions belonging within it. In short, this is the origin of all that science which would account for phenomena by an *à priori* theory, as when the motions of the planets were explained on the theories of Ptolemy or of Tycho Brahe. The common people from their stand-point could account for the occurrence of erratic blocks only on the theory that they were fragments of giants' clubs broken in battle, or that they were dropped by giantesses out of their aprons.† The explanations given by Playfair and Venetz lie quite beyond the popular apprehension.

So much therefore is clear, that the undeveloped understanding will of necessity connect in causal relation a number of objects which do not in reality stand to each other in the relation of cause and effect, reason and consequence. The question for such a mind is, to which of the objects of its consciousness it shall specially attribute causality.

The cause, as being the producer, will naturally be regarded as strong, powerful, effective, and so gifted with peculiar attributes: for only that which is possessed of power can produce. Whatever therefore we regard as preëminent in its kind, whatever appears to us as specially notable, peculiar or important, we rate as the cause of other phenomena which we regard as its effects, if only the circumstances of time and space permit such a view. This perception of causality the mind must get from objects within its own range. Now, as we have already seen, the narrower the mind's range, the higher will be its estimate of objects. Therefore, the more restricted the field of consciousness, the more inconsiderable will the objects be which pass for causes —inconsiderable in our view, though of high moment in that of the savage. If we now recall to our minds what has been already observed with regard to the savage's anthropopathic apprehension of objects, the following example will be readily understood, while at the same time it will serve to illustrate the preceding remarks. An iron anchor must be regarded by the savage as a very strange and peculiar object, for he could never mold such an instrument, nor does he see the like every day. "A Kaffir broke a piece off the anchor of a stranded vessel, and soon after died. Ever after the Kaffirs regarded the anchor as something divine, and did it honor by saluting it as they passed by, with a view to propitiate its wrath." * An anchor is, in the eyes of the savage, something so remarkable and so strange, and he is so utterly ignorant of the use it serves, that there was a concourse from all sides to see it, and all were filled with admiration. Their interest was as great as that of an astronomer when he discovers a new planet. That any man should have the hardihood to break off a piece of this singular object was no less matter of astonishment for the Kaffirs than the anchor itself. Well, the man died suddenly. What caused his death? They could find no natural cause : but there was the anchor, and this man had broken off a piece of it. Here were facts which spoke for themselves. So the anchor, the injury done to it, and the death of the Kaffir were without more ado ranged in the order of cause and effect, and the anchor was advanced in the estimation of the savages. The anchor had been injured and outraged and would have its revenge : here we have a specimen of anthropopathic apprehension of an inanimate thing. It slew the impious wretch : here we have an object that appears to be of some importance viewed as the cause of something else, viz. : the death of the transgressor. Henceforth that anchor is a dread and mighty Thing ; so they greet it as they pass, to keep it in a good humor.

---

* Grimm, Deutsche Mythologie, I. Aufl. S. 306–7.

* Alberti, die Kaffern, S. 72 ; Lichtenstein, Reise, I. 412.

We find in this example four factors. First, the consideration of this strange object as something altogether peculiar, singular and important, simply *because* it is strange. Second, the anthropopathic apprehension of this object as something that lives, feels and wills.[*] Third, the establishment of the relation of cause and effect between this object and other things. Fourth, the apprehension of it as something mighty, which is therefore to be treated with reverence, to the end it may be friendly; or, in other words, as something which, in virtue of the inner nature attributed to it, becomes an object of veneration. We are now in a position to understand what is meant by a fetich. When an object is viewed in the fourfold manner above set forth, it is then a fetich, and fetiches are therefore objects in which these four factors are united.[†] The objects here are all sensible objects.

We have now empirically demonstrated that these are the necessary consequences of the savage's intellectual status, viz. : an over-estimate of inconsiderable objects, an anthropopathic apprehension of objects, an erroneous perception of causal relations, and the veneration of objects supposed to be causes. So the fetichistic mode of apprehending things flows quite naturally and inevitably from natural and empiric grounds. Granted only a contracted and undeveloped intelligence, and you have fetichism as the inevitable result. The mental status of the savage finds its natural expression in fetichism : fetichism is its System of the Universe, its philosophy, its religion ; and hence fetichism, as being such System, Philosophy and Religion, finds its explanation when we have gained anything like correct notions of the savage intellect.

We will cite a few more examples to show how fetichism is made up of our four factors. " A negro of some distinction, an acquaintance of Römer's, was about to take refuge in a Danish fort, with his family and his valuables, to escape from the attack of a merciless enemy. On quitting his hut in the morning he stumbled on a stone with such violence that he suffered considerable pain. This accident caused him to regard the stone as a fetich. He at once picked it up, and never more parted with it, as through it he succeeded in escaping from the dangers which had threatened him."[*] "An American savage chose the crucifix and a little image of the Virgin that had come into his possession, for his Manitus. He never parted with them, after he had found, as he believed, that they protected him sundry times against the arrows of his enemy."[†] "As the Yakuts first saw a camel during an outbreak of the small-pox they pronounced that animal to be a hostile deity who had brought the disease among them.[‡]

The taboo of the South Sea Islanders is by many writers supposed to resemble the fetich, and even to be identical with it. Still the two things do not appear to be identical, if we accept the account which Gerland gives of the taboo. (Waitz's Anthropologie, Band. 5.) Waitz gives an excellent

---

* Bastian, S. Salvador, S. 227.
† The first writer to employ the word fetich was De Brosses in his work " Du culte des dieux Fétiches," which appeared in 1760 anonymously, and without the name of the place of publication. As to the origin of the word he says: " . . . certain deities, whom Europeans call Fetiches, a word formed by our traders in Senegal, out of the Portuguese term Fetisso, *i.e.* enchanted, divine, oracular. It is from the Latin root fatum, fanum, fari." Winterbottom, in his "Account of the Native Africans in the Neighborhood of Sierra Leone," derives the word from the Port. Faticeira, witch, or Faticaria, witchcraft. The Negroes borrowed not only this but also another word, gree-gree, from the Portuguese. According to Bastian (S. Salv. S. 95) the universal name in West-Africa for a fetich is Enquizi. Another name is Mokisso, or Juju (*Ibid.* 254, 81); also Wong (Waitz, II. 183); among several Amer. tribes, Manitu.

* L. F. Römer's Nachrichten von der Küste Guinea. Kopenhagen, 1769, S. 63, 64.
† Charlevoix, Journal historique d'un Voyage de l'Amérique septentrionale. Paris 1774, p. 387.
‡ Wuttke, Gesch. d. H. I. 72.

·definition of the fetich : A fetich, says he, is an object of religious veneration, wherein the material thing and the spirit within it are regarded as one, the two being inseparable. As we have already said, the fetich is any object whatsoever, viewed anthropopathically, or regarded as endowed with human characteristics. Taboo, on the other hand, according to Gerland, is an object which receives religious veneration because it is the temporary abode of a spirit or of a Deity. "We know," says he, "the meaning of the taboo, the religious ban of Polynesia, and the question arises whether the same custom prevails also in Micronesia ? It does; but though in the latter islands the belief in taboo is as universal as in Polynesia, still the taboo has not there so extensive a range of objects. (Gulick, Micronesia, in the *Nautical Magazine*, 1862, 417.)" The taboo attaches to meat and drink ; and the notables of the Ladrones will not eat eels : the isolated inhabitants of Ponapi, the Marshall and the Gilbert Islands, etc., will not eat the flesh of this or that animal ; the common people on those islands must not eat the kava, and on the island of Kusaie they must abstain from the cocoanut, etc.; several trees also are taboo, *i.e.* forbidden (Mertens, Recueil des Actes de la Séance, publ. de l'Acad. imp. Scientifique de St. Petersburg, 29 déc. 1829, 177); the rain-conjurers must not eat the blooms of the pandanus. Also places, temples and persons, *v.g.* great princes, are taboo for the commonalty. Whoever would go a fishing must be continent for the space of twenty-four hours. In conversing with women certain words were taboo : and hus we might go on rehearsing an interminable list of such prohibitions. The word taboo also is used in Micronesia (Kotzebue, Entdeckungsreise, II. 59; Hale, Ethnographie, in his Tarawa vocabulary, s. v. Tabu ; Pickering, Memoir, s. v. Tabu, etc.), and in the isle of Morileu the word *pennant* is employed in the same sense. Thus a tree, or a locality, etc., would be *pennant* (Mertens, 134). Nor were the ceremonies employed in Micronesia to lift the taboo less imposing than those in use in Polynesia. Thus Cheyne describes a very protracted festival which he saw observed on the isle of Eap, the chief ceremony consisting of prayers addressed by the priests to the Sea-god, to induce him to quit a vessel that was taboo, and return to his native element. (Cheyne, " A Description of Islands," etc., 157 seq.) From this narrative we learn what is the meaning of Taboo. The god enters a thing and thus withdraws it from common use. The chieftains being of divine origin, their person and property are taboo to the commonalty, as is also whatever they are pleased to declare taboo.* This view of the taboo is very probably the correct one ; yet we must not suppose that in Polynesia and in Micronesia the taboo is not also regarded in another light, and apprehended as a fetich. On the isle of Nukunono Fakaafo worship used to be paid to the Tui Tokelau, or Lord of Tokelau ; and this was a stone wrapped up in matting and held so sacred that only the king durst view it, and even he only once a year, when it assumed a fresh suit of matting. (Turner, " Nineteen years in Polynesia," 527.) This stone idol, which was ten feet in height, stood in front of the temple, and was, at the time when Hale saw it, ten feet in circumference, owing to its thick wrappages of matting. (Hale, 158; Turner, 527.) It was the Tui Tokelau that caused disease, so whoever was attacked would have a new mat wrapped about the god, to propitiate his wrath by means of this rather costly offering.† As this stone was considered so sacred, it was natural for the people to identify it with the deity. Whatever offerings they made to the stone, were made to the god : whatever petitions they had to address to the god, were addressed to the stone. Which is here the god,

* Waitz, Anthrop. Bd. V. Abtheil. 2 ; Gerland, S. 147.

† Waitz, Anthrop. V. Abth. 2, S. 195.

the stone or the deity? The better class of the islanders, those best instructed by the priests as to their religious belief, would perhaps regard the stone as only the habitation of the god, and consider the latter as distinct from the stone. But would the more ignorant sort make such a distinction? If not, the taboo was for them a fetich.

Here we have an observation to make. The so-called Religion of Nature, i.e., the religion of the savage, has two aspects, which must be sharply defined and kept separate if we would have clear conceptions on the subject. Under one aspect sensible objects are worshiped; under the other, worship is paid to spirits. It is not asserted that either of these branches of Natural Religion arose prior to the other: they are both perfectly natural phenomena, springing inevitably out of an undeveloped state of intellect. The worship of sensible objects is founded on the relation subsisting betwen the mind and such objects: the worship of spirits is founded on the relation between the mind and the souls of the departed. These two systems run parallel to one another, and here and there unite their currents to form a single stream. This subject I propose to consider in another place. At present we have to do only with the worship of sensible objects, i.e., with fetichism, and we purposely omit the consideration of the other branch of Natural Religion. We do not assert that the only religion of the Negro, for instance, is fetich-worship, though we study the Negro here only in so far as he is a fetichist. Just as in the higher grades of intelligence one individual will surpass another in mental development, so too will one savage excel another, and attain a higher grade of religious development, however contemptible his very highest grade may appear to be in our estimation. Thus the savage has already made one step in advance, as soon as he perceives that the object of his worship is not a being possessed of anthropopathic properties, that it cannot of itself perform those acts which he formerly attributed to it, or when he recognizes as *inhabiting* the object, a spirit separate from the material thing. Fetichism becomes thus elevated by means of the belief in spirits, and the fetich is advanced to the higher grade of the taboo. As the South Sea Islanders are raised above the very lowest stage of intelligence, the taboo is better adapted to them than the fetich. For the same reason, intelligent Negroes regard their fetich as taboo. Halleur gives the following as a specimen of Negro intelligence : " I wished to make a Negro understand the folly of offering to the fetich—a tree, for instance—food, drink, lemons, and palm-oil, as he himself must know that the tree made no use of them. ' Oh,' said the Negro, ' it is not the tree that is the fetich. The fetich is a spirit, and invisible, who lives in the tree. To be sure, he does not consume the material food, but he enjoys its spiritual portion, and rejects the material, which we see.' " [*]
Here is the fetichist become a tabooist, supposing that the description of tabooism heretofore given is correct.

CHAPTER IV.

FETICHISM AS A RELIGION.

1. *The Belief in Fetiches.*

ACCIDENTAL coincidence determines whether or no an object shall be regarded as a fetich, as we have seen in the foregoing examples. The savage, however, cannot entertain a doubt as to the power of his fetich, for he has had evidence of this, and with his own eyes has seen how such and such an object brought about such and such an event : how the anchor slew the man, how the camel brought the smallpox. It is only after he has found

----

[*] Halleur, S. 39.

his fetich powerless in a considerable number of instances that he is undeceived. But it is a very difficult thing for him, owing to the obtuseness of his intellect, to suspect that the true cause may lie outside of his fetich. Even if his faith is shaken, it is impaired only so far as regards one special fetich, while it remains firm as to all others. He bases his judgment on the most superficial grounds. Thus, a plague broke out in Molembo soon after the death of a Portuguese; the two things were arranged in the order of cause and effect, and as long as the memory of the plague lasted the people of Molembo were very careful that no European should die within the limits of their country.[*] When cases occur, wherein the savage, according to his way of judging, directly sees the action of his fetich, his belief is confirmed. "In a clearing in the woods," writes Bastian, "I observed on the side of the road a fetich-house, and wished to examine it more closely, but my black carriers could not be induced to carry me to the spot. As I alighted, to go on foot, they almost resorted to violence to withhold me from executing my purpose, and I read in their eyes, when I came back to them, that they regarded me as certain to die very soon. . . . Weary, I reached Quimolenzo toward night, when suddenly my sight failed me, and I felt myself sinking powerless to the ground. A violent fever raged in all my veins, and this continued through the entire night. The following day it was the same, and I was so weak I could not rise from the bed. My people exchanged knowing looks, as much as to say: The spell of the fetich is working; and they were quite sure they would have to bury me before night." [†] "In front of the American's house (in Shemba-Shemba, West Africa) there was a crowd of people assembled, in the midst of whom a fetich-priest was running up and down with loud cries, jerking

hither and thither a wooden puppet decked with tatters of every color, and beating it with a switch on the face and shoulders. I learned that a knife had been stolen from one of the Negroes, and he had applied for its recovery to this priest, who was the owner of a fetich in high repute as a detective of thieves. The unfortunate god appeared to me to have paid dearly for his reputation, seeing that he got a merciless whipping to begin with, to teach him the necessity of attending seriously to his business. The priest having wrought himself up to a high state of prophetic clairvoyance, announced to the spectators, in a tone of perfect assurance, that the next morning they would find the knife alongside the fetich, which he posted in front of the factory. In the morning there lay the knife, for the merchant, disliking a continuance of these ceremonies for an entire week, chose rather to confirm the infallibility of the fetich, than to expose his property to the risk of being plundered, if the people continued to flock around his establishment." [*]

The savage has never a doubt as to the efficiency of his fetich, and his faith is all the stronger because ever since he was a child he has seen every one entertaining the same belief, and so his mental fiber is, so to speak, saturated with it. Every one knows the force of early impressions; how the great mass of mankind never emancipate themselves from their influence, and how it is only after many a painful inward conflict that a man escapes from their dominion. But this absolute faith of the savage in the power of his fetich, disposes him to view it with dread; this dread in turn serves to exaggerate the apparent efficiency of the fetich and so to confirm more and more the man's belief in its power. "When a Negro has anything stolen from him he entreats some great fetich to discover the thief. The pomp of ceremony attending the consultation of the fetich oftentimes

---

* Bastian, S. Salv. S. 104.
† *Ibid.* S. 50, 53.

* Bastian, S. 61.

so fills the thief with consternation that he surrenders the property." * The thief being also convinced that the fetich has power to hurt him, gives back what he has stolen, or confesses the theft. "The rich frequently employ a Kassa potion to make their domestics confess their thefts." † In Great Bassam they merely lay a fetich-stick upon the body of the accused. If he is guilty, he is sure to confess; his fears will extort the admission.‡ Beneath the threshold of the king of Dahomey's palace is set a charm which causes his wives internal pains whenever they are guilty of misconduct, and so they often find themselves constrained to make a voluntary confession of their guilt.§ To this category of beliefs belongs the so-called *Judgment by the Lizard*, which is in vogue among the inhabitants of Senegal. A smith beats upon a lizard with his hammer; the fear of incurring the evil fortune which is supposed to follow from this performance is expected to bring the thief to a confession, and it usually does.‖ Many similar delusions are recorded in books of travel. But especially noteworthy is the Obeah of the West India Islands, particularly Jamaica, a baneful superstition for the eradication of which the most stringent enactments of law have proved insufficient. Its influence upon the minds of the Negroes is so great that at one period it notably increased mortality among them; at another, stirred them up to mutiny, by impressing them with a belief that they were invulnerable.¶

Thus fetiches serve for ordeals, which among the Negroes usually consist of poisonous potions, or of emetics and drastic agents.* The fetich has power to punish the guilty: the innocent he will not hurt. As the fetich must come into bodily contact with the subject of the ordeal, the latter is required to drink fetich-water,† or water in which the bark of the wild manioc, or some other substance has been steeped. According to Halleur, "fetich-water is prepared from the bark of the tree odum. It is supposed that, as this tree is always a fetich, when a person accused of crime drinks the water in which its bark has been steeped, the fetich enters into him and thus discovers either his guilt or his innocence. If the accused party vomits, it is a sign that the fetich has discovered his innocence, and is quitting his body: but if the fetich-water is retained, then the fetich has discovered his guilt, and will not quit him until he has been punished." ‡ "The accused may, under certain conditions, send a slave to take the questionable potion in his stead. Many, however, of their own accord apply to have the fetich-water administered to them, to be purified by the ordeal." § Very often the accused has the magical potion given to him without his knowledge, so that the savage lives in constant fear lest any one should employ this redoubtable form of fetich against him. The power of this spell may be estimated from the fact that the trading-post of Bimbia, between the Calabar and the Cameroons, and opposite to Fernando Po, which was at one time a missionary station, has become almost entirely depopulated, owing to the employment of the fetich-water during many years by the notables of the place on every slight occasion. ‖ Nor is the ordeal by fire or that by water unknown in Africa. In Mada-

---

* Proyart's Geschichte von Loango, Kakongo u. s. w. Aus dem Französischen. Leipzig, 1777, I. 167.
† Bastian, S. Salv. 61.
‡ Hecquard, Reise an die Küste und in das Innere von Westafrika. Leipzig, 1854, S. 48.
§ Forbes, Dahomey and the Dahomans. Paris, 1851, p. 55.
‖ Boillat, Esquisses sénégaliques. Paris, 1853, p. 102.
¶ Bryan Edwards, Hist. des Colon. Anglaises, p. 266; Waitz, II. 190.

* Winterbottom, p. 172; Köler, Einige Notizen über Bonny. Göttingen, 1848, S. 127 seqq.; Cavazzi, Histor. Beschr. der Königreiche Congo, etc., 1694, 94, 108 seqq.; Proyart, S. 141.
† Bastian, San Salvador, S. 84, 306. cf. S. 203.
‡ Halleur, S. 34.
§ Bastian, S. Salvador, S. 85.
‖ Ibid. S. 306.

gascar the accused person has to undergo the ordeal of red-hot iron.[*] Among the Malay Lapongs the glowing iron is applied to the tongue of the accused,[†] while among the Antaymours the ordeal requires him to swim across a stream inhabited by caymans.

If a fetich which first owed its distinction to accident, displays its power again on another occasion, it may easily transcend the rank of being one man's fetich and be adopted by an entire family, or even by a larger aggregation. For in America, Africa, and Siberia,[‡] each individual has his separate fetich; each family, and even each tribe, their respective fetiches. The fetich of a tribe is honored with more pious and constant devotion than the inferior fetiches, as having for a longer period shown his efficiency.[§] Thus there are Grand Fetiches, which are regarded with profound awe, and which, in the shape of mountains, trees, rocks, etc., protect the chiefs or the territory of the tribe.[‖] The fate of mankind is by the American Indian thought to depend upon the belt of wampum. The chief of the Muemba is Chiti Muculo, "the Great Stick, the Great Tree," The center of religious and political life among the Wanikas is the Muansa, in whose honor the tribe celebrate roaring festivals, and which is to be approached only by the chief. This holy of holies is a wooden instrument which emits a peculiar buzzing sound.[*] The Grand Fetiches have their mysterious influence intensified, by being, as far as possible, withheld from the gaze of the profane. "The Grand Fetich," says Bastian, speaking of one in Congo, "dwells in the midst of the bush, where no man sees him, or can see him. When he dies, the fetich-priests carefully collect his bones, in order to reanimate them; and supply them with nourishment, so that the Fetich may anew gain flesh and blood."[†]

Nor do the Negroes regard the Christian religion as anything but the worship of a Grand Fetich. Thus San Salvador (called by the natives Congo dia Gunga—the tones of the bells—on account of the great number of its churches and convents) was widely known and feared throughout South Africa, as the home of a powerful fetich.[‡] The negro is so rooted in this mode of apprehending things, that he is ever returning to it, or rather, he never quite gives it up. "It has ever been the study of the missionaries to check the abominable practices of fetichism, and with the aid of the civil power they have succeeded in abolishing the worst features of this Moloch worship, though not in substituting any other religion in its place, and the Negroes have advanced only so far toward conversion as to use salt." [§] The only reason however that induced them to go even thus far was, that they thought salt would cause their children to grow fat. But they soon refused salt again, first because the ceremony cost too dearly, and secondly, because, as they

---

[*] Leguével de Lacombe, Voy. à Madagascar (1823-30). Paris, 1840, I. 233.
[†] Waitz, Anthrop. V. Abth. I. S. 149. *Cf.* II. 523.
[‡] Charlevoix, p. 344, 346. Lettres édif. Nouv. Ed. VI. 174. De Bry, Descriptio auriferi Regni Guineæ in Part VI. of India Orientalis, VI. 21. Oldendorp, Geschichte der Mission der evangelischen Brüder auf den caraibischen Inseln St. Thomas, St. Croix, und St. Jean, herausgegeben von J. J. Bossonet. Barby, 1777, I. 320 ff. Des Marchais, Voyage en Guinée, Isles voisines et à Cayenne en 1725-27 par le P. Labat. Amsterdam, 1731, II. 131, 152. Georgi, Beschreibung, S. 384.
[§] J. B. Müller, Mœurs et Usages des Ostiakes, in the Recueil des Voyages au Nord. Amst. 1731, Tom. viii, 413, 414: "Les Ostiakes ont beaucoup plus de vénération pour leurs idoles publiques, qu'ils ne dépouillent pas et n'abandonnent pas comme les autres; mais ils les estiment au contraire, et les révèrent comme étant d'ancienne date et d'une autorité reçue et avérée.
[‖] De Bry, vi. 21. Des Marchais, I. 297: "Les rois et les païs en ont d'autres qu'ils appellent les grands Fétiches, qui conservent le prince ou le païs : telle est quelquefois une grande montagne, un gros rocher, un grand arbree," etc.

[*] Waitz, Anthrop. III. 190; II. 422, 424.
[†] Bastian, S. Salv. S. 82.
[‡] Bastian, S. Salv. S. 173.
[§] *Ibid.* S. 96.

said, the elephant grows fat though he uses no salt. "In Congo, where the ruins of churches have served to perpetuate the memory of the Christian religion, the natives account for their ignorance of Christianity by saying that the Desu of the Portuguese is too mighty a fetich for common folk, and so was reserved for the king alone, while his subjects had more comfort in worshiping fetiches of the time of Chitome, Guardian of the Sacred Fire.* A Christian priest is for them only a fetich priest practicing peculiar fetich ceremonies. "When the slaves, torn from family and friends, were put on shipboard in chains, to drag out a miserable existence over sea beneath a foreign sky, and in foreign lands, the pious bishop of Loanda sat on the stone seat at the end of the wharf and assured them, with his apostolical benediction, of a future replete with joys unutterable, with which the brief period of their probation here below durst not be compared. The poor Negroes understood nothing of the ceremony but this, that the white man's fetich now deprived them of their last hope of ever again seeing their native place. Their names however were registered in the account presented to the Pope by the society de propaganda fide, to be by him duly authenticated and submitted to St. Peter."†

As all the savage's thoughts and the whole conduct of his life are governed by fetichism, he regards his fetiches as absolutely necessary to his existence. Any rude shock given to this system of ideas and usage, causes emotions in the mind of the savage, as painful as those aroused in men of other beliefs by the act of sacrilege, and the hatred of the blacks for the whites is largely owing to the disregard of this fact on the part of the latter, and to the daily and hourly insults which they thus offer to the black man's religion. Bastian wished to take a bath in a river near a certain Negro village. As he was

on his way he was met by the Mafooka, the oldest man in the place, accompanied by the entire population. "On inquiring what he wanted, I found that he desired me not to go any nearer to the water; and he promised that my name should live for all time in the songs of that valley, if I would yield to his most humble entreaty. I scarce thought it worth while to pay any attention to the absurd request, which I judged to have been made simply with a view to deprive me of a pleasure I had long coveted, so I told the gabbing old man to betake him to a warmer region than his own country, and ordered my carriers to go on. This however it was impossible for them to do, for screaming children in swarms grasped them by the legs, and threw themselves upon the ground before them, to block up the way. In heart-rending tones of wailing the Mafooka, in the mean while, struck up a song of woe, the effect of which was increased to the most painful degree by the chorus, in which all joined. The expression of blank despair was visible on every countenance. Poor people! Small wonder it was so: for the next day, on further inquiry, I learned that had I looked upon the stream, its sources would have been dried up forever, and their only supply of water cut off! Rather than bring upon my soul the guilt of so great a catastrophe, I preferred to return unrefreshed..... As we came near another village, my carriers halted, and the interpreter said my coming must be announced beforehand. I therefore dispatched him to make the announcement. On his return he informed me that the usages of that country did not permit any one to pass through the village in a hanging-mat. To avoid delay, I submitted to the regulation: but when he insisted on my going through the same formalities at the next village I ordered the bearers to move on. They hesitated, and only resumed the journey after repeated commands. Scarce had we reached the first hut, when with wild cries the entire popu-

* Bast. S. 96.
† Ibid. S. 98.

lation, armed with spears, sticks and muskets, surrounded my mat-palanquin and began to belabor the carriers. In the mean time I had distributed among my coolies the guns I had with me for presents, and, alighting at the moment of the attack, we soon had an unobstructed passage. I passed through the villages thereafter without difficulty, and so I saved much time which else had been wasted in the observance of ancient customs. Wherever I observed that this disregard for ceremony gave very deep offense, I distributed a few gifts among the seniors to appease them."*

Thus the savage is the abject slave of customs which to us appear ridiculous; and so little doubt has the Negro as to the truth of his fetichistic religion, that many of them ascribe the contempt of Europeans for the fetiches to the natural stupidity of the white man.† Every Negro, even the sternest autocrats and despots, bow in reverence before the fetich. "Every year the Duke and Duchess of Sundi were required to wage a symbolic contest with the chief fetich priest, by the sacred tree in Gimbo Amburi; they were always worsted, and obliged to acknowledge the fetich's power." ‡ Even if the Negroes do now and then admit the absurdity of their faith and worship, still they cling to them because tradition vouches for them and they themselves know of nothing better.§

2. *The Range of Fetich Influence.*

The efficiency of the fetich is, for the savage, beyond all question, and there is no limit assignable for its influence. I do not mean to say that each individual fetich possesses this unlimited power, but that there is nothing which is not subject to one fetich or another. The question for the savage is what kind of objects

may be employed as fetiches to meet various contingencies. Not to speak of the daily discovery of fetich power in new objects, there are sundry things which have long been known as *fetich* for certain defined purposes, and which, as such, are received by all. Now a fetich may be either friendly or hostile toward me. First, he shows himself friendly toward me when he confers a benefit, or when he preserves me from evil. The Cabinda Negroes always carry their little idols (Manipancha) about with them; commune with them in a state of high nervous excitement; counsel with them as to the future; obtain from them news about home and family, and have firm faith in the revelations which they suppose they receive from their fetiches.* Some American Indians carry similar figures, carefully wrapped up, in their medicine-bags. On solemn occasions they are taken out and treated with great reverence.† In short, no action of any moment is commenced, whether the chase, or fishing, or war, without first consulting the fetiches as to its ultimate success and as to the best mode of commencing it.‡ As in the ordeal, the fetich here appears as a Being that knows hidden things: in the ordeal, things past, here things to come. This is the original of the Oracles. On the Gold Coast the most renowned Oracle is at Mankassim.§ But the fetiches confer other benefits, besides revealing the past and the future. They bring "luck;" and for this purpose they are carried on fishing and hunting expeditions and when the tribe goes to war. There are fetiches for river fish and for sea fish; for favoring winds; for a cheap market; for health; for clear sight, etc.‖

---

* Bastian, 60, 108.
† Livingstone, Missionary Travs. (Germ. Trans.). Leipzig, 1858, II. 83.
‡ Bastian, 204.
§ Bosmann, III. 281.

* Bastian, S. 81; Tams, Die portug. Besitzungen in S. W. Afrika. Hamb. 1845, S. 89.
† Schoolcraft, Information, etc., V. 169.
‡ Cf. Meiners, Allg. Krit. Gesch. d. R. Bd. I, S. 176.
§ Cruickshank, Eighteen years on Gold Coast (1834), p. 227.
‖ Bastian, S. Salv. S. 80; Des Marchais, II. 130 seqq., 152 seqq.; Bosmann, 179 ff.;

" The usual form of a fetich specially intended for those on a journey is a ball of red cloth, within which the fetich priest encloses some powerful medicine, generally the extract of some plant (milongo). Further, the Negro suspends all about his person cords with most complicated knots, roots, bullets, and in a word any object that strikes his fancy. The Bushman who acted as my guide in Shemba-Shemba had an image three feet long dangling from his belt, which he never would think of removing. In fact, the heavier the load with which you burden a Negro, the greater the number of fetiches he in turn will add, to make things even." [*] The ordinary fetich is generally a very unpretentious object—often a couple of leaves from a tree.[†] " The poorer Negroes of the interior are often quite content if they only have a cord to tie around the calf of the leg. Frequently this cord is of matebbe, which, like plumes in the hair, gives invulnerability. The Kroo Negroes almost universally wear this cord around the shank, but more loosely than the Caraibs. The Catholic missionaries were for a while much elated with the thought that they had rooted out this particular form of fetichism, by substituting for the common cord one twisted out of palm-leaves blessed on Palm Sunday."[‡] Among the Kaffirs the warriors are rendered invulnerable by means of a black cross on their foreheads and black stripes on the cheeks, both painted by the Inyanga, or fetich-priest. This contrivance makes the warrior invisible, while it deprives the enemy of his sight and fills him with terror.[§] The Negro's faith in his fetich which renders him invulnerable and disables

his enemy's arm is so strong, that he will court danger, suffer arrows to be shot at him, and allow his arms and legs to be hewn off.[*]

But yet some discretion is to be used in the choice of the material which constitutes the fetich, and the savage will very naturally suffer his choice to be determined by the value of the object he selects. The natives of Siberia prefer metallic fetiches to all others. these being, as they suppose, by reason of their great age, possessed of a longer experience and a higher wisdom than are possessed by other materials less durable by nature.[†]

In warding off evil the fetich does but exhibit the other side of his beneficent disposition. There are fetiches against thunder; to extract thorns that have penetrated into the feet; against wild beasts; to save one from missing his path, etc.[‡] By being employed against disease, the fetich becomes medicinal, and thus also the fetich-priest is at the same time necessarily a medicine-man, or physician.[§] " When on Fernando Po contagious diseases break out among the children the skin of a snake is fastened to a pole in the middle of the market-place, and thither mothers bring their infants, to touch this fetich. In the village of Issapoo the renewal of this snake-skin in the Reossa (market-place) is the occasion of an annual festival, and it is first touched by the infants born during the preceding year." [||] The savage, being ignorant of the real cause of disease, attributes it directly to the action of a hostile fetich, and always judges death to

Proyart, I. 167 ; Oldendorp, I. 324; Georgi, S. 384; Voy. au Nord. VIII. 410–414 ; Charlevoix, p. 340, 348 ; Lettres édifiantes, Nouv. Ed. VI. 174 seqq.
* Bastian, S. 80.
† Halleur, 19. Cf. Waitz, II. S. 186.
‡ Bastian, S. 79.
§ Döhne. Zulu-Kafir Dictionary. Cape T. 1857, p. 303.

* Proyart, p. 192; Bowdich, p. 364 seqq.; Köler, S. 127.
† Voyages au Nord. VIII. 414. " Ils ont beaucoup de confiance en elles, surtout quand elles sont d'airain, cela leur donnaut, à ce qu'ils imaginent, une sorte d'immortalité, parce qu'elles ont resisté à la corruption du temps immémorial, et qu'elles ont acquis, pendant tant d'années, beaucoup de lumières et d'expérience.
‡ Bastian, 80.
§ Ibid. 81, 138.
|| Bastian, 318, 319.

be brought about by witchcraft.[*] Against such a power naught can avail, save counter charms, to be obtained by the priest or magician from their more potent fetiches. It is true, the Mandigoes employ many wholesome medicinal agents—herbs, potions, infusions—but yet they generally make only external applications of them.[†] As a lock of hair, or a few drops of blood, may be so enchanted as to throw a spell upon the person from whom they were taken, the Kaffirs, in order to avoid the suspicion of such practices, are always very careful to restore such articles—vermin included—to the owner, so that he may secretly bury them out of sight, or destroy them. [‡] "In case of sickness they call in a male or female conjurer; and of these there is one specially qualified to deal with each special class of diseases. The conjurer undertakes to blow counter to the evil wind sent from a distance by some enemy: if, however, he is unsuccessful in this, nor yet can prevail with the aid of music, then he gives up his patient to the wicked dæmon." [§] "When a Negro falls sick," says Halleur, who describes the scene more particularly, "his relatives apply to the fetich-priest. After he has got their offering of rum and cowries (for without these gifts the holy man is quite inaccessible) he inquires of his fetich, who it is that has bewitched the sick man: for they believe that disease is caused only by witchcraft. The priest next fashions out of clay an image of the conjurer named by the fetich and carries it into the forest." This same course is followed by the medicine-men among the American Indians. They stab the image with knives, or shoot arrows into it, where-

by the witchcraft is turned against the conjurer himself. It frequently happens that he who is the bewitched actually regards himself as held by a spell, and soon dies of profound melancholy.[*] "But," continues Halleur, "if the spell is obstinate, and refuses to give way, then the rum-offering and the ceremonies of disenchantment must be repeated, and the patient treated with remedies prescribed by the fetich, and prepared by the priest. This treatment is followed up till the sick man either recovers, or succumbs to the power of the over-strong spell. The corpse is borne about the entire village previous to its interment in its former home. Oftentimes the bearers, when passing the house of one they dislike, or on meeting such a one on the street, halt suddenly, pretending that the corpse refuses to go any further. The priest asks of the dead man the reason of this unwillingness to proceed, and gets for answer that the occupant of the house or the passenger in question is the conjurer that bewitched him. The man is at once arrested and held to prove his innocence, after the funeral is over. This proof is made by the administration of the fetich-water. The punishment is death, in case the suspected murderer cannot prove his innocence, or if, when proved guilty, he cannot purchase life for a considerable sum." [†] "When the draught of fetich water proves fatal to the party accused, the priests search for the seat of the enchantment in the dead body, and exhibit to the people portions of the viscera forcibly torn from their place and now unrecognizable, as *corpora delicti*, just as the medicine-men pretend to extract a splinter or a stone.[‡]

Among the Bambarras, if one of the highest caste of the Kubaris fall

---

[*] *Ibid.* 91 ; Halleur, S. 32 ; Waitz, II. 188, 503.

[†] Park, Voyage dans l'interieur de l'Afrique. Paris, an VIII. II. 27 seqq.; Cord.-Laing, Voyage dans le Timani, le Kouranko et le Soulimana (1822). Paris, 1826, p. 350.

[‡] Steedman, Wandering and Adventures in the Interior of Africa. London, 1835, I. 266.

[§] Bastian, 87.

[*] De la Potherie, Hist. de l'Amér. septentr. Paris, 1722, II. 30; Keating, Narr. of an Exped. to the Source of St. Peter's Riv. London, 1825, II. 159.

[†] Halleur, S 32 ff.; Vignon in N. Ann. des Voy. 1856, IV. 299; Waitz, II. 189.

[‡] Bastian, 85.

sick, the presumptive cause of his disorder is, that someone has, whether purposely or unawares, touched one of his wives. The offender, who must be discovered, and who is discovered by the great oracle of the Buri, is either banished or put to death.[*] It may, however, appear to the priest that the disease was due to the patient's own transgression, in having forsworn, or omitted the customary offerings.[†]

The fetich has power to heal bodily diseases; a draught of fetich-water can discover in the heart the proofs whether of guilt or of innocence; and it is therefore but natural that it should have also power to banish moral ills. During the festival of the First Fruits the men of the Creek tribe of American Indians used to take, after a prolonged fast, the war-medicine, being strong emetics and drastic agents,[‡] while the women bathed and washed themselves. All offenses, with the exception of murder, were thus blotted out.[§] It is beyond question that the idea of purification from sin attached to these ceremonies, but especially to the bath and the drinking of the "black draught" as it was called, an infusion of dried cassine-leaves. The taking of this draught was accompanied with peculiar rites; and it was intended also to "give courage and cement friendship." The Cherokees used a similar potion, "to wash their sins away," as they said.[‖] "Though the superficial observer might here suspect a reminiscence of Christian doctrine, still if we look at the matter more nearly it will scarcely appear probable that so important and mystic a rite should have had such an origin, especially as we seek in vain among these tribes for any evidence of their having been ever in contact with the Christian religion."[*]

The savage attributes to fetich influence not alone disease and death, but every phenomenon he is unable to account for, as, for instance, storms and the changes of weather. He is thus furnished with an explanation for everything; and this explanation is entirely satisfactory to him. It is plain that this fact of the savage having ever ready at hand such unquestioned "ultimate reasons" to account for everything must check the development of his mind, or, in other words, must retard his progress toward civilization. For he knows *à priori* the cause of phenomena, and the means by which they are produced: hence it never occurs to him to study their natural causes and conditions: consequently he does not recognize the natural relations between things, and fails to discover that the supposed cause is no cause at all. His mind accordingly makes no advance, but is ever under the tyranny of hallucination. And every *à priori* principle has the like tendency to check the mind's development; for here it is all one whether it is the Negro that says: this is the work of the fetich; or whether it is the Mohammedan that says: this is Allah's work. A formula explains everything for them both, and by its very explanation leaves everything unexplained.

Fetiches also ward off evil spirits. When the women in Shemba-Shemba have occasion to quit their fields for a time, they strew them with fragments of pottery, for else the malign spirits would trample down the crop.[†] The Negroes of Whida post fetich images, five or six inches in height, at either end of their fields, at the doors of their houses, in their apartments, court-yards and cattle-stalls, being fully convinced that else evil-minded spirits or men would do them

---

[*] Raffenel, Voy. dans l'Afrique occid. (1843-4). Paris, 1846, I. 318.
[†] Bosmann, II. 184.
[‡] Schoolcraft, Information resp. the History, Condition and Prospects of the Indian Tribes. Phila. 1851, V. 685.
[§] Adair, Hist. Amer. Indians. Lond. 1775, p. 105, 120; Schooler. V. 266 seq.
[‖] Memoirs of Timberlake. Lond. 1765, p. 78.

[*] Waitz, Anthr. III. 209. Similar rites among the Kaffirs, II. 414.
[†] Bastian, S. 62

injury.[*] The same custom is followed by the Polynesians of New Zealand, Hawaii, Nukahiva and other islands.[†] Burying-places, too, are protected by potsherds and little images.[‡] A low, thin hedge encircles Negro villages, at a distance of about 100 paces from the huts, and this serves to keep aloof evil spirits.[§] A line of twisted bast forms a cordon of defense round about a Boobie village in Fernando Po. Here also the natives employ mussel shells as fetiches. When the devil would come to do them harm, his feet are lacerated by the angular points of the shells.[‖] Seeing that spirits have such fear of the fetiches with what dread thieves must regard them! "Over the doorway of the Negro hut are suspended roots and cast-off rags, and often broken egg-shells, as guardian fetiches. Others employ a block of wood with the likeness of a human face cut in it, and this they plant within the doorway of the hut, or in their fields; yet most of them are contented with a rather smoothly-dressed pole, on which they set a snail's shell, as a most potent fetich." "In a village near S. Salvador I saw wooden fetiches with lofty plumes, set up as guardians in front of the houses ; in front of the main entrance to another village I saw an empty pot supported on a forked stick." "They have no locks to their doors, nor do they need them, for but rarely is there found a thief so foolhardy as to pass the fetich posted near the threshold." [¶] "The Negro avoids touching them, lest a curse should come upon him."[*] The following will show how dangerous a thing it is merely to touch a fetich. Captain Rytschkow, having entered a hut in a certain Wotiak village, observed lying on a board that was fastened to the wall something which he took to be dried grass. He approached to examine it, but scarcely had he taken it in hand when the owner of the hut and his wife, with loud cries of distress, ran to where he stood and begged him piteously not to touch their Modor, or household god. They explained to him how the most grievous misfortune would befall them if even one of the family, to say nothing of a stranger, were to touch the Modor. This Modor consisted of some sprigs of fir, which a certain aged Wotiak had alone the right to touch and to distribute among the several families.[†] But the guardian power of fetiches goes farther still : to them indeed the appeal is made, *Videant ne respublica detrimentum capiat.* They are the Protectors of the country [‡] and of its laws. "To give due sanction to a law, it is placed under the special protection of a fetich, whose duty it then is to punish violators of it, as also the one who, knowing of a violation, does not lodge a complaint against the offender." Furthermore, "when a priest administers an oath, he gives to both parties a draught of the *bitter water,* and this, laden as it is with the fetich's malediction, will slay the one who proves false."[§] The Orang-Benuas in Malacca have similar usages, and indeed they prevail throughout the entire Malay race, being practiced especially when they form alliances. They drink some liquid mixed with blood, in which a dagger or the points

---

[*] Des Marchais, II. p. 153. Ce sont pour l'ordinaire des petits marmousets de terre rouge ou noire de cinq ou six pouces de hauteur; ils les mettent à la tête et à la queue de leurs champs, aux portes de leurs maisons, dans leurs chambres, dans leurs cours, dans leurs parcs à cochons, dans leurs pouliers ; . . . ce sont pour eux des gardiens, des sauve-gardes à qui ils se croyent redevables du bien qu'ils ont, et d'être à couvert des malheurs qu'ils craignent. *Cf.* also Römer, Guinea, S. 38.
[†] Gerland, *ap.* Waitz, Anthr. V. 2, 225.
[‡] Bastian, S. Salvador, S. 107, 124.
[§] Halleur, S. 23.
[‖] Bastian, S. 316, 348.
[¶] *Cf.* Waitz, II. 422, 502.

[*] Waitz, 79, 186, 316, 78, 348. The same is related of the Loando Negroes by Proyart, I. 168, 169.
[†] Rytschkow, Tagebuch über seine Reise durch verschiedene Provinzen d. Russ. Reiches in. den Jahren, 1769–71, S. 166, 167.
[‡] Des Marchais, I. 297.
[§] Bastian, 293, 90 ; Waitz, II. 157 ; Meiners, B. I. 176.

of arrows have been dipped ; these will kill the perjurer.[*] The Burats pay special worship to a lofty rock on the shore of Lake Baikal. They who take an oath must ascend this rock, and on its summit perform the usual rites. It is the firm belief of the natives that whosoever profanes by perjury the sacred mount can never come down again, and that the mountain slays him.[†]

Among the Africans, too, as among the Malays, alliances are consecrated and confirmed by being placed under the protection of a fetich. "At the conclusion of the meal, each Macota comes and kneels before the Yaga, who puts into the mouth of each a piece of human flesh reserved from the banquet, so that by partaking in common of the viand they may be all bound together by an indissoluble fetich. In Great Bassam, after the feticeros have ascertained the portents betokened by the entrails, the heart and liver of the victim sacrificed at the forming of a new village, together with the flesh of a hen, a she-goat and a fish are baked all together in a pot, and the entire community is required to eat of the mess, under penalty of dying within the year.[‡]

The fetich, by punishing perjurers, maintains the stability of oaths and of alliances. The fidelity of the savage depends upon his fear of the fetich : and were he to lose this fear, he would be free from every obligation. When therefore he would renounce these obligations, he must deprive the fetich of all power to do him injury, and break its ban if that can be done ; or in case this is impossible, he must only disregard the obligations, and then depend upon gifts and sacrifice to appease the wrath of the offended deity. And either one or other of these two courses the savage in reality adopts. The spell of a mighty fetich may be broken by that of one mightier still; and an offended fetich may be appeased by gifts.[*] The priest undertakes to make the offering acceptable to the fetich, or to render him harmless. According to Cavazzi, the Ganga Nzi gave release from a sworn obligation, by erasing it, as it were, from the tongue, with the fruit of the palm-tree. Often, too, a fetich may be deprived of the power to hurt, by being imprisoned.[†]

The power of the fetich is great; great also is the fear which he inspires. Now, just as my fetich can do injury to other men, so may their fetiches injure me. The consequence is that I must be in a state of constant anxiety, and ever on my guard, for how can I say but that some one is possessed of a fetich hostile to me, which he may employ against me? "The savage anxiously scans a stranger, as the latter may perchance be the owner of a formidable fetich. He will be inclined to run away; or, in case he thinks himself strong enough, he will try to make away with the newcomer."[‡] In this point of view the following occurrence is characteristic. One of Bastian's suite was attacked and robbed. "I sent a force to the Elder of the nearest village ; and on his refusing to come of his own accord, they compelled him to come to me. As the attack took place within his jurisdiction, I held him accountable, and required him either to discover the robbers or himself to make reparation for the outrage. He protested his ignorance of the affair and his inability to comply with my demand. As I could not delay, I took out my note-book, to make a memorandum of the name of the place. So soon as I set pencil to paper he fell into a violent convulsive tremor, and prostrate at my feet, entreated me not to undo him with my fetich-

---

* Newbold, Account of the British Settlements in the Straits of Malacca. Lond. 1839, II. 395.
† Isbrand, Voy. au N. Tom. VIII.; Pallas, Mongol. Völker, I. 218.
‡ Bastian, S. 154.

* Bosmann, II. 54; Monrad, Gemälde v. d. Küste von Guinea (1805–9). Weimar, 1824, 37, note.
† Waitz, Anthr. II. 185.
‡ Bastian, S. 104.

book, for that he was ready to perform whatever I should require."[*]

Accordingly there are many tribes which have gained for themselves a certain degree of impunity through the terror inspired by their fetiches.[†]

"The ointment *magya sambo*, invented by Tumba Demba II., daughter of Donghi, and which was prepared from the body of an infant brayed in a mortar, made her warriors invulnerable, and so wrought on the fears of her enemies as to make them powerless."[‡]

The fortunate possessor of such a "Grand Fetich," which domineers over the fate and fortunes of others, will prize this more than all his other property. A woman held a fetich of this kind, owned by her, dearer than all her children, and refused the offer of five slaves, which was made to her for it.[§]

The hostile fetich may be concealed anywhere, and may be carried anywhere by an enemy; so that a man is never secure from danger. If the Negroes would take vengeance of any one, they get a feticero to bewitch a piece of meat or other food; and this they set in some place likely to be visited by their adversary, who will thus infallibly come by his death.[||] Accordingly the Negro, ever in dread of witchcraft, at every turn pronounces a counteracting charm. "The host must always first taste of a dish before it is passed to his guests, so as to 'extract the fetich,' and this custom is universal throughout Africa."[¶] There are also other fetiches to meet this danger. "To guard against fetich-water, the more wealthy provide themselves with cups made of rhinoceros horn, which pass here, as also in India, for sure reagents against poison. In Bimbia the natives protect themselves against poison-water by burying in some remote valley of the interior a twig with which they mystically connect the duration of their lives, hoping thus to have placed the latter beyond the power of any fetichman."[*] Nor are fetiches themselves secure against one another, and so quite naturally you will see a fetich with a number of other fetiches attached to him, for protection.[†]

3. *The Religiosity of Fetich Worshipers.*

The fetich being possessed of such powers, the bestower of so many benefits, the defense against so many ills, it will be the duty of the savage without delay to choose a fetich for his guardian. Accordingly the life of the new-born babe is immediately placed under such tutelage, and the fetich thus chosen as guardian of the infant watches over him through life. But the fetich will not care for his ward except on condition that he receives service in return. He requires of his charge submission, obedience; he exacts a vow,[‡] and imposes a command, which his protégé is expected to perform with all fidelity. So long as he is faithfully served, the fetich preserves his ward from danger and misfortune; while, on the other hand, disobedience brings down his wrath, and is surely punished: "In sundry parts of Africa the babe is tattooed on the abdomen immediately after its birth, as a sign of its consecration to some fetich."[§] "Within a few days after it is born the child is brought to the Ganga (fetich priest), who imposes on it one or more vows; and the mother takes care to accustom her child, from its earliest years, to the performance of those vows, and gives it such instruction as to their obligation as will make it easier in after life to

* *Ib.* 225.
† *Ib.* 129.
‡ *Ib.* 234.
§ Cruikshank, 241 seqq.
|| Bosmann, Guinea, S. 179.
¶ Bastian, 135.

* *Ibid.* 85, 306.
† Oldendorp, I. 324 ff.
‡ For the Amer. Indians, v. Charlevoix, 349; for the Negr., Moore, Travels into the Inland Parts of Africa, 91; for the Siberians, Georgi's Reise, 599 seqq.
§ Bastian, 77.

discharge them. In some tribes, however, this mystic union with the Mokisso is delayed until the critical period of youth, that of puberty, when, in Africa, the boy-colonies, who then begin to be visited by the ideal dreams of youth, retire into the woods, and when the Indian lad climbs his solitary tree. Important occurrences in one's life are also occasions for acknowledging the power of the fetich."[*]

Among the American Indians a youth's "life-dream" is of high importance for his successful transition from boyhood to manhood. During this dream he receives a special guardian spirit, his "medicine," which he ever after carries about with him, in the shape of some animal's skin. The youth of 14 or 15 years retires into solitude and there abstains from all food for a time, so that he may dream the better. His dream discloses to him his future destiny and his fortunes through life; and the celestial admonitions which are thus conveyed to him direct his course down to the day of his death.[†] Many curious names owe their origin to these dreams: "Hole in the Sky" was the name of an Indian whose guardian spirit appeared to him in an opening in the heavens.[‡] It is essential that this guardian spirit be seen; and the fasting and dreaming must be continued until some animal makes its appearance. After the dreamer awakes, he tracks an animal of the same species, kills it, and carefully preserves the skin, or at least that part which was specially observed in the dream, and this he always carries about with him. To lose it would earn for him the ignominious title of "Man without medicine," and bring upon him untold misfortunes in later years.[§] Families

and tribes of Indians have also their guardian fetich in the shape of some animal, as a bear, a buffalo, a hawk, an otter, etc., and the Algonquins called this fetich the Totem.[*] The whole species represented in the totem was exempt from pursuit. Its name was adopted as that of the clan, and when an individual was questioned as to his own name, he would generally, with a sort of family pride, give that of the totem. Marriage was not to to be contracted between those of the same totem, just as the Negroes of Aquapim regard two families whose fetiches bear one name as related, and so forbidden to intermarry.[†]

The vows taken in honor of the fetich are of course very simple, and have reference merely to external acts. As specimens of different vows taken in Loango, Dapper gives the following, in addition to a series of minute directions as to costume:[‡] Not to eat such or such flesh, birds, fishes; such or such herbs, fruits, etc.: or if one ate of them, to do so all alone and afterward to bury the bones. Others bound themselves never to pass over water, even were the same in small quantity, or had fallen in the shape of rain, or had come from any other source. Others again were not to cross a river in a boat with their shoes on, though they might wade or cross on the back of an animal. Some were required to wear the hair of the head unshorn, others might cut off that as well as the beard, while others still were allowed to cut off only the one or the other. Some were not permitted to eat fruits, while others were required to eat all they got, and to refuse a share to any one,

---

[*] Bastian, 254.
[†] See examples of such dreams in Kohl, Kitchi-Gami, oder Erzählungen vom oberen See. Bremen, 1859.
[‡] Schoolcraft, II. 160.
[§] Catlin, Letters and Notes on the N. A. Indians, 4th Ed. Lond. 1844; Waitz, Anthr.

III. 118; Charlevoix, p. 346; Hist. Buccaneers of America. Lond. 1741, I. 116; Lettres édifiantes, VI. 174.
[*] Waitz, Anthr. III. 119.
[†] Bas. Miss. Magazine, 1852, IV. 327.
[‡] Cf. Dupuy, Journ. of a Resid. in Ashantee. Lond. 1824, p. 239; Bosmann, II. 66; Proyart, 195; Bowdich, 362, 524; Tuckey, Narr. of Exped. to explore Riv. Zaire in 1816. Lond. 1818, 124, 223.

no matter how much they had.* The Yagas (a tribe of warlike African savages) imposed upon themselves, according to Cavazzi,† strenuous practices of abstinence, similar to those found among American Indians, with a view to render themselves the worthy champions of the sacred Quixilles; and they thought that they entered the strife in earnest only after the first captive had been put to death as an atonement for the sins of the tribe. The sanctity of the royal palace was so rigidly maintained among them, that when once a baptized infant was by its mother brought within the enclosure, the chief ordered the palace to be torn down, burnt, and leveled with the ground, for such a profanation necessitated the erection of a new one. The flesh of swine, elephants and snakes was forbidden to the Yagas, and they would no more touch it than would the Australian touch the flesh of his kobong. Unfavorable seasons were ascribed to the indignation of the gods on account of the people's sins. Thus these savages, who sucked the brains out of the heads of their living foes, and who, by public licentiousness, cannibalism and infanticide, inviolated every article of the moral code, even they had an ideal which they called Virtue.‡ When on the Gold Coast the members of a family separate from one another, and they can no longer worship in common the family fetich, then the priest destroys the latter and prepares from it a draught, to be taken by them : and so the fetich enters their bodies. At the same time certain prohibitions as to food are enjoined, the observance of which is a religious duty.§

Thus each savage has his special guardian fetich and his own peculiar vows ; thus, too, each has a religious belief peculiar to himself, and the principles governing his conduct in sundry contingencies are the reverse of those held by his neighbors. Consequently he must regard his neighbor's conduct as smacking of heresy, and his neighbor's person as a thing unclean. "The diversity of Mokissos made it necessary in the great caravanserai in the market-place of Loango that each person should bring his own cup from which to drink the palm-wine, so as not to be exposed to the danger of drinking unawares out of a heterodox cup." *

"In what manner soever the Mokisso has been selected, the whole after life of his worshiper is bound up in him. This is the source of all true contentment for the savage, and here he finds the solution of all those anxious questions which arise in his mind no less than in that of other men, who would be but ill content, however, with the very simple solution accepted by the Negro. The vow he has undertaken is for him the sum total of religion. So long as things go pleasantly for him, he is happy and contented under the guardianship of his Mokisso ; he feels strong in the assurance of divine approval ; ascribes to the divine complacency, his days of sunshine ; indeed his judgment is strictly controlled by his wishes and desires. But if unintentionally or involuntarily he breaks his vow, the whole course of providence in his regard is at once and irrevocably altered. Then misfortune overtakes him ; he is quickly overwhelmed with calamities, and his only escape lies through death and oblivion : for him there is no hope, no path leading to reconciliation and deliverance. The luckless wretch need not, in Africa at least, go far in search of death. The fiends who surround him, in the shape of fellow-men, quickly trample him to death, and with the last breath of the fetich-worshiper expires a System of the Universe, in smallest 12 mo. With the man perishes the god he himself made, and both go back into the night of Noth-

* Bastian, 253.
† *Ib.* 205 ff ; Cavazzi, Relat. histor. de l'Ethiop. occid., trad. d. l'Ital. par le P. Labat. Paris, 1732.
‡ Bastian, 205 ff. ; Cavazzi, *ubi supra.*
§ Cruikshank, 220.

* Bastian, 258.

ingness. Here, too, is shown the might of inexorable Fate. The devotee made the Mokisso what it was : but the Mokisso was bound to avenge the infraction of his commands; he annihilates his worshiper, and with him annihilates himself." *

But let us suppose that the savage observes his vow. "By studying the Negro when swelling with pride at his good fortune, we can get an insight into many other features of this kind of worship. His good Genius makes him overweening of himself, and he looks down upon his fellows with disdain; but he may attain a still more exalted degree of eminence, when by his virtues he attracts to his service still other Mokissos. With this view he assumes new vows, and enters into covenants with one Mokisso after another. His faith increases his courage and audacity, and *fortem fortuna adjuvat*. But now his rôle becomes hazardous, as it is difficult to perform the numerous vows he has taken:" † soon it will be quite impossible. · But if he omits any, he offends and enrages the slighted fetiches, and the upshot of the matter will be, that he must follow the course we have already described.

The greater the number of the fetiches to which a savage is devoted, and the greater the number of his vows, the more will his time be occupied in paying them reverence. Thus only freemen, the rich and the powerful can afford to have many fetiches or to bind themselves by many obligations. The slave must bestow all his time and attention in his master's service, and the poor are sufficiently occupied in procuring a livelihood. neither of them have leisure for anything beyond the simplest devotions. The higher, therefore, a Negro's rank, the more fetiches he will possess, the more vows he will have to observe, and the more difficult will it be for him to live without offense. Römer fell in with a Negro who owned nearly 20,000 fetiches, many of which, however, he kept merely because they had belonged to his ancestors.* "The princes of Loango receive several years' schooling in a complicated form of fetich-worship, assuming new vows for each degree of initiation; and thus only are they qualified to rank among the Eligible Princes, who alone can ascend the throne. When an adult person is to adopt a new Mokisso, the Ganga is not governed by his own private inspiration, as he is when he imposes a vow on the new-born infant; but he puts himself in sympathetic *rapport* with the postulant, and hearkens to the words spoken by the latter in an ecstasy; and these words determine his choice." † Nor is this of little importance for the postulant and his future happiness. The Ganga might impose on him a vow entirely uncongenial to his tastes and inclinations. In that case, he would soon transgress against his obligations, and incur guilt. But the adult postulant has a well-defined character (if we may so speak of a savage) and the Ganga adapts to this the new fetich and the new vow, thus securing a good understanding between the fetich and the devotee, and insuring the happiness of the latter. Furthermore, "in the fact that the Ganga, in selecting a Mokisso for the new-born infant, takes into account the character of its parents' Mokisso, and seeks to establish between the two a sort of organic connection, we see the earliest effort toward a system transcending the individual." ‡ The power of the savage increases in proportion to the number of vows he faithfully performs, and of the fetiches who give him protection and strength. "Whenever the Ruling House succeed, by means of their fetiches, in establishing a strict line of separation between themselves and the rest of the tribe, they soon assume

---

* Bastian, 254, 55.
† *Ib.* 256.

* Römer, Guinea, S. 62. ·
† Bastian, S. 257.
‡ *Ib.* 65.

the most unlimited prerogatives. A prince of the blood may then at will enslave and sell an inferior, whenever he is in want of money."[*] "In the king of Loango, as being the personification of supreme human felicity, resides the most unlimited authority over the Mokissos, which are themselves the very expression of unbounded Might. It is his will that causes the sun to shine ; by his command vegetation proceeds : a word from him were sufficient to annihilate the universe."[†] On the White Nile, as also in Benin and in Dahomey, a like opinion prevails.[‡] For this reason certain exceptionally powerful fetiches, the Sea, for instance, are reserved for those who govern. "The king of Quinsembo has his palace, or Banza, some three miles inland, on the bank of the river Quinsembo, back of a line of sandhills, and he never passes beyond that line of hills seaward, lest the sea should come within the range of his vision, and he should see it. Were he to behold the sea, the consequence would be his death, and the destruction of the kingdom, as he is forbidden by the fetich to look upon the sea. Many other kings along the coast are similarly restricted, while others will eat only the products of their native soil, and eschew all foreign articles of luxury in their attire."[§]

The savage puts fetters upon himself, in proportion to the number of vows he undertakes. Thus, the greater his power, as the owner of many fetiches, the more numerous the restrictions put upon his liberty : and so the very fact that he holds unlimited power curiously enough proves in the end his destruction. The dignity of kingship, for instance, involves the service of many fetiches and the performance of many vows.

Should the king prove unfaithful, he brings disaster upon himself and upon his kingdom. In Congo if the king's white fez fell off his head, the accident foreboded evil to the state, just as the Japanese Dairi, should he happen by a shake of the head to alter in any way the position of his royal crown, would thereby alter the heavenly course of the sun, whose representative he was. Accordingly, all watch with the eyes of Argus, to see that the ruler discharges his vows. Wo to him if he be negligent ! Then those over whom the despot once tyrannized would in turn become his tyrants. Of him may be said what Bastian affirms with regard to the entire Negro race : " No magistrate can by his prohibitions restrict him in the pursuit of his favorite enjoyments ; but he will voluntarily take upon himself the shackles of his fetich. No tyrannical despot may prescribe a code of laws to govern his conduct. He makes his home wherever he pleases, and does as he likes, provided only he does not transgress the bounds set by tradition, or depart from the customs handed down from his own ancestors. But *hic hæret aqua :* for these customs surround him like a system of intricate snares, which it is not easy to escape. The slightest offense, when proved against him in a Palaver, is sufficient ground for irrevocably adjudging himself, his family and all his goods confiscated to the king, and the latter will have no scruple in selling him as a slave to the first trader that comes that way."[*] On the ·White Nile, when the rain fails, the king is put to death.[†] Among the Banyars, too, the king, who is also the high-priest—*i.e.*, chief conjurer—is held accountable for national calamities ; yet he does not pay the penalty with his life, escaping with a sound pommeling.[‡]

---

* *Ibid.* 256.
† *Ibid.* 256 ; Proyart, 120 ; Brun-Rollet, in Bulletin de la Soc. géogr. 1852, II. 422.
‡ Palisot-Beauvais *apud* Labarthe, Voy. à la Côte de Guinée, 1803, p. 137 (German tr.).
§ Bastian, 33.

* Bastian, 64.
† Proyart; Brun-Rollet, *ubi supr.*
‡ Hecquard, Reise au die Küste und in das Innere von W. Afrika. Leipz. 1854, S. 78 ; Waitz, Anthr. II. 129.

In this slavish obedience of the savage to his fetich we may recognize an important educational element. The savage imposes duties on himself—he curbs his passions. Herein he renounces, to a very slight degree, 'tis true, his natural willfulness. His motive is no doubt selfishness. With a view to power, he lays upon himself the burden of obligations. Yet it is a selfishness that is under restraint.

4. Worship and Sacrifice.

Such being the power of the fetich, whose good-will brings prosperity, but whose wrath is fatal, the chief study of the savage must be to propitiate him, to gain his favor and to avoid his anger. Now the savage can pay to his fetich only such homage as he is wont to render to those who claim his respect and submission. He shows obedience to his fetich, by performing his vow. He resorts to flattery, prayers, gifts: in other words, he adores his fetich, and offers to him sacrifice.

A man offers prayer and sacrifice, either in order to obtain the blessings of prosperity, or in thanksgiving for benefits received. The desire of a tranquil life is the direct expression of man's natural instinct of self-preservation. This instinct remains unchanged, whatever may be his grade in point of development and whatever may be the means which he chooses for the attainment of tranquillity. All men desire εὖ πράττειν, if not in this world, at least in the world to come. Knowledge, however, varies and grows. With the advance of knowledge, the objects which in a ruder age were worshiped as conferring εὖ πράττειν are changed for others. Hence the objects of worship in the different degrees of mental development vary widely: thus we have fetiches, the stars, gods, etc.; and yet the expression of the natural desire of prosperity is ever the same, viz., prayer and sacrifice, though in outward form there may be wide diversity, according to the degree of intellectual and moral culture.

The savage pays worship to his fetiches. The Negroes testified their respect for the anchor. The Ostiaks do honor to illustrious mountains and trees by shooting an arrow at them as they pass by. The Daurians planted rough posts in the center of their huts, winding around them the intestines of animals, and the occupants of the hut never passed by the fetich without a prostration and a prayer.[*] The Circassians slay a goat at the grave of a dead kinsman, consume the flesh, hang the skin on a stake, and make it an object of worship.[†] The offerings made to the fetich are often of very trifling value, being proportioned to the wealth of the devotee. Thus the Negroes and the *early* Peruvians, as also other American natives,[‡] and the Siberians [§] seldom offer anything but potsherds, worthless rags, and worn-out boots and shoes. The Ostiaks clothe in silk their fetiches, which are made to resemble the human form, and to one side of the head they attach a bunch of hair, to the other a dish, into which they every day pour broth, which then flows down either side of the idol.[||] As a sign of their gratitude, the natives of Cabende eject from their mouths upon the fetich the first morsel of food they take at a meal, having first chewed it: and the idol is left unwashed and in this pitiable state until the meal is at an end.[¶] Many fetiches have also localities specially assigned to them, where they receive offerings, and we find fetich altars of various descriptions.

Offerings are made to the fetiches with a view to obtain benefits from them. Thus the Negroes offer to their fetiches empty jugs when they wish

* Voy. au Nord. VIII. 103.
† *Ib.* X. 447. Isbrand affirms the same as to the Burats. Voy. au Nord. VIII. 64.
‡ Acosta, Hist. natur. et mor. des Indes occidentales. Paris, 1606, p. 206, 227; Charlevoix, 348.
§ Georgi, Russ. Völk. S. 389.
|| Isbrand, Voy. au Nord. VII. 38.
¶ Bastian, 81. *Cf.* Halleur, 32.

for rain; swords or daggers when they are going to war; fish-bones when they are bound on a fishing-expedition; small shears or knives when they desire store of palm-wine.* The savage is most liberal of his homage and of his gifts when he is in straits, but often times the fetich is utterly neglected in time of prosperity.† Finally, offering is made to the fetich, in thanksgiving for benefits received, after a successful fishing-expedition or warlike foray; after a prosperous chase or harvest; after the birth of a child; after recovery from sickness, and escape from danger.‡

Animals and even human beings § are offered to the fetiches. On perilous routes and rivers the American Indians make offerings of birds or of dogs, sometimes binding the legs of the latter together, and leaving them suspended from a tree to meet their fate.‖ To such fetiches as bears or deer they offer maize; and to a maize-fetich they offer bears' flesh.¶ "In Bonny the most beautiful maiden is annually offered to Ihu-Ihu, or Yoo-Yoo**—a name denoting priest, temple, or place of sacrifice, as well as any guardian deity. Probably it here stands for the Sea, to which an offering is ever made on a fixed day. The maid chosen to be offered to the god has her every wish gratified, and whatsoever she touches becomes her property.†† The priest who performs the human sacrifices, bites a piece out of the neck of the victim, while life still remains. When captives are sacrificed, their heads are arranged in a row in front of the Yoo-Yoo house, and the remainder of the bodies are cut up, boiled in a cauldron and eaten.* The Kroos also occasionally sacrifice prisoners of war to their fetich-tree.† "They have many festivals whereon sacrifice is offered to the fetiches. Even days become fetiches for them, some being regarded as lucky, others as unlucky. In Ashantee there are but 150 or 160 lucky days in the whole year, when an enterprise of moment may be commenced with any hope of success.‡ On the Senegal Tuesday and Sunday are *dies atri*, but Friday is a still more unlucky day, and hence a certain Bambarra king had all children born to him on a Friday put to death.§

As a mark of respect for the fetiches their worshipers build houses to shelter them, temples. The Wotiaks ‖ and the Ostiaks ¶ build for this purpose miserable huts, but the Abipones** and the Negroes affect some small regard for ornament. Bastian gives the following description of an African fetich-house: "The temple was quadrangular, constructed of straw matting, the entire front being of wooden framework, with three arched doorways. Each of the two side-doorways was surmounted by a pyramid, while over the middle one rose a cupola; and the door-posts were adorned with figures in black and green. Within was a simple mound of earth, on which stood three forked sticks painted red and white in alternate stripes."††

The Yoo-Yoo house in Bonny is 40 feet in length and 30 in width. At one end stands an altar 3 feet high, and a small table with a vessel holding *tombo*, a kind of spirituous drink.

* G. Loyer, Relat. du Voy. du Royaume d'Issiny. Par. 1714, p. 248.
† Charlevoix, 347; Bosmann, 445.
‡ De Bry, VI. 20; Loyer, 248; Charlevoix, 348; Georgi, 389; Valentyn, Oud en Nieuw-oost Indien. Amsterdam, 1724, III. 10.
§ Charlevoix, 118; Georgi, 338; Valentyn, III. 10.
‖ Charlevoix, 118, 348. Cf. Waitz, II. 207.
¶ Loskiel, Gesch. der Mission der evangel. Brüder unter den Indian. in N. Amerika. Barby, 1789, S. 53.
** Holman, Voyage round the World (1827–32). Lond. 1834, I. 378.
†† J. Smith, Trade and Travels in the Gulf of Guinea. London, 1851. p. 60, 68.

* *Ibid.* p. 82.
† Waitz, Anthr. II, 197 seq.
‡ Bowdich, p. 363 seq.; Dupuy, 213 *note*.
§ Raffenel, p. 183; Mungo Park, Sec. Journey (in Bütner's translation). Nordhausen, 1821, S. 315. Cf. Waitz, II. 201.
‖ Rytschkow, Tagebuch, S. 166.
¶ Voy. au Nord. VIII. 103.
** Dobrizhofer, II. 99.
†† Bastian, 50.

There is abundance of wine and rum in glasses and flagons, and on the walls hang pictures, chiefly representing the Guana lizard. The foreigner is waited on by a priest; for in Bonny strangers have ready access to the temple, whereas elsewhere he is excluded. The priestly attendant mutters a few unintelligible words, makes a mark with moist clay between the visitor's eye-brows, and rings a bell. A glass of tombo is then handed to the stranger, and thus he is admitted to the mysteries, and initiated.* These fetich-houses are in many parts of Africa, asylums, especially for runaway slaves; † and in the medicine-huts of the American Indians even an enemy's life is safe.‡

Having done due honor to his fetich and made to him such offerings as his means allowed, the savage counts with certainty on a return. For though he stands in great awe of his fetich, still the relation between the two is not such as to make the devotee in all cases the bounden slave of the object he worships; nor is the fetich, when the worst comes, the superior of the man. The savage is too wild and passionate to submit to such absolute control: and the moral character which he attributes to his divinity is not such as to make the latter a paramount Destiny. A man's apprehension of another being cannot transcend the sum total of his actual conceptions. He cannot conceive of a being as possessed of attributes of which he has never formed any notion. Consequently the savage's fetich will be what the savage is himself. Now the savage is given to falsehood and treachery; he is usually cruel, selfish and wayward. From what he is himself he judges of human nature, and these same data make up his conception of the fetich. From a moral point of view the fetich is no better

than himself; like his worshiper, the fetich is a savage, and on occasion is to be treated as a mere savage. So, if despite prayers and gifts he refuses to grant what is asked of him, then he is to be handled roughly till he yield to force what he denies to entreaty. We have already seen how the fetich is pommeled in order to make him attend seriously to his business.* If the Ostiaks are unsuccessful in the chase or in fishing, they inflict severe chastisement on their fetiches for having led them away from the game, or for having failed to render assistance. The punishment over, they become reconciled again with the unfortunate culprits, give them a new suit of clothes and other gifts, in the hope that they will now do better. During the prevalence of an epidemic the natives of Kakongo entreated the fetiches for relief; but as the pestilence continued, they threw their fetiches into the fire.† The same was done by a Lapp who had in vain prayed to his fetich to preserve his reindeers from disease.‡

As the savage renounces fetiches which prove of no account, so he strives to get possession of those whose power is known. The fetich thus becomes an article of commerce and barter; and numerous instances might be cited of such articles being sold, exchanged, or even stolen.§ It is chiefly the priests that carry on this traffic: ‖ and both in Africa and in America the price of valuable fetiches is very high; indeed their owners are rarely willing to part with them at any price.¶

---

*J. Smith, p. 60.
† Bowdich, p. 361; Monrad, 44.
‡ McCoy, Hist. Baptist Ind. Missions. Washington, 1840, p. 195; Perrin du Lac, Reise in die beiden Louisianen (1801–3). Leipz. 1807, I. 171.

---

* The Cingalese have the same custom. Vide Knox, Histor. Relation of the I. of Ceylon. Lond. 1681, p. 83. Also the Madagascans. Flacourt, Hist. de la grande I. de Madagascar, 1658, p. 181; the Easter Islanders, Georgi, 385; the Ostiaks, Voy. au N. VIII. 413.
† Proyart, 310.
‡ Hoyström, S. 319. Cf. Waitz, Anthr. II. 185.
§ Bosmann, S. 99; Atkins, Voy. to Guinea, Brazil and the W. Indies. Lond. 1737, p. 104; Charlevoix, p. 347. Cf. Waitz, ubi supra.
‖ See following section.
¶ Cf. Waitz, III. 214.

5. Fetich Priesthoods.

Starting from small beginnings, but gaining strength as it advances, fetichism at last extends its influence over the whole life of the savage. We have soon no end of fetiches and fetich usages, the knowledge and understanding of which requires study, and can be acquired only by the initiated and those who devote their lives to this special branch of learning. The mere layman is quite inadequate to treat of so complicated a subject without making fatal errors. Only wise men are competent to expound so abstruse a science. The man who knows all the fetiches and the entire ritual, is by this very knowledge distinguished from the profane and ignorant multitude · he is an eminent and reverend personage, as being master of many recondite arts all unknown to the generality. Thus if we take into account the low intellectual status of the savage, we shall see that those possessed of this mystic science will necessarily come to be regarded as priests, magicians, medicine-men, etc., or in short fetichmen—for all these terms have that one signification. The fetichman's importance and. dignity are the natural corollary of the system to which he belongs.

The feticeros are sages. They understand the entire system, and are familiar with all the fetiches and the mode of preparing them, their respective powers and their names. In America it is the *Jongleurs* * (conjurers), in Siberia, the Shamans, † in Africa, the Gangas ‡ (different titles for fetichmen) that supply all the fetiches. That the trade in fetiches is remunerative we may judge from the fact that each Indian village has twenty or more fetichmen and women who thence get a living. In Africa, too, this trade yields a fair income.§

The fetichmen are also familiar with the ceremonies to be used in order that the fetich may be induced to exert his full power. They "know all the potent formulas for blessing the elements." * The safest course to pursue, therefore, is to have the feticeros themselves apply the fetich. Hence, the priest's influence is coextensive with that of the fetich. In assigning powerful fetiches for the cure of disease, and in applying these, he acts the part of a physician. When by his fetiches he constrains thieves, the winds, the clouds, spirits, etc., to do his bidding, he becomes a conjurer, or magician. Finally, inasmuch as he has special control over religious rites and sacrifices, and thus comes into close relations with the fetiches, he is strictly a priest. Yet at bottom all these functions are identical and are all implied in the one title of *fetichman*. The distinction, therefore, sometimes made between the fetich-priest and the conjurer is merely a relative one, as Bastian has well observed.† Hence among some inconsiderable Eskimo tribes a single priest will combine in his own person the various functions of the feticero, being at once physician, conjurer and priest, while under other conditions a division of labor takes place, determined by chance or by inclination. Thus in Negro tribes one fetichman devotes himself to the medicine-fetiches, and is a physician; another professes the art of rain-making, or some other branch of conjuring; a third is devoted chiefly to the ceremonies of religion. In North America the Jongleurs give counsel as to the manner of appeasing the fetiches or gaining their good-will, but do not offer sacrifice. This function is discharged by the chief on behalf of the tribe, and by the father on behalf of the family.‡ The same is stated as to the Tcheremissians and other Tartar tribes.§ On the other hand, in

* Charlevoix, p. 346; Lettres édif. VI. 174.
† Georgi, S. 384.
‡ Des Marchais, I. 296.
§ Waitz, II. 196, III. 213.

* Bastian, 85.
† *Ibid.*
‡ Charlevoix, Journ. Hist. d'un. Voy. de l'Am. Sept. p. 364.
§ Rytschkow, S. 92, 93.

sundry tribes of Siberians,[*] Kirghis[†] and Negroes[‡] the conjurers offer sacrifice. The Calmyks[§] and many Negro[||] tribes recognize a distinction between conjurers and priests, while in some African and American tribes[¶] the conjurers assume all the functions of priests, and *vice versa*.

Of all the feticeros, those who are priests are usually held in the highest consideration. "Among the Yagas the Gangas have precedence of the Scingilli, or Rain-makers, and it is their duty, when a warlike expedition is to set out, to paint the Grand Yaga red and white, as he awaits the inspiration of the Mokisso, and to hand him his battle-ax, after he has banqueted off the body of an infant slain in sacrifice. When victory is proclaimed the Gangas obtain the trophies of the fallen enemy. At the period of the New Moon they offer the five-fold sacrifice, when, after the sacrificial fire has been sprinkled with the blood, the whole tribe join in a boisterous feast the victims' bones being carefully preserved for magical purposes; as is also the custom among the Tohungas of New Zealand. The Gangas have also to guard from profanation the Quilumbos, into the inner recesses of which no woman is ever admitted; and to expose in the woods the new-born children, as the army, like the corps of Mamelukes, is made up only of young slaves."[**] Cavazzi, whose sojourn of 14 years in Angola and Congo gave him the best opportunities for acquiring a knowledge of Negro customs, describes a number of different classes of fetichmen with distinct functions pertaining to each class. The children of a man killed by lightning applied to the *Ganga Amaloco*, to get for themselves protection against a like visitation. The

Mutinu-a-maya (Lord of Water) divined by means of a calabash cast into a stream. The *Molonga* prognosticated the issue of disease from boiling water; and the *Neoni* from revelations conveyed to him from his idol, through the mouth of the Nzazi. If these prophecies proved false, the priest laid the blame upon his Familiar Spirit, and procured another. The *Ngodi* professed to give speech to the dumb. The *Amabundu* could shield from harm seed sown in the ground. The *Ganga Mnene* could prevent evil spirits from eating up the grain after it had been harvested. The *Ganga Embugula* could by whistling overpower his enemies. The *Npungu*, the *Cabanzo* and the *Issaen* were associated together in the work of shielding the warriors from wounds, and took one another's places whenever one of themselves happened to be wounded. The *Ngurianambua* could charm elephants into the toils; the *Abacassu*, stampeded cows; and the *Npombolo*, all kinds of wild animals. The wealthy brought their deceased relatives to the *Nganga Matombola*, who by means of his magical figures caused them to rise from the bier, to move their limbs and to walk about.[*] "On the Gold Coast the *Wongmen* differ from the priests, properly so called. The Wongmen are possessed by the fetich, Wong, and any man may become a wongman provided he has learned to dance to the sound of the drum, to chant the songs which are sung when the oracle is consulted, and to perform the ritual of the medical art. There is another class of fetichmen, the Otutu-men, who also profess the art of healing, and who attend to the Ordeals. Then there are the Gbalo, or Talkers, who summon the spirits and question them. Finally there are the Hongpatchulo, who sell charms to people that wish a curse or an enchantment to befall their enemy. Besides priests some tribes have also priestesses. In the northern Negro countries, where a

---

*Gmelin, Reise durch Sibir. i. d. Jahren, 1733-37. Gött. 1751, II. 359, 360.
† Pallas, Reisen durch versch. Provinzen d. russ. Reiches. Petersburg, 1771, I. 393, 394.
‡ Oldendorp, I. 339.
§ Pallas, I. 359.
‖ Oldendorp, I. 339.
¶ Acosta, V. c. 26, 248; Cavazzi, I. 253 seqq.
** Bastian, 95.

---

* *Cf.* Bastian, 201.

nominal Mohammedanism prevails, there is not to be found such a variety of priests and conjuring physicians. Here we find the Marabouts, who, in addition to their priestly office, practice divination and drive a trade in Gree-Grees, though among these are many who have nothing to do with such jugglery, and whose study it is to gain a name for piety and beneficence. Hence the Joloffs make a wide distinction between the true Marabouts and the Thiedos (Unbelievers, Atheists, mercenaries), who believe in nothing save their gree-grees." *

Among the Kaffirs, too, the Conjurers, Inyanga, are divided into several classes, the highest being that of the Izanuse, or "Smellers," who extract the witchcraft from the sick by sniffing; while the inferior classes embrace the cow-doctors, the farriers and the fellers of timber.†

The conjurer-doctors, or medicine-men, who are common to Africa, Asia and America, either blow their breath upon that portion of the patient's body where the fetich locates the disorder, or rather the enchantment; or they resort to suction, friction or pressure on the diseased part, until finally they drive out the spell, which makes its appearance in the shape of hair, splinters of wood, thorns, bones, snakes' teeth, and the like.‡ They prescribe for their patients formidable remedies and regulate their diet. Should the sick man die they throw the blame upon him, as not having exactly carried out their prescriptions. If they see no chance of a patient's recovery they prescribe a course of treatment which he cannot possibly follow, such as violent jumping, or dancing,

and thus they escape all responsibility for his death.* The Hottentot poison-doctors are famous. No snake can sting them, and not alone can they heal the bites of serpents by their sweat, but they can confer on others the same power.† A priest-physician in Congo had in his establishment five women to treat various diseases. His pharmacopœia, however, had but few medicaments for any complaint save for the *Mal Francez;* but abundance of magical formulæ.‡

As a matter of course, the fetich-priests are soothsayers, and the mouthpieces of the oracles. The Lappish and Siberian Shamans divine by means of a ring which they place on the head of a magical drum. They beat a certain number of taps on the instrument and then observe on which one of the figures painted on the drum-head, the ring stands. Each figure has a special significance; and as this is known only to the priests themselves, the response will be whatever they choose to make it. Teleutian, Sajanian and Abinzian soothsayers divine by means of 40 small rods thrown upon the head of a magic drum; the Tungoos from the whir of arrows shot from the bow, or from the vibrations of a tense bowstring.§ The N. American Jongleurs set fire to pulverized cedar charcoal, and divine from the direction in which the fire travels.‖

In Africa, the Npindi conjured the weather at the intersection of road-ways. "The Rain-makers have at all times, and among every people, acted an important part, and many African populations invested their princes with this dignity, which was often as

---

* Waitz, II. 199.
† *Ibid.* 412.
‡ Greenlanders, Cranz, S. 270–74; Am. Ind., Charlevoix, 264-268; Hennepin, in Voy. au N. V. 293; California Ind. Begert, 142; Natchez, Petit, Relations, etc, in Voy. au N. IX. 26; Caribs, Biet, p. 387; Gumilla, hist. de l'Orinoque Avigum, 1708, II. 185; Du Tertre, Hist. gen. des Antilles, II. 366 seq.; Brazilians, Lery, p. 242-47 *Cf. supra,* Section II.

* Charlevoix, p. 368. Des qu'ils voyent un malade tourner à la mort, ils ne manquent jamais de faire une ordonnance dont l'exécution est si difficile, qu'ils ont à coup sûr leur recours sur ce qu'elle n'a pas été exactement suivie.
† Steedman, Thompson, v. Meyer, Reise in S. Afrika (1840). Hamb. 1843, S. 158; Kretzschmar, S. Afr. Skizzen. Leipz. 1853, 167 ff. *Cf.* Waitz, III. 213.
‡ Bastian, 202.
§ Georgi, Beschreib. S. 395.
‖ Charlevoix, p. 363.

full of danger for them as was the power over the harvests for the ancient kings of Sweden. The Emperor of China devolves upon his subjects the responsibility for his lack of power in this regard, assigning as the reason their wickedness. The hair and nails are plucked from the body of the Mani of Jumba, after his death, and preserved as infallible rain-makers. The Makoko of the Anzikos wished to get for the like purpose one-half of the beard worn by the missionaries, and would even agree to undergo the ceremony of baptism as the price of so potent a charm, just as the despot of Benin agreed to pay the same price for a white wife." [*] Bastian thus describes the manner of conjuring the rain; "The sky was overcast and the thunder rolled above the mountain-tops; but when I expressed my fears of a storm, my guide assured me that I need have no apprehension, as one of the officials who accompanied me was an accomplished rain-conjurer, and he had promised that he would not permit a single drop to fall. I was fain to accept the assurance, and the more so, as I saw my Zeus Aetherius rise to his feet, shake his raven locks, extend his hand menacingly toward the clouds, and point with his finger in every direction. My carriers, who looked on devoutly, thought the ceremony was now at an end, and made off with the tipoja (mat-palanquin): but scarce had we left the tree, beneath which I had hoped to be sheltered from the rain, when the floodgates of heaven were opened, and in an instant I was drenched to the skin." [†] Rain-makers are to be found everywhere in Africa, as, for instance, among the Bushmen [‡] and the Kaffirs,[§] who at first took the missionaries to be a new kind of rain-makers.

"The wind-maker, too, is an important personage ever since the Negroes have become accustomed to use European manufactures; as any delay in the arrival of the merchant-vessels may occasion suffering to the natives. Inasmuch as they do not themselves tempt the deep, the conjurer could find no market among them for Lappish Æolus-sacks: and instead, he retires into his hut, which smokes and rocks while he is engaged inside with his redoubtable incantations, conjuring up the favoring breezes which shall conduct to their shores the fleets of the white men." [*]

Such is the power which the feticero possesses over Nature, over Spirits, men and beasts.[†] The common people have full faith in this power; and as the priest himself is no less a savage than they, his faith is the same. Should his incantations fail to produce the desired effect, he accounts for the failure by supposing that counter incantations have been at work, or that the ritual has not been strictly observed, and this explanation satisfies not alone others, but also himself. There are even at this day plenty of people in civilized Europe who tell fortunes, who practice necromancy, who profess to cure diseases by the imposition of hands and other similar means; and who are themselves no less deceived than those who employ them. The records of courts of justice and the reports of asylums for the insane are sufficient evidence of this. "The Cazembe now in highest repute regards himself as immortal by reason of his magic arts, and says that his predecessor's death was due to a want of precaution. He is possessed of such an excess of magic power that its superabundance would at once annihilate whosoever should come in contact with him; and there is accordingly a curious ceremonial to be observed, in order to avoid such consequences. This ceremonial would almost appear as though plagiarized from the animal-magnetizers. In their system it is called

* Bastian, 116, 117, 118.
† Ibid.
‡ Lichtenstein, II. 102.
§ Campbell, 2nd Journey. 230, 236, 238; Thompson, Trav. and Adv. in S. Afr. I. 180.

* Bastian, ub. supr.
† Waitz, V. 1, 178.

Dorsal Manipulation, and its purpose is to re-isolate the somnambulic subject."[*]

Undoubtedly the priests are the first to detect the imposture and to discover the impotence of their idols and of their own arts. Still, lest the people should be shocked by the publication of this discovery, the priest will keep it to himself, henceforth acting the part of a conscious deceiver, from motives of selfish interest and ambition. With this view he will surround himself with a veil of mystery, and resort to all manner of tricks and fraud.

"The only kind of historic record to be found among African tribes is the traditional narrative of important events, and this is handed down from one fetich priest to another as a secret of the craft. Accordingly, when application is made to the priests for counsel, the knowledge which they possess of the past history of the various families of the tribe, gains for them the credit of inspiration."[†] They alone are privileged to hold converse with the great dread fetich who dwells in the recesses of the forest, and to tread the floor of his home, without being torn in pieces.[‡] They are not men of the common mold their origin is enveloped in mystery. Among the Dakotas the medicine-men and medicine-women first come into the world in the shape of pinnate seeds, something like the seeds of the thistle. Then they are driven about by the winds and thus come into relations with mighty spirits, whose preternatural science and power they make their own. Next they gain entrance into the womb of a woman, and in due time are born with human bodies; though after death they return to the society of the gods. After they have four times run their career in human shape they are annihilated. They may likewise be transformed into wild beasts.[§]

They can also cause ghosts to appear on occasion, to inspire the vulgar with due respect for the fetich and for his retreat in the woods. "The village was situate on the edge of a dense forest, and on learning that in the forest there was a fetich-house, I directed my men to advance by a circuitous foot-path leading to it. They stoutly refused, saying that not one of them could come back alive: and it was only by repeated threats that I could induce them to move. But as soon as the villagers were aware of my purpose, they surrounded my mat-palanquin *en masse*, entreating me not to expose myself to destruction: and threw themselves before the feet of my carriers, to prevent their advancing—a very unnecessary thing to do, as the carriers themselves showed no disposition to go forward. However, as I longed to examine a second fetich-house, I paid no attention to their entreaties, pushed back those that stood close around my palanquin, and repeated my command to move on, with some emphasis. The whole multitude then uttered the most pitiable cries. The women tore their hair, and beat their breasts, and the seniors rolled themselves in the dust alongside the palanquin, invoking the power of heaven and earth to check my progress. I was at length obliged to yield. As we went up the ravine which skirted the forest there went up a fearful bellowing, which seemed to issue now from one quarter, again from another, and which imitated all manner of indescribable noises. The Negroes, terrified by this outburst of fetich indignation, ran in all speed from the locality, to escape from the wrath of the god· for there great Pan is not yet dead."[*] The Great Spirit of the Shekani and the Bakele dwells in the bowels of the earth. At times he comes forth, and takes up his dwelling in a great house which has been built for him, and there he utters such frightful bellowings that

* Bastian, 293.
† *Ibid*. 100.
‡ Lettres édif. IX. 95; Dobrizhofer, II. 99.
§ Waitz, II. 180, 504; V. 2, 178.

* Bastian, 193.

women and children tremble with fear.*

The priests are deeply versed in the science of ghostly apparitions. "The Spirit-seers of America might get from African professors many practical rules for the converse with Spirits, which they could readily turn into hard cash. But they must make haste, for the courts of justice at Cape Coast Castle are beginning to shed light upon the mystic cloud of secrecy which involves Negro spiritism, and have already condemned more than one unmasked fetichman as an impostor. As society assumes definite shape in the colony, the more dangerous fetich practices are more and more brought under the control of the law; and the peaceable citizens adopt the policy of favoring and strengthening the Mylah ceremonial in opposition to that of the Obeah: thus, in the words of S. Augustine, patronizing *theurgy* in order to discredit *goety*." †

Nor must we omit to take note of the ceremonies performed by the feticeros. These are usually conducted in the most fearful style of wild and boisterous frenzy. In proportion as the rational faculty is developed, a man controls more and more the external bodily signs of emotion. His power of speech has attained that degree of perfectionment, that he can readily convey to others by that means all his sensations: he uses *language*. But the lower the grade of mental development, the weaker is the power of expressing in words the sensations and emotions of the mind. Clowns and children speak by means of gesture, and their whole body seems to express their emotions. With the savage accordingly, whose language is fragmentary, the lack of verbal expression must be made up by violent gesticulation. When the King of Dahomey would do honor to a foreign guest by chanting a song of praise, he must also give proof at the same time of his saltatory skill. When Bastian was entertained by the king of Shemba-Shemba, that potentate simply kept up a movement of the feet *a tempo*, and made frequent genuflections, in performing which he would slip partly out of his seat, and give his little cap of bast a graceful toss on his poll. Several nations resort to the mimic hieroglyph language of the dance.* It need not occasion surprise, then, if the savage, when under the stress of violent emotions, finds expression less in language than in cries and shouts, wild gestures, leaping and rolling on the ground. We have already seen many examples of this.† But whence does the priest or the conjurer derive his power over the objects against which his conjuring arts are directed? This power comes from his fetiches. They must endow him with the power they themselves possess and must in his person make display of it. Accordingly the conjurer becomes transformed, and possessed of unwonted strength. He has to manifest the presence and efficiency of the Power which possesses him, and the expression which he gives to it, is the same as that by which he gives utterance to every strong and passionate emotion, viz., the wildest and most violent convulsive movements of the body. Maniacs are by savages regarded with great alarm, as being possessed by spirits.‡ It is perfectly natural, therefore, that the conjurer, when possessed by the spirit of the fetich, should become for the time being a maniac. When the priest has wrought his mind into the last degree of frenzy, he is judged then to have attained the height of his magic power, and to manifest to its full extent the dread might of the fetich. It is therefore the business of the priest to know how to arouse himself to this state of frenzy. If nature qualifies him for the task, so much the better; and for this reason the

---

* Wilson, Western Africa, etc., p. 391.
† Bastian, 101, 85.

* Bastian, 56.
† Cf. Waitz, II. 205 seq. 223.
‡ Georgi. Beschreibung, S. 376. Gmelin. IV. 105.

priests select children who are epileptics, to be trained to the priestly functions.* "The Shamans pass into the state of madness by a super-excitation of the motor system, and at the same time often become the subjects of hallucination, accompanied by complete mental alienation, owing to spiritual excitement. By careful training, children of feeble nervous constitution are educated to pass readily into this state of alienation and phantasy, and so attain in this art a degree of perfection unattainable under any other conditions. Just as jugglers perform feats of skill which fill us with astonishment, though an anatomist will show you, from the arrangement of the muscles, how such sleights are rendered possible : so the Shamans are a kind of psychical jugglers, who have in childhood been trained to perform several abnormal mental operations, which we neither can nor would imitate, or even countenance. On the contrary, we suppress all tendencies in that direction as quickly as they manifest themselves. But there may even be *normal* mental operations well-developed in the savage, which we lack; just as we lack some of his physical accomplishments, for in stance, the power of employing the toes in place of the fingers, for the purpose of weaving, grasping, etc. : a faculty possessed by the Coch-in-Chinese, Polynesians and other races." †

This faculty of psychical jugglery is enlarged by hereditary transmission. Inasmuch as epilepsy is heritable, it is not unusual for the office of Shaman to be handed down from father to son for from four to six generations, and a Shaman is esteem-ed in proportion to the antiquity of his Shaman ancestry.* The dexterity of the Shamans in performing their feats of psychical jugglery we may learn from the account given by Carver. He saw an elderly member of "the Friendly Society of the Spirit," which is an association of fetich-priests, throw at a young man who was to be elected into the society, a bean, or something that had the shape and color of a bean. "Instantly he fell motionless, as if he had been shot." He remained insensible for a considerable time, until he was brought to his senses by means of very violent friction and even blows. And even then, consciousness returned only after he had passed through a series of the most fearful convulsive fits.† The witches also, in the middle ages, fell to the ground, as though dead, when forced to anoint themselves with their witch's salve.‡ In pro-portion as the priestly office, having taken root in society, becomes a herit-able privilege, and as the nervous pre-disposition, which at an earlier period determined the selection of the candi-date, is lost under the influence of prosperity, the more difficult does it become to bring about the state of ecstasy by means of convulsive opera-tions, and then resort has to be made to sundry contrivances, viz. · deafening music, violent jumping, inhalation of narcotic vapors, the repetition of mo-notonous sounds, excessive transpira-tion, protracted abstinence from food, partial strangulation, etc. These methods are universally employed by fetich-priests, to attain their purpose. The Jongleurs of the American Conti-nent practice such contortions of body, and utter such hideous cries, that not alone the spectators are filled with consternation,§ but even women and

---

* As to the Siberians, Georgi, *ub. sup.*; Patagonians, Falkner, Descr. Patagon. Lond. 1774, p. 117 : "They who are seized with fits of the falling sickness or the Chorea Sancti Viti, are immediately selected for this employment, as chosen by the demons themselves : whom they suppose to possess them and to cause all those convulsions and distortions common in epileptic paroxysms ; Greenlanders, Cranz, S. 268, 270.

† Bastian, Die Seele u. s. w. S. IX.

* Gmelin, III. 331.

† Carver, Trav. through the Inter Parts of N. America. Lond. 1778, p. 271, 274.

‡ Bodin, de la Demonomanie des Sorciers. Paris, 1581, p. 96-99 ; Malleus Malefic. Lugd. 1669, II. 69.

§ Charlevoix, p. 361 seqq.: On les y voit entrer dans des convulsions et des enthousi-asmes, prendre des tons de voix et faire des

children at a distance are thrown into convulsions of terror.* By means of similar contortions and shouting the Shamans of Siberia and the African feticeros work themselves up into the state of ecstasy.† To expedite matters they drink tobacco-juice, or resort to exhausting vapor-baths.‡ The Shamans of Siberia drink a decoction of toadstools or the urine of those who have become narcotized by eating that plant.§ The highly excited nervous condition produced in the conjurer by his fearful bodily exercitations is so exhausting that many refuse to go through them, even on promise of a considerable reward.‖ This artificial frenzy has such a serious effect upon the body, and more particularly the eyes, that many of the Shamans become blind: a circumstance which enhances the esteem in which they are held.¶

Among the means employed for the purpose of inspiring the beholders with awe we must reckon the attire of the fetichman. And first we have the conjurer's mantle and his magic drum,—apparatus which appear to be wanting to the Shaman men and women of Kamtschatka alone of all the Shamans of Siberia. The drum is a simple sieve, a sheepskin being drawn over one rim, and the inside of the frame having a lot of jingles and little idols suspended from it. The real purpose of this instrument—viz., to deaden the senses by its noise—is very different from that assigned by the Shamans. They assert that the gods and the spirits have a liking for this fearful music, and are

attracted by it.* They therefore keep up a drumming until those beings make their appearance; i. e. until the drummer himself, by his violent exercise, has passed into the state of ecstasy. The drum is sometimes replaced by a staff hung with bells, or by some other noisy instrument.† The Dakotas, besides the drum and the clappers, employ a notched bone, with which they saw upon the edge of a tin dish: and thus they produce shrill, ear-rending sounds.‡ Isbrand gives the following description of the Shaman's leather conjuring mantle: A sort of long coat (casaque), adorned with pendent figures of iron, representing all kinds of birds, fishes, and wild beasts: arrows, saws, hammers, swords, clubs—in a word, every conceivable thing that is calculated to inspire fear.§ A mantle of this description is so heavy that a strong man can scarce lift it with one hand,‖ and when the Shaman, clothed in this garment, leaps and jumps about with all his might, there arises such a clangor that you might well imagine you had before you some fiend in chains.¶ And the remainder of his equipment is perfectly in keeping with his mantle. his headdress, the plumage of the owl and the eagle, the snake-skins and horns suspended here and there for effect, and the gloves, resembling the paws of a bear. African feticeros trick themselves out with the skins of tigers and lions. They daub their faces with white paint, and the rest of their bodies with other colors; or else they give themselves a true coat of tar and feathers. Then they suspend from their persons a number of little bells, animals' heads, wings and claws; drums, weapons, horns, herbs, roots, etc.** Thus weighted they

---

actions, qui paraissent au-dessus des forces humaines et qui inspirent aux spectateurs les plus prévenus contre leurs impostures une horreur et un saisissement, dont ils ne sont pas les maitres.
* De Lery, Hist. d'un Voy. fait en la Terre de Brésil. Genève, 1580, p. 242-47, 298.
† Georgi, Beschr. S. 320, 377, 378; Gmelin, Reisen, I. 285, 397, 398; Isbrand, in Voy. au N. VIII. 56 seqq.: Römer, 57, Bosmann, 260.
‡ Charlevoix, p. 361, 362.
§ Georgi, S. 329.
‖ Charlevoix, p. 362.
¶ Georgi, ub. sup.

* Georgi, Beschr. S. 378 and S. 13; Gmelin, II. 49.
† Georgi. S. 13, 378; Gmelin, I. 289.
‡ Schoolcraft, Illustrations, Pl. 75.
§ Isbrand, p. 56; Georgi, Beschr. S. 377; Gmelin, I. 397, 399; II. 83.
‖ Ibidem.
¶ Gmelin, I. 398.
** Ibid.

dance, howl, scream, and foam, as is related of the conjurers of Thibet: saltitant, torquentur in omnes partes, fremunt, furunt, strident, ululant, etc.* These operations they perform in the mystic gloom of some darksome hut, or in total darkness.† These conjurers often perform tricks of common jugglery. Thus they will perform a trick called " washing with fire," where they dexterously separate the fire from the ashes, suffering only the latter to touch their bodies ; or they will tread barefoot upon hot coals, pierce their bodies with arrows, or knives, etc.‡

By such artifices as these the power and influence of the feticeros, which were already secured to them in popular estimation by their intimate converse with the fetiches, are enhanced enormously. The assistance of the fetich priest is indispensable on all occasions, whether public or private, and is always invoked. Hence at Fernando Po the Chief Priest, or Botakimaon, is " a weighty man in the state." Each village has its own Buyeh-rup, who gives counsel in domestic concerns. This Buyeh is, however, a far less important personage than the Botakimaon, at whose residence the Negroes assemble in the season of the Ripe Yams to celebrate the "Custom." It is the Botakimaon who crowns the king. According to Consul Hutchison (in his interesting work, Impressions of Western Africa), "the Botakimaon, previous to the ceremony of coronation, retires into a deep cavern, and there, through the intermediary of a Rukaruko (snake-demon) consults the demon Maón. He brings back to the king the message he receives, sprinkles him with a yellow powder called tsheoko, and puts upon his head the hat his father wore. Having once ascended the throne, the use of cocco (arum acaule) and of the flesh of the wild boar and the porcupine is interdicted to him."* The priest is also a jurist, giving judgment on cases where the individual comes in conflict with the laws of the state. "The only concession made in a primitive condition of society to the common weal by the Negro (who in all other respects is absolutely independent), is this, that he accepts the ancient traditions, and acknowledges their binding force : but now, even while he is determined that these shall place the least possible restriction on his liberty, he assigns to them a weight of authority which soon removes them beyond his control. He studies to keep them as far as possible in the background ; he never meditates upon them, never strives to determine precisely what they are. The consequence is, that he is soon caught in the toils, and can extricate himself only by the aid of those who are skilled in legal technicalities, i.e., the priests. He thus is at their mercy, and becomes their slave."† In his capacity as jurist the priest administers oaths and conducts the ordeals. This latter function is in their hands an engine of boundless mischief. "As every case of death whose cause is in any way obscure, is ascribed to witchcraft, and the kindred of the deceased are obliged to avenge his death; the priests who conduct the ordeal are invested with formidable powers. The cause of death being obscure, the kinsman of the deceased has no course left, save to follow the directions given by those who are eminently fitted to be his guides. He accordingly applies to the fetichman and inquires of him what foe has done this deed. The priest ascertains dur-

---

* Cavazzi, II. 183, 196, 251. Same account given of the savage inhabitants of the isth. of Darien, California and Brazil by Wafer, Voyages où l'on trouve une description de l'isthme de Darien (Apud Dampier, Voyages, Tom. IV.) p. 176; Lery, 242, 247, 298; Begert, Nachrichten von Californien. Mannheim, 1712, S. 142, 159, 165.
† Alphab. Thibet. p. 243, 244.
‡ Gmelin. II. 87 ; III. (Vorrede) S. 7 ; III.
72

* Cf. Bastian, 318, 319. Tsheoko is a vegetable product, obtained, according to Hutchison, by collecting a creamy coat that is found on the waters at the mouth of some small rivers, evaporating the water and forming a chalky mass of the residue.
† Bastian, 167.

ing sleep or in a trance the response he is to make, and names the offender. Next the Ordeal-Water; or the body of the deceased, as the bearers halt before his hut; or the discovery of buried talismans, will put the guilt of the accused beyond question. By decree of the Palaver he is arrested, bound hand and foot, and hewed to pieces: for it is a religious duty, incumbent on every member of the community, to take part in the execution of the culprit. The tyrants of the Zulus availed themselves of this dogma, to further their political aims. On the faith of oracles which accorded with their own desires, they extinguished almost the entire aristocracy of their nation, and grew rich by confiscating the herds of the condemned." *

The priest obtains knowledge of what is to come by inspecting the entrails of victims, or by revelation from the fetich. He may, at his pleasure, predict a favorable or an unfavorable issue for an enterprise; and thus may put a stop to measures of which he disapproves. It is to him also that the fetich makes known his wishes as to what he would have done; and then the priest can forward what enterprise he will. "It is the will and command of the fetich:" such is the formula in which the priest's own desires find expression; and thus they become a law for the deluded people. This exaggeration of the fetich priestly power is specially exemplified in the family of the high-priest of Whida, and in the Chitome of Congo. The Negro of Whida worships, as his greatest fetich, the sacred serpent, of which we will speak in another place. It is death to refuse anything to the priests and priestesses of this fetich. They may carry off for their fetich whatsoever they will — cattle, men, treasure. The high-priest rules supreme, the king being only the chief of his servants.† But this absolute priestly power attains its highest development in the Chitome of Congo. He is not honored as the principal minister of the gods or fetiches: he is himself a god, a fetich. His person is incomparably more sacred than that of any king in Africa: his power greater, and his house more jealously guarded against profane intrusion. He may commit what crimes he will, but no man can so much as call him to account, far less seize his person or inflict punishment. Without his will and assent the king can undertake no business of importance, and no minister of the king can assume office. Newly-appointed governors visit, with a great retinue, the palace of the Chitome, and with all humility beg of him his gracious permission to enter on their duties. The prayer is never granted in the first instance, the Chitome obliging them to wait his pleasure until they have backed up their petition with a respectable amount of gifts. At length he comes forth out of his palace, sprinkles the suppliants with water, strews dust upon them, and orders them to lie on their backs upon the ground. He then treads several times on their bodies, to signify that they are his servants; and exacts from them an oath of implicit and prompt obedience to every command of the Chitome. The humbled governors consider themselves in luck if the high-priest gives them a brand from the sacred fire, which he keeps ever burning. Such brands he sells for the healing and prevention of disease. A portion of all the products of the field belongs to the Chitome. It is by his power that the universe is upheld — but here, too, unlimited power has its peculiar disadvantages. For since the universe is upheld only by the Chitome, and, were he to die, would undoubtedly go to destruction, therefore the Chitome must never die. Accordingly, when he falls dangerously sick, his successor forces his way into the palace, provided with a club and a halter; with the one or the other of which the Chitome is dispatched, as

---

* Bastian, 91.
† Bosmann, 458 ff.; Des Marchais, II. 144, 153.

he himself may elect. The old Chitome, having been by this act of high-handed violence put out of the way, his assassin is now Chitome, (le roi est mort: vive le roi!) and the universe is safe.* The Chitome is himself a fetich: all other fetich-priests base their authority upon the fetiches they possess, as do those of Whida, for instance, upon the Holy Serpent. Among the Kramantees a priest's successor is always that one of his sons who has the courage to take out of his dying father's mouth certain kernels, and to put them at once into his own.

Since the priests, by their conjuring arts, can do what they please, the people, when want or calamity oppresses them, attribute all their woes to the malice of their spiritual rulers. If they can but make away with the assumed cause, they believe that the effect will cease: and thus the belief in the power of the priest, which before brought him only advantage, now turns to his injury. The princes of the Kaffirs put to death all the conjurers they can lay hold of, whenever the country is visited by an obstinate and dangerous epidemic.† The Chiquites of Paraguay, having discovered that the priests do more mischief than good, exterminated them *en masse*. Still they continued in the belief that all diseases are brought on by magical arts. Lest, therefore, the people should be deprived in sickness of the assistance which used to be rendered by the conjurers the chiefs now practice the healing art, using the same forms previously used by the priests.‡ The extraordinary power wielded by the priests, makes them very bloodsuckers and tyrants, and the only remedy against their despotism is when the downtrod-

den people break their fetters, and take a fearful revenge. The arrogance of the priests of Whida led them to form a conspiracy against the king. But now the people forgot that a priest's person is sacred: the magnates of the kingdom, with one accord, rose to defend their prince, and a general and bloody persecution of the guilty priesthood was commenced.*

But the influence of the priest extends not alone to great affairs but even to the trifling concerns of private life. A man cannot take possession of a hut until it has first been exorcised of the powers of evil by the priest. For this purpose he must dwell in it for a season, purifying it by thurifications, and consecrating it to some guardian fetich.† In Congo he gives his sanction to marriage by giving to the pair two hens, to be dressed by bride and bridegroom respectively; that dressed by the bride to be eaten by the groom and *vice versa*.‡ When the wife finds herself *enceinte* she places herself and her unborn child under the protection of a fetich. "In Western Africa she makes an offering to the priest of a flagon of rum, and a certain quantity of cowries, and in return he fastens around her arm a bracelet made of the tail-feathers of a parrot." § "Between the 10th and the 12th year of their age the children are consecrated by the fetich-priest. The children to be consecrated assemble around the fetich-tree of their neighborhood, and then the priest offers to the fetich a white hen, by cutting off its head and suffering the blood to drop on the ground. He then distributes the feathers among the children, who form a circle all round, and lights a fire to prepare the hen for the fetich. The fetich gets a small portion and the remainder is taken to the house of the priest. With shouts and songs they then proceed to the

* Cavazzi, I. 254.
† Sparmann, R. nach dem Vorgebirge der guten Hoffmung im Jahre, 1772 (tr. from the Swedish). S. 198, 199. The Patagonians acted in like manner, on the outbreak of the small-pox: Falkner, p. 117; Barrere, Beschr. von Guiana, Götting. Samml. v. Reisen. II. 159.
‡ Lettr. édif. Nouv. Ed. VIII. 339-345.

* Bosmann. S. 463 seq.
† Bastian, 78.
‡ Bastian, 88. *Cf.* Loyer, p. 152.
§ Halleur, S. 29.

bathing place, where the priest washes the neophytes and marks each with a white stripe. The ceremony concludes with shouting and singing." [*] Education, such as it is, is altogether controlled by the priests. "Every year the priests assemble the boys who are entering the state of puberty, and take them into the forest. There they settle, and form an independent commonwealth, under very strict regulations, however: and every offense against the rules is sternly punished. The wound given in circumcision commonly heals in one week, yet they remain in the woods for a period of six months, cut off from all intercourse with the outside world, and in the meanwhile each receives separate instruction how to prepare his medicine-bag. Forever after each one is mystically united with the fetich who presides over his life. Even their nearest relatives are not allowed to visit the boys in this retreat; and women are threatened with the severest punishment if they be only found in the neighborhood of a forest containing such a boy-colony. When the priest declares the season of probation at an end, the boys return home, and are welcomed back with great rejoicings." [†] The children are subjected completely to the power of the priests, and the latter appear sometimes to give this power a highly mystical expression. Bastian thus recounts what he heard in Quindilu from the lips of an interpreter:

"In the country of Ambamba each person must die once, and come to life again. Accordingly when a fetich-priest shakes his calabash at a village, those men and youths whose hour has come, fall into a state of death-like torpor, from which they recover usually in the course of three days. But if there is any one that the fetich loves, him he takes into the bush and buries in the fetich-house. Oftentimes he remains buried for a long series of years. When he comes to life again, he begins to eat and drink as before, but his reason is gone, and the fetichman is obliged to train him, and instruct him in the simplest bodily movements, like a little child. At first the stick is the only instrument of education, but gradually his senses come back to him, and he begins to speak. As soon as his education is finished the priest restores him to his parents. They seldom recognize their son, but accept the express assurance of the feticero, who also reminds them of events in the past. In Ambamba a man who has not passed through the process of dying and coming to life again is held in contempt, nor is he permitted to join in the dance." [*] Bastian adds that the Batheniers of the Sheikh Al-Gebal, in Bamba, are subjected to a similar course of treatment.

Nor are adults exempt from the power of the priest. When the fetich demands the consecration of persons to his service these may be chosen, as in Loango, in the following manner: In that kingdom "annually a stated number of men, women, and children, 12 years of age, are dedicated by the chief of the Gangas to the fetich Maramba. These then keep a fast for several days in a dark hut, and are then dismissed with the admonition to observe strict silence for eight days. Torture is employed to test their resolution: but if this fails, and they refuse to open their mouths, the Ganga conducts them to the presence of the idol, and there making a crescent-shaped incision on the shoulder, requires them to swear, by the blood which flows from the wound, that they will be ever true to Maramba. He forbids them the use of certain meats, imposes upon them certain vows, and hangs around their necks, as a token of their consecration, a little case containing relics." [†] Persons thus devoted to

---

* *Ib.* 30. *Cf.* Waitz, I. 365.
† Bastian, 85.

* Bastian, 82.
† *Ib.* 86.

the fetich are, according to Halleur, inviolable : "They may do what they please, and may take what they wish : it is death to refuse them anything." The only drawback is that every year a few of them are offered in sacrifice.*

The priests are the Sages. Their science expatiates over the entire field of fetichism and gives the rules for the preparation and application of fetiches ; the formulas of incantation ; the methods of performing juggling tricks ; the doctrine of souls and spirits and the rites of worship. Finally, their science embraces a knowledge of history and of jurisprudence, as we have seen,—a difficult course of study for the dull brain of the savage, who strives dumbfounded to grasp the profound thoughts, and the lucid definitions of his Master. Thus, e.g. "the distinctions between Spirit and Soul ; their relations with the body, their pre-existence and their future existence are as nicely defined, as the functions of the three Spiritus familiares in Cornelius Agrippa." † As is ever the case when the mind is constantly occupied in the contemplation of one object, the priest, who is ever engaged with his fetich, enlarges and develops the primitive conception of the thing. He originates a multitude of new fetiches, and proposes them for the veneration of the common people, who take them up greedily. He elaborates distinctions and definitions, classifications and systems : in his hands the popular belief assumes scientific shape. It cannot be uninteresting to study minutely this dogmatic theology of the savage : but we must not expect to find here anything like logical consequence ; for the savage, even though he dogmatize, is still a savage, and consequently his most elaborate system will be simply no system. As was to be expected, the various systems of Africa and Amer-

ica differ very widely from one another. Of course also the adherents of the different schools do not reduce their controversies to a courtly war of words, as is our custom ; they prefer to demonstrate their theses by hard knocks. Such debates are not infrequent, and many a skull is cracked in the heat of argument. Thus, during Cavazzi's stay in Congo, two schools of doctors, the Macusa-Matamba and the Ngulungu-Nbazi, were continually at war, because they adhered to two different systems of medication.* Similar disputes divided the doctors of the Abipones, as also the piaches (conjurers) of the Caribs.†

The common people, of course, know nothing of fetichistic science. The notions peculiar to that science are as little comprehended by them as the nice points of dogmatic theology are understood by the masses here. Hence the very terminology of the savage *savant* is unintelligible to the savage layman. The feticeros among the Negro tribes, as also the Angekoks of the Greenlanders are said to have a language peculiar to themselves, which is entirely, or in great part, unintelligible to lay folk.‡ Even our common people do not understand the language of the learned. The Dakota priests use a peculiar language ; the words are those of the common language of their nation, but employed in a sense different from that commonly given to them. The chiefs also use this esoteric language, in order to keep the common folk out of their secrets.§ In New Zealand, Tahiti, Hawaii and

---

* Halleur, 32.
† Bastian, 83, *Aum.*

* Cf. Bastian, 202.
† Dobrizhofer, II. 84; Du Tertre, II. 386 : S'il arrive, qu' une personne invite plusieurs Boyez (pioches) et qu'ils fassent venir chacun leur dieu, c'est pire que la diablerie de Chaumont : car ces diables s'entredisputent, et se disent mille injures, et même, au dire des Sauvages, s'entrebattent si rudement, etc.
‡ Römer, S. 80 ff.; Cranz, 273; H. Egede (Bishop of Greenland), Beschr. von Grönland, S. 122. Cf. Bastian, 153.
§ Rigg's Grammar and Dict. of the Dakota lang. Washington, 1852. Cf. Waitz.

Mangareva we find also a sacred language—the priests use this language, though they now understand it only imperfectly.*

To propagate the knowledge of fetich science, the priests are "usually attended by a number of disciples, who prepare the fetiches, and who expect to succeed their masters." "Women who have long been barren, or who have lost their children, are wont to dedicate to the service of the fetich the unborn fruit of the womb, and to present to the village priest the new-born babe. He exercises it, at an early age, in those wild dances with deafening drum-accompaniment, by means of which he is accustomed to gain the requisite degree of spiritual exaltation; and in later years he instructs his pupil in the art of understanding, whilst his frame is racked with convulsions, the inspirations of the demon, and of giving fitting responses to questions proposed." † The Shamans, too, have their disciples; and Negro priests receive fees for instruction in their magical arts.‡

This priestly science, which makes its possessors men of redoubtable power, is kept a secret among themselves. It is only for the Initiated. Having thus doctrines in common, and being attached to one system, the priests constitute a society apart, a fraternity; an order, whose secrets are known only to the initiated, and whose mysterious power inspires the uninitiated with fear and terror. Such secret associations of priests are found in the organized priestly classes of Cabende and Loango.§ "To the South of Congo, we find a complete fetich-system only in Bamba. The king of Bamba, who was once the generalissimo of the kingdom of Congo, now lives in an almost inaccessible mountain district, entirely isolated from Portuguese influence, and permits no foreigner to enter his banza. Here is found one of those systems of religious mystery which exercise so fearful an influence along the western coast from Cameroons as far as the Gambia." The central object in this system is the Grand Fetich, already mentioned, who lives in the heart of the bush, perfectly inaccessible to all, who "usually conceals the mysteries of his worship in some remote cavern, but who also reserves to himself some localities lying near the highway, so as to remind terrified wayfarers of his power as often as they see the tokens of his occupancy." * In America too similar mystic fraternities are found.

New members are admitted only after a noviceship and probation of from one to ten years. When the candidate has given evidence of his fitness for promotion, by his observance of protracted fasts, by the performance of the frantic dances, by the violence of his convulsive paroxysms, and by drinking tobacco-juice, he is advanced by due degrees to full membership. Among the Caribs, the disciples of the Piaches receive full consecration as priests only after they have attained the age of 30 or 35 years.

The brethren form an alliance for mutual protection and defense, and their fidelity to one another is assured by the fact that the apostate is pursued with unrelenting hate.† The Dakota Indians have similar associations, whose mysteries consist of dances known only to the initiated.‡

The barbarous style in which these mysteries are celebrated, and instruction conveyed to the candidates, may be seen from the account which Bastian gives of the Yagas: "So soon as the death of the Yaga at Cassange became known throughout the country, the people and the Maquitas gathered around his corpse, which was

* Thomson, Story of N. Zealand. Lond. 1859, I. 80; Chamisso, 46; Moerenhout, 273; Voy. aux Îles du grand océan. Par. 1837, I. 484. Cf. Waitz, V. 2, 226 ff.
† Bastian, 85, 100.
‡ Cavazzi, II. 220, I. 294.
§ Bastian, 81.

* Ib. 82, 50.
† Vide Carver, p. 272; Charlevoix, 363; Du Tertre, II. 367 seq.; Biet, III. IV. 386, 387; Lafiteau, I. 336–344.
‡ Keating, I. 283.

seated on a high throne, arrayed in the feather-ornaments proper to a prince, and holding in its hand the Rilunga. They begged him to name his successor. Amid the din of uproarious music, the spirit of the deceased entered into the representative of the family of the Tendallas, who was lineally descended from the brother of the founder of the kingdom, and, in the ecstasy of wild inspirations, guided his hand to select the Chosen One out of the entire assembly. At once all the priests surrounded the Yaga-elect, and carried him off into the gloomy recesses of a distant forest, into which a layman could penetrate only at the cost of his life. In the mean time Magnates attended to the funeral rites of the dead Yaga, and after breaking out a tooth, which was regarded as something holy, they immured the body together with two of the favorite wives of the deceased, in a sepulchre previously drenched with the blood of a boy and a girl. The new Yaga, while receiving instructions in the fearful mysteries of the Catondos, was obliged to witness dark deeds of murder, so that his heart would not shudder at the contact of death, and was taught the poisonous and medicinal properties of herbs. At the end of one year he entered upon his office. All workmen who understand anything of the builder's art assemble to erect for him a palace. But before the work can be commenced, blood must be shed, to give firmness to the foundation-stone, and the one who is chosen to be the victim has his eyes and mouth carefully bandaged, lest a look or a cry should excite the compassion of the Yaga—for the slightest emotion of human feeling would break the spell, and bring down upon his head the wrath of his forefathers. His breast is steeled against pity; the head, as it is struck off, rolls into the stream, and the Yaga walks four times through the pool of blood which has flowed from the victim, and washes therein his feet and his whole person. He then plants his banner on the spot where his throne is to stand, and work on the palace begins. When it is completed, the new Yaga shows himself to the people, who receive him with loud cheering. On the evening of the third day the prince (Yaga) summons the magnates to his residence, and then takes place that banquet, of which we have already made mention, where by partaking in common of human flesh they are bound to one another by an inviolable fetich." *

Among the American Indians the religious mysteries of the various orders and secret associations of the priests are held in the highest veneration; but they lay most stress upon the art of conjuring spirits. Schoolcraft mentions three such associations, the Jossakeed, the Meda (Meday, Midé) and the Wabeno; the second of which is best known. "To the Meday belong individuals of different tribes and tongues: all are admitted without distinction to the assembly (of the order) provided they are acquainted with the Meday ritual.† The chief festival of the order is the Medawin, which, however, the Sioux keep in a manner slightly different from the Chippeways. The songs sung at this festival are preserved in symbolic pictures which form a secret written language. These writings can be deciphered only by the initiated, who are acquainted with the true signification of the pictures and who know the songs by heart, the symbols serving merely to suggest their general tenor. The right of membership in this association, which is granted even to young children, is conferred in a hut specially built for the purpose. On this occasion a priest makes an oration upon the goodness of the Great Spirit; then follows a procession of the members in a circle, with their medicine-bags, and the candidate receives in the face a puff of air from out of the bags. The power of the conjuring-

---

* Bastian, 150–154.
† Copway, Traditional Hist. of the Ojibway Nation. Lond. 1850, p. 168.

devil thus prostrates him as though he were dead : but another puff restores him. He then gets a medicine-bag of his own ; with it is conferred on him the power of a Meday ; and he at once puts his power to the test, touching others with the medicine-bag, which causes them to fall prostrate. When the candidate is a child he is set before each of the medicine-bags in turn, and he gets a new name in addition to his own, which he ever after bears as a member of the society." [*]

The power of these secret associations is so great that, like the Vehmgericht, their judgments and their penalties, which are ever executed with promptness and vigor, affect not alone their own members, but the people in general. They constitute an invisible police, that with its thousand eyes beholds every hidden thing, and in the face of which no man considers himself secure. The effectiveness of the police of Old Calabar, administered by the Egboords, has sometimes led European police-captains to seek admission into the lower grades ; [†] for all, even slaves, may purchase admission, though the latter can enter only the inferior grades. On the great festival of Egbo, masked men go about the streets, armed with whips, drag offenders forth from their hiding-places and inflict punishment. On that day women are not permitted to quit their houses. The power of the order is felt along the Gold Coast and the Slave Coast.[‡] The terror of the Vehmgericht of the Belli-Paaro was spread throughout the old kingdom of Quoja. Now members were adopted only every twenty-five years, to keep up the association. Those who were cited to appear before this tribunal appeared thickly veiled, for a fearful death awaited whosoever with unhallowed eyes looked on the spirits who surrounded him there. When after three years of novitiate (con-

cerning which the most direful stories were current among the common people) the new adept was for the first time suffered to quit the gloomy forest and to see the light of the sun, he made himself known to the Masters of the Society as a Brother by executing the figures of the Belli dance. He then took the brotherhood's "oath of vengeance."

We cannot determine whether, or how far, the African Purra and Semo associations are of a religious nature. Waitz gives this description of them : " Among the Mandingoes, especially those in the region of Sherbro, the Veis, the Timmanis and other tribes, the Purra association takes a very important part in the administration of justice. The Purra is a secret society, the nature of which is still obscure : so much however is known, that it is a kind of secret police, a secret tribunal, punishing theft, witchcraft and other secret misdeeds. Its ministers go masked, and surprise and seize culprits by night. Naturally this occasions grave abuses, still no man durst make any resistance. The society requires absolute obedience from its members and is made up of warriors divided into sundry classes. If any one by chance comes to a knowledge of their secrets, he is adopted a member by a terrible ceremonial, and threatened with death, should he divulge anything. Two parallel lines tattooed on the body are the insignia of membership. The Purra has also been described as a common federal tribunal having jurisdiction over different nations, and whose judgment is invoked in case of quarrels. The Purra then acts as judge or as mediator, and taking sides with one or other of the parties, decides the quarrel. The Semo among the Susus appears to resemble the Purra, and to have a similar purpose. The Semo has a sacred language peculiar to itself. Though Caillie [*] has written a long account of this associa-

---

* Schoolcraft, V. 430 seqq. ; Kohl, I. 59, 11. 71 ; Waitz, III. 215.
† Bastian, 294.
‡ Holman, I. 392.

* Caillie, Journ. d'un Voy. a Temboctou, etc. (1824-28), I. 228.

tion, still we know absolutely nothing of its true nature."* (Waitz, II. 135.)

6. Fetichism among Non-Savages.

The human mind, in its various stages of progress, must always exhibit phenomena answering to the degree of development to which it has attained. Even where a higher grade of intelligence generally prevails, still the lower grades will not be entirely excluded, for the whole community will not have reached the same degree of development, individuals differing from one another very widely in this respect. Even in civilized countries you will find those who are essentially no better than Bushmen or Negroes in point of mental culture, albeit in outward seeming they differ as widely from the savage as our world differs from that of the Bushman. The difference between the fetich-worshiper κατ ἐξοχήν and the fetich-worshiper as he is found in civilized countries is just this: the former is simply, or at least primarily, a fetichist, but the latter is primarily something different, though secondarily he is a fetichist. He would be as thorough a fetichist as the other, were it not that he is something else besides a fetichist, and so his energies cannot all tend to fetichism. Our next chapter will

---

* Winterbottom, 180 seqq.; Golberry, R. durch das W. Afr. (1803) I. 56; Laing, 88 seqq.; Forbes, Six Months in Sierra Leone (Ger. Tr.) S. 84. Cf. Cæsar, B. G. VI. 13, 14: Fere de omnibus controversiis publicis privatisque constituunt; et si quod est admissum facinus, si cædes facta; si de hereditate, de finibus controversia, iidem concernunt, præmia pœnasque constituunt.... Hi certo auni tempore in finibus Carnutum, que regio totius Galliæ media habetur, considunt in loco consecrato: huc omnes undique, qui controversias habent, conveniunt, eorumque decretis judiciisque parent. Si quis aut privatus aut publicus eorum decreto non steterit, sacrificiis interdicunt. Hæc pœna apud eos est gravissima. . . . Druides a bello abesse consueverunt, neque tributa una cum reliquis pendunt; militiæ vocationum omniumque rerum habent immunitatem. These Druids were also soothsayers, physicians, conjurers, etc. Cf. Tacitus Ann. XIV. 30; Hist. IV. 54; Germ. 7, 11; Plin. Hist. Natur. XXX. 4.

treat of the fetichism which prevailed among our heathen forefathers.

Here are a few examples. Suppose a hunter has repeatedly met with extraordinary good-luck in the chase when he wore in his hat a conspicuously beautiful feather, and that, on a few occasions when the feather was wanting, he had no success at all. He will in the future, for luck, plant such a feather in his hat. Now the hunter will have his faith in the potency of his fetich increased in proportion as his assurance of good luck, which he gets from the sight of the feather and his conviction of its efficacy, increases his confidence in himself, and so adds to his dexterity: *possunt, quia posse videntur.* Some people take an umbrella with them, *so that it may not rain.* In short we need but run over the list of our popular superstitions, in order to see how far the fetichistic apprehension of object still endures amongst us. Thus, for instance, on every page of the Appendix to Grimm's "Mythologie" we meet with fetichism displaying all its characteristic features. I select only the following instances:

Useful fetiches: "If a man finds a horseshoe, or a piece of one, he is in luck.* He who takes in a large sum of money must mix with it a quantity of chalk, and then wicked people cannot take it back. (The fetich as caretaker.†) If a man eats a raw egg on Christmas morning, he will be able to carry heavy loads. Swallows' nests and crickets bring good luck to a house. If one finds a treasure, he must not cover it over with any garment used to cover the body, or he is a dead man: he must cover it with a pocket handkerchief, or with a crust of bread. Chase a hen thrice around a table, and mix with her food fragments of wood from three corners of a table, and she will stay at home. Fetich-medicine: Rain-water will make children speak at an early age. A pulled tooth is to be driven into a

---

* Grimm, D. M. Anhang. Nr. 129.
† Ib. Nr. 5.

young tree, and covered with the bark. If the tree be cut down, the ache comes back. If you break a twig off a willow, and drive it into the aching tooth until the blood comes, and then restore the twig to its place, drawing the bark over it, the toothache goes away. The head of a mouse, bitten off from the body, or cut off with a knife of gold, assists a child in teething, when it is hung about his neck. If one is troubled with catarrh, let him drink a glass of water with a three-pronged fork. To cure debility in children: their urine is to be caught in a new pot: into this is to be put the egg of a coal-black hen bought without chaffering: the egg to be pierced with nine holes: the pot, wrapped in a linen cloth, to be buried after sunset, in an ant-hill that has been discovered without search. If any one afterward find the pot, he must not make any use of it, else he will take the complaint that was buried. Maleficent fetiches: It is unlucky to walk over *sweepings*. Fetich oracles: the grave-digger's mattock rattles when a new grave is to be dug. Charms and counter-charms: If one goes out of doors unwashed, he is easily bewitched. Never throw into the street hair that has come out in combing, or you will be always in danger from witchcraft. Old women often cut out a sod a foot long that has just been trod by their enemy: this they hang up in the chimney, and so cause their enemy to pine away. The whirlwind is caused by witches: throw a knife into the whirl and you will see them at work. Witches can produce rain and thunder: they can also raise winds to carry off linen that is bleaching, and hay that is curing in the sun. In the springtime when the cattle are first driven afield, axes, hatchets, saws and other iron implements are placed before the door of the barn; thus the cattle are guarded against witchcraft. When water is bewitched, and will not boil, place under the pot three sticks of different kinds of wood. A shirt spun by a girl of five to seven years of age is a sure protection against witchcraft. If your beast has been bewitched, go to the stable at midnight, and you will find on its back a straw: put the straw in a sack, call in the neighbors and give the sack a thrashing; the sack will then be seen to swell and the witch will utter a shriek. Our ancestors did not compare very favorably with savages: their treatment of witches was more cruel than the ferocity of any savages toward their conjurers; and the blazing fires of the Christian middle ages, lighted for the torturing of witches, were supposed to be the ministers of a Holy Spirit. Such blasphemy as this cannot be imputed to the savage. When we call to mind the rude and undeveloped state of intellect in which fetichism takes its rise, what a fearful light is thrown by these medieval phenomena upon the intellectual status of our forefathers whom it is still, in some quarters, the fashion to praise and to admire! Shall I recount the pitiable absurdities, the gossip of the dairy and of the spinning-room, which were held by judges who pored day and night over their musty folios evidence sufficient to justify them in tearing away from the bosom of their families, in torturing and putting to death with every circumstance of cruelty, weak old women, idiots and children? Need I recite the frantic harangues which called for the kindling of fires in the market-places of university-towns, and which occasioned the death of hundreds of thousands of innocent victims? As late as the year 1783 the portentous gleam of these fires was to be seen in Germany." * And who is to assure us of their final extinction; and that there are not beneath the ashes concealed fires, still living and full of danger, which may burst forth in flames afresh, carrying desolation throughout the land? For we still have mighty fetiches, and these act in Europe precisely as they do in Africa.

Plutarch relates that the Dictator

---

* Bastian, 93.

Sulla had no such faith in any god, as in a little image of Apollo which he constantly wore upon his breast. Suetonius says that Nero was Religionum usquequaque contemtor, præter unius deæ Syriæ. Hanc mox ita sprevit, ut urina contaminaret, alia superstitione captus, in qua sola pertinacissime hæsit. Siquidem icunculam puellarem, cum quasi remedium insidiarum a plebeio quodam et ignoto muneri accepisset, detecta confestim conjuratione, pro summo Numine trinisque in die sacrificiis colere perseveravit: volebatque credi monitione ejus futura prænoscere.*

The amulet differs from the fetich in this, that here the sensible object is not regarded as possessed of a power of its own (for then it would be a fetich), but only as the representative symbol of some higher power, which is the real efficient cause. The amulet therefore points back to a train of ideas which lie behind it: the fetich stands upon its own merits. Thus, for instance, in the Arab's amulet—a verse from the Koran on a strip of parchment—it is not the parchment and the ink that produce the effect he desires, but the omnipotence of Allah, of which the writing is regarded as the sensible sign. But yet the people, who wear such amulets as a protection against the powers of evil, very readily forget this distinction, confound the two things, and regard the sensible object as the efficient cause. Thus the amulet becomes a fetich. The Mohammedans of Senegambia write the potent verse on a tablet, then they wash off the inscription, and drink the water.† Thus again, so soon as the working of miracles is associated with the image of a saint, that image of necessity becomes a fetich; and will receive from its worshipers precisely the same usage, which other fetiches receive at the hands of savage devotees. In mediæval times it was no uncommon thing

for people, when a saint withheld his assistance in time of need, to renounce his service, to break his image in pieces, or to cast it into a river or a swamp.* As late as the middle of the 17th century some Portuguese sailors pronounced dire threats against St. Antony of Padua during a calm: they would have bound him hand and foot, were it not that some one came to his assistance. At length they set his image on the tip of the bowsprit and thus addressed it, kneeling: "S. Antony, be so good as to stand there ever till you give us a favorable wind, to continue our voyage."† A Spanish ship's captain fastened a little image of the Virgin to the mast, saying she should remain in that position until he got from her a favorable wind.‡ The Neapolitans once called S. Gennaro *vecchio ladrone, birbone, scelerato*, because he had not checked a stream of lava. They even cudgeled the saint.§ Some Spanish peasants, during a protracted drought, threw the Virgin into a pond, and called her witch, wench, etc.‖ When Russian peasants would do anything unbecoming in the presence of the saints' pictures, they cover the latter with cloths, to prevent their witnessing the deed.¶ A Russian peasant, who had harvested a poorer crop than his neighbor, borrowed from the latter his holy image, and mounted it on his plow, expecting thus to have better luck.** To this day Russian peasants whip saints' images; to this day images of the Virgin are put in prison by Italian peasants, precisely as the Negro does with his fetiches, when he would punish them, or keep them from harming him.††

---

* Meiners, I. 181.
† Della Valle, Voy. VII. 409; Meiners *ub. supr.*
‡ Frezier, Rel. du Voy. de la Mer du Sud, p. 248.
§ Kotzebue, Reise nach Rom. I. 327.
‖ Spanien, Wie es ist. 1797, II. 117.
¶ J. J. Straussen's Reisen, Amst. 1678, S. 84.
** Weber, Verändertes Russland, 1721, II 198.
†† Waitz, II. 185.

---

* Suet. Nero, c. 56.
† Bastian, 197; Waitz, II. 187.

CHAPTER V.

THE VARIOUS OBJECTS OF FETICH-WORSHIP.

ANYTHING may become a fetich. An intelligent Dakota once said that "there is nothing that the Indians do not worship as a God."[*] For the Negroes of the Gold Coast, *Wongs* (objects of worship) are, first, the gods dwelling betwixt heaven and earth, who beget children, die, and come to life again. These deities are divided into distinct classes, which get their names from the functions they discharge, and these names are taken from the vocabulary of Negro state-craft. But then Wong is also, 1, the sea, with all its contents; 2, rivers, lakes, fountains; 3, certain enclosed areas of land, and all termite-hills; 4, the otutu (a little heap of earth raised over a buried sacrifice) and the drums belonging to a quarter of a town; 5, certain trees; 6, certain animals—the crocodile, ape, serpent, etc., while other animals are only sacred to the Wongs; 7, images carved and blessed by the fetichman; 8, certain combinations of cords, hairs, bones, etc.[†]

1. *Stones as Fetiches.*

All Nature is endowed with life: the savage mind apprehends even stones anthropopathically. The Lapps transfer to stones the domestic relations of Father, Mother and Child: they even fancy that stones roam about at night, after the manner of the "Roving Bell."[‡] It is not only in Ovid's Metamorphoses that men are changed into stones; the natives of the Marianne Isles have a belief that the first Man was metamorphosed into a rock, which is still pointed out as an object of veneration.[§] The worship of stones is to be found in all quarters of the globe; but in Africa it prevails most among the Gallas.[*] Men swear by stones and by rocks; for instance, the Somali in Africa,[†] not to speak of other nations. The ancient Germans and Gauls, as also the Celts, who, according to Grimm, were stone-worshipers *par excellence*, did the same.[‡] Nullus Christianus ad fana aut ad petras, vel ad fontes, vel ad arbores luminaria faciat, aut vota reddere præsumat,—such is the exhortation given by S. Eloy in a sermon.[§] The church in the middle ages never tires of condemning the "votum vovere ad lapidem, vel ad quamlibet rem."[||] Offerings were made to stones by anointing them with oil, blood or wine.[¶]

The pagan inhabitants of Canaan worshiped stones in this manner.[**] De Brosses, in His work in the Bætylia shows that all the great nations of antiquity, not excepting the Greeks and Romans, worshiped stones. The inhabitants of Pharæ worshiped 30 square stones. Τούτοις σέβουσιν οἱ Φαρεῖς, writes Pausanias, ἑκάστου θεοῦ τινος ὄνομα ἐπιλέγοντες. Τὰ δὲ ἔτι παλαιότερα καὶ τοῖς πᾶσιν Ἕλλησι, τιμὰς θεῶν ἀντὶ ἀγαλμάτων εἶχον ἀργοὶ λίθοι.[††] In a higher state of intellectual development, when the notion of gods gained the ascendency, it was very easy to establish relation between some god and a stone, which previously had been worshiped on its own account. The Sacred Treasure of Jupiter at Tegea was a rough quadrangular stone. Meteoric stones were a special object of worship, being often regarded as incarnate rays of

* Waitz, III. 191.
† Bas, Missionary Magazine, 1856, II. 131; Waitz, II. 183.
‡ Requard, Voy. en Lappland, in Voy. au N. VI. p. 321.
§ Le Gobien, Hist. des Isles Mariannes. Paris, 1700, p. 197.

* Rochet d'Héricourt, Voy. dans le roy. de Choa. Par. 1841, p. 167.
† Burton, First Footsteps in E. Afr. Lond. 1856, p. 113.
‡ J. Grimm, D. M. S. 370.
§ Vita Eligii by Andoenus Rotomagensis (d. 683 or 689), pub. by Achery, Spicileg. t. v. Paris, 1661, p. 215-219; Grimm, D. M. Anh. S. XXX.
|| Grimm, D. M. Auh. S. XXXIII. XXXIV. XXXV.
¶ Meiners, Gesch. d. R. S. 150; De Brosses, Les Pierres Bætyles, 110, 123, 133, 135.
** Cf. Merx, s. v. Abgötterei, in Schenkel's Bibellexikon.
†† Pausan. VII. 22, VI. 22.

the sun.* Such ἀγάλματα διϊπετῆ (Bæty-lia, abadir) are the Stone Symbol of Diana, at Ephesus; of the Sun-God Elagabal, at Emissa, in Syria; of Mars, at Rome, and the Black Stone, the Kaaba, at Mecca.

Many savages regard stones as the children of Mother Earth,† for they have also an anthropopathic conception of the earth, and so worship her. According to Dapper, the King of Alé and his grandees used to hold council together, previous to a war, in a pit dug in the midst of the forest. The deliberations at an end, the pit was carefully filled up again, lest it should betray their secrets. The Iroquois and other Indian tribes believed themselves to be the children of Earth : they would never sit upon the bare ground, but always first covered the spot on which they sat, with a little grass, or with a branch of a tree.‡

Nam neque de cœlo cecidisse animalia
    possunt
Nec terrestria de salsis exisse lacunis :
Linquitur, ut merito maternum nomen adepta
Terra sit, e terra quoniam sunt cuncta creata.
            Lucretius de R. N. v. 793 seqq.

2. *Mountains as Fetiches.*

Mountains are for many reasons objects of fetichistic worship. At one moment their summits are veiled in clouds, the next they are radiant in the fierce blaze of the sun; out of their caverns the winds issue forth, and down their sides are poured the torrents which fall from the rain-clouds enveloping their heads. All these phenomena are regarded by the untutored mind of the savage as produced by the agency of the mountain itself, and he accordingly pictures to himself the latter as endowed with a human will, and acting from human motives. In this respect he is a poet. He does not imagine any such thing as a Spirit of the mountain, a being merely inhabiting it; no, it is the

Mountain itself, this tellurian mass that he worships. It is true, the fetichist sees in it something more than a heap of earth and rock. For him the mountain forms the clouds, and sends the storms. But why? From such motives as move men to action : now he is terribly wrathful; anon he is all smiles. So his worshipers will study to appease him, and for this purpose will make offerings to him.

The worship of mountains is found among several Siberian tribes, among Negroes and American Indians.* The Ural was worshiped by the nations dwelling around it. We must distinguish between this fetich worship and that respect paid to mountains, on the ground of their having once been the seat of a certain cultus, or the home of some god. In that case it is not the mountain but the god that is worshiped : and of this kind of veneration we do not treat here. As Jacob Grimm did not study fetichism in its psychological aspects, he doubted whether men ever could pay adoration to a mountain, and discredited all accounts which state that such a worship exists. I extract from his Deutsche Mythologie the passages which have a bearing on this subject, as so many proofs for the reality of Mountain-fetich worship.† "Many were the Sacred Mounts and Hills : but yet they do not appear to have been worshiped directly, but to have been venerated merely on account of the god who inhabited them (Wotan's and Donner's Berge). Though Agathias speaks of λόφοι and φάραγγες (hills and ravines) as being objects of worship, without any mention of any other object, we may suppose that he was an inaccurate observer, and that he failed to notice a worship of water or of fire having its sanctuary on the mountains. We might look for the worship of mountains among

---

* Bastian, Die Seele, u. s. w. S. 9.
† *Ibidem.*
‡ Tanner, Mémoires trad. pas E. de Blosseville. Paris, 1835. I. 250; Waitz, III. 184.

* The Yakutes, Sarytschew, I. 27; the Burats, Georgi, 318; Negroes, De Bry, VI. 21, Römer, 65; Peruvians, Acosta, 206; Mongolians, Isbrand, p. 111.
† Deutsche Mythol. S. 369.

the Goths, in whose language *fairguai* signifies *mountain*, if the explanation we have already * given of this word is correct. Dietmar of Merseburg gives an example of Sclavic mountain-worship (p. 237): Posita est autem hæc (civitas, i. e. Nemzi, Nimptsch) in pago Silensi, vocabulo hoc a *quodam monte*, nimis excelso et grandi, olim sibi indito: et hic *ob qualitatem suam et quantitatem*, cum execranda gentilitas ibi veneraretur, *ab incolis omnibus nimis honorabatur*. The commentators are of opinion that this mountain is the Zobtenberg."

3. *Water as a Fetich.*

Jacob Grimm gives a very full account of the worship paid to Water in the spring, the brook, the river, and the sea, and describes the religious observances of the people, as they "offered their prayers, lighted lamps, or made their sacrifices on the banks of the stream, or on the margin of the spring;" and these usages he traces from the remotest antiquity down into the Christian era.† "The pure, flowing, bubbling, evanescent water; the flaming, glowing, dying fire; the air, perceptible, not to the eye, but to the ear and to the touch; the Earth, which maintains all things and to which they all revert: these have ever been regarded by man as sacred and worshipful, and through them he has been wont to bestow a solemn consecration upon the customs, the pursuits and the events of his life. Their action upon the entire universe being steady and constant, the untutored mind pays them worship for their own sake without any reference to a deity residing in them." The anthropopathic apprehension of rivers, springs, and the sea is found among all savage nations. Many of the populations on the banks of the Niger regard its tributaries as the wives of the main stream.‡ In Acra a pitcher used to be cast into a pond which was thought to be the messenger of all the rivers in that country: the pond was then entreated to go abroad with the pitcher and purchase water of other ponds and streams: on returning home it was expected to bring sufficient water to irrigate all the fields.* The spring is regarded as the seat of all the river's life. Strangers must not come near it.† The Negro savage believes that the presence of the white traveler may enrage the River Spirit, or do him hurt, or even deprive him of life. Rivers are an object of worship not only in Africa,‡ but also in America § and in Northern Asia.‖ Whenever the Kamtchatdales sail across a dangerous whirlpool they cast into the water little pieces of wood neatly carved, and tobacco, and excuse their temerity by saying: " Be not angry with us for sailing over thee, as though we had forgotten our reverence for thee. We are not without reverence, but the Russians oblige us against our will to make this navigation." ¶ The ancient Russians worshiped the Don, the Dnieper (worshiped as the Borysthenes by the Scythians) and the Wolga—streams on which they depended for their existence. The ancient Mongolians would appear also to have been given to river-worship.** According to Agathias the Alamanni too worshiped rivers: Δένδρα τε γάρ τινα ἱλάσκονται καὶ ῥεῖθρα ποταμῶν καὶ λόφους καὶ φάραγγας, καὶ τοῖτοις ὥσπερ ὅσια δρῶντες.†† Herodotus makes a similar statement as to the Persians :

---

* Deutsche Mythol. 116.

† D. M. 326–340.

‡ Clapperton, Tageb. seiner, zweiten R. p. 414.

* Allg. Gesch. der R. IV. 180; Waitz, Anthr. II. 177.

† Laing, p. 310; Bastian, 59 f. "In 1641 Hans Ohm of Sommerpahl built a mill over the brook : and as the succeeding year proved disastrous to the crops, everybody assigned as the cause, the profanation of the sacred brook, which was indignant at having been checked in its course. So they attacked the mill, and utterly destroyed it." Grimm, D. M. 338.

‡ Cavazzi, I. 363.

§ Charlevoix, p. 348.

‖ Georgi, Reise, S. 318 ; Steller, S. 21.

¶ Steller, S. 19.

** Wuttke, I. 214. Cf. Barrow, Trav. in China. Lond. 1804, p. 509.

†† Agath. 28. 4.

Ἐς ποταμὸν δὲ οὔτε ἐνουρέουσι οὔτε ἐμπτύουσι, οὐ χεῖρας ἐναπονίζονται, οὐδὲ ἄλλον οὐδένα περιορέουσι, ἀλλὰ σέβονται ποταμοὺς μάλιστα. *

Seneca says of the Romans: Magnorum fluminum capita veneramur: subita et ex abdito vasti amnis eruptio aras habet. Coluntur aquarum calentium fontes: et stagna quædam vel opacitas vel immensa altitudo sacravit.† The honor which the Hindus pay to the Ganges does not belong to this category. The Hindu apotheosis of Nature is pantheistic, not fetichistic. "O Mother Earth, Father Air, Friend Fire, Brother Water, I now in all reverence and for the last time address my prayers to you: I am about to enter into the Supreme Brahman, for owing to the surplus of good works which I have laid up during my intercourse with you, I have attained to immaculate knowledge and have so cast aside all power of straying from the Truth."‡ We must however here remember that in the hands of the common people the amulet easily becomes a fetich.

The natives of Sumatra and of the Philippines worship the sea, as well as those of Africa. By the ancient Peruvians, before the time of the Incas, the sea was regarded as the supreme deity.§

The Kaffirs make offerings to a stream, of entrails, animals and millet, to secure immunity against disease.‖ Roman naval commanders offered sacrifice to the sea before setting sail.¶ Even in the last century Christian Greeks made offerings to rivers; and Turks regarded it as perfectly natural to throw overboard Christians and Jews, in a storm, to appease the wrath of the sea.** A tempest having broken up the first bridge of boats, Xerxes ordered three hundred lashes to be given to the Hellespont, and chains to be cast into it. Again he presented an offering on a dish of gold, and this, together with a golden goblet, he threw into the waters of the strait. Herodotus is undecided whether this was done in honor of the Sun, or to appease the offended Hellespont.*

4. Wind and Fire as Fetiches.

"The hurricane (called by the Congo Negroes, 'the Horse of the Boonzie') is regarded as a ravening, devouring monster—a giant like the Jötunns—whose wrath may be appeased by casting meal into the air. I regard this," says Jacob Grimm, "as a primitive superstition."† "In the popular traditions of Russia the four winds are the sons of one mother, and in the ancient Russian song of Igor the Winds are addressed as Lords, and are said to be the grandsons of Stribog, whose divine nature is implied in his name. In like manner in Oriental tales, and poems the wind is represented as speaking and holding converse."‡ Of the Payaguas of S. America Azara § says: "When a storm overturns their huts or casas, they take a brand from the fire, and run against the wind for some distance, threatening it with the brand. Others strike terror into the storm, by pummeling the air soundly." In Asia the Tcheremis used to make offerings to the winds.‖ In ancient times the same custom was in vogue among the Greeks and Romans, as well as other nations.¶

In every quarter of the globe we meet with the worship of Fire, that "mysterious element, ever restless,

---

* Herod. I. 138.
† Senec. Ep. 41; Cic. de N. Deor. III. 20.
‡ Otto Böhtlingk, Indische Sprüche, B. II. S. 97 (1 Aufl.).
§ Bosmann, S. 168; Atkins, Voy. to Guinea, Brazil and the W. Indies. Lond. 1737, p. 119; Snelgrave, Nouvelle Relation de la Guinée. Amst. 1735, p. 69; Marsden, 256, 258.
‖ Alberti, S. 72.
Cicero, de N. Deor. III. 20.
** Shaw, Travels, or observations relating to sev. parts of Barbary and the Levant. Lond. 1757, p. 333; Guys, Voy. littéraire de la Grèce. Par. 1776, I. 466; Kleemann, Reisen in die Crimm. II. Wien, 1771, S. 113.
* Herod. VII. 34, 35, 54.
† D. M. 363. Cf. S. 360-368.
‡ D. M. 361.
§ Azara, II. 137.
‖ Rytschkow, S. 86.
¶ Herod. VII. 178, 189; Pausan. II. 12; Cic. de N. Deor. III. 20.

ever consuming, ever brightly flaming Power of Nature." "Our Northern student lights his lamp with a match, spreads out before him the volumes written in the past, and traces in Hephæstus the root Phtha, or compares Vesta, Behram and Agni with one another. As I take it, this is commencing at the end and not at the beginning. The student does not consider that friction-matches are a very recent invention, and that anciently the production of fire was a very difficult process: as we may still see in the case of savages who often spend hours in getting fire.* The *lucifer* which has become for us a thing so familiar that we never stop to think about it, was once one of the most mysterious of wonders, a wonder which must have all the more forcibly impressed men's imaginations, inasmuch as it not alone promoted man's comfort, but even made life endurable, especially in cold climates. Hence we can understand why the Sacred Fire always burned in the shrine; why faithful guardians were appointed to care for it, and why this worship of Fire was recognized in public legislation, as well as in the concernments of private life."† "Fire, like water, is regarded as a thing of life;" ‡ and by many savage tribes it is held to be an animal. Tὸ πῦρ θηρίον ἐμφυχον, says Herodotus, describing the beliefs of the Egyptians (III. 16), and Cicero has, ignis animal. (De N. Deor. 3. 14.) Among the Damara, one of the rudest of savage tribes, who can scarcely count beyond the number three, and to whom the institution of marriage is unknown, the daughters of the chiefs are charged with the duty of keeping up the Sacred Fire, for Vestals are to be found in several religious systems, the duty of keeping up a sacred fire being an easy one, and best suited for women. When a family separated from the tribe and emigrated they took with them a brand of the sacred fire.

Whenever the fire went out, on rekindling it, sacrifice was offered.* The Sioux called themselves Potowatomie, which means, we make fire,† and, like the Ojibways and other nations, they kept up an undying fire, as the symbol of their nationality.‡ According to Adair the word Cherokee is derived from Cheera, fire. The Muscogees gave to fire the highest Indian title of honor, *grandfather;* § and their priests were called "Firemakers." The chief ceremony of their principal festival, "the First Fruits," was the Renewing of the Fire, a performance which, among the Mexicans, was repeated every 52 years. The old fires were then all extinguished, and it was only after they had practiced purificatory rites and fasted for the space of three days that the people supposed they had received the consecration which was needed for the kindling of the new Fire.‖

With the worship of fire that of Lightning and Thunder is closely allied. Perhaps among all the phenomena of Nature the worship of Thunder and Lightning is the most widely diffused. It is found among the rudest populations—the aborigines of Brazil, for instance.¶ The Betchuana worship the rain as it falls from the clouds. As their country is arid and barren, and their great curse drought, they hold Rain to be the Giver of all good. They begin and end every solemn discourse with the word *Puhla,* rain, and they have the greatest veneration for their Rain-makers.**

In some countries it is not the Rain itself but a Rain-giver that is worshiped, not the Thunder, but a Thunderer, who ranks above all other spirits by reason of the dread power of his voice and the awful, death-dealing force of his shaft, the Lightning.

---

* *Cf.* Grimm, D. M 341 ff.
† Bastian, 343.
‡ D. M. S. 340.

* Anderson, Reise in S. W. Afrika bis zum Ngami. Leipz. 1858, I. 239.
† Keating, I. 89.
‡ Schoolcraft, II. 138.
§ Waitz, III. 208.
‖ *Ibid.* 208.
¶ M. v. Neuwied, S. 144.
** Thompson, I. 180; Campbell, 2d Journey, 230.

The Damara regard as their supreme deity Omakuru, the Rain-giver, who dwells in the distant North.[*] Some of the Damara even claim for themselves descent from the Rain, while others would have only birds, fishes and worms reckoned as Rain's progeny.[†] In the island of Ponapi the supreme Being vents his wrath in the thunder:[‡] and in the northern Sagas Lightning is called God's *Beard-speech*, for when Thor mutters words behind his red beard, the lightnings flash through the sky. Zeus shakes his ambrosial locks, and the heavens are moved. In the isle of Morileu navigators adored the rainbow, or perhaps the spirit of the rainbow.[§]

After the mind has attained some degree of development, the old objects of worship still remain, but they are then subordinated to the new, and pass for the symbols of the latter. As Zeus was thus connected with lightning and thunder, so among the Israelites Jehovah was connected with fire, as his appearance in the Burning Bush, in thunder and lightning on Sinai, and in the Pillar of Fire, clearly shows. Vulcan came into relation with the sacred fire of Vesta through the column of flame which shot up from Etna.

5. *Plants as Fetiches.*

" Heathendom regarded all Nature as living," says Jacob Grimm.[||] This view of Nature is very clearly expressed in the northern myth of Baldr. To ward off from the beloved God all danger, Frigg exacted an oath from Earth, from stones, water, fire, plants, beasts, birds, worms, and even from Pestilence, not to injure him. Only the young and and tender Mistletoe was by the goddess thought so weak and powerless that she did not require of it the oath. But when afterward Hödur, at the prompting of Loke, with this plant compassed the death of Baldr, all creatures wept—plants, beasts and men.

If inanimate stones are regarded as living beings, we are not to be surprised if plants are also thought to have souls, for their whole process of development, in growing and blooming, in bearing fruit and in withering, has many analogies in human life. This anthropopathic apprehension of plants is very evident in the belief entertained in popular superstition as to the powers of the magical plant Mandrake, which is mentioned under the name μανδραγόρας by Hippocrates, Xenophon, Plato, Theophrastus and others. It is described as shaped like a man. When it is plucked from the earth it utters a cry, a groan of pain so terrible as to cause the death of the one who plucks it out. But if it be displaced by a special manipulation of the surrounding earth, it must be then washed in red wine, wrapped in white and red bandages of silk, bathed every Friday, and vested in a fresh, white garment at each new moon. If questioned it will make known future and hidden things tending to the welfare and prosperity of the questioner, and if a piece of gold lies beside it through the night there will be found in the morning two: but its good-nature must not be imposed upon, however. The water in which it has been washed is to be poured upon the doorsill, or upon the cattle, and so the house and the stock are preserved from ill-luck. If barren women drink of it, they will be blessed with progeny. If a man wears the mandrake about his person he will always in suits at law defeat his opponent.[*]

This mandrake is of human origin,

---

[*] Anderson, I. 237.
[†] Rh. Missionsber, 1852, S. 235; Hahn, Grundzüge einer Grammatik des Herero. Berl. 1857, S. 152.
[‡] Michelewa y Rojas, Viajes cientificos en todo el Mundo (1822–42). Madrid, 1843, p. 197.
[§] V. Kittlitz, Denkwürdigk. auf einer R. n. d. russ. Am., Mikrones. und Kamtsch. (1826 ff). Gotha, 1858, II. 105.
[||] D. M., S. 371.

[*] Meiners, II. 600.

springing from a chaste youth's semen fallen to the ground. But on the other hand, men also spring from plants. There is a Micronesian story to the effect that Tangaloa's daughter, while yet the earth was parched and barren, assuming the form of a snipe alighted upon the earth, and made her home on a rock. From the rock a creeping plant sprung forth, and as this died away it produced at first worms, then men.[*] Some of the Damara tell of the descent of man and the larger beasts from a sacred tree, which they worship. In the German Song of Alexander (Alexanderlied) by Pfaff Lamprecht, "megede rehte vollencommen"—perfectly beauteous maidens —are spoken of as springing from flowers.

> "Si giengen unde lebeten
> Menschen sin si habeten."

As they spring from the flowers, with them they perish:

> "Die blûmen gare verturben
> Unde die scônen frowen sturben."

Daphne was changed into a bay-tree. In speaking of the worship of plants, trees and woods, I do not give it Ovid's interpretation:

Stat vetus et multos incædua silva per annos,
Credibile est illi numen inesse loco.[†]

On the Coral Islands of Polynesia the *crinum* and the *dragon's blood* are held sacred. The Dayaks of Borneo worship also the *dragon's blood*, together with the *pancratium amboinense*.[‡] Generally, however, it is large trees that are worshiped, such as the mighty *adansonia*. In Whidah the sick apply to the sacred trees, for the cure of their complaints.[§] On the Zaire the public and the domestic council of the prince meet beneath the holy *ficus religiosa*,[*] a tree which plays an important part in the history of religion. In Congo it is planted in all the market-places, as an object of worship: its bark has fetich-craft: and any injury done to the tree is punished as a crime. The Somali worship certain trees,[†] and the Galla specially the wanzey-tree, though in the south of Shoa they regard the *wodanabe*-tree as their national Palladium, their "great Fetich." [‡] This same tree-worship is found in N. America and Northern Asia, for instance, among the Ostiaks, Wotiaks and the Tsheremis.[§] The savages of Acadie worshiped an ancient tree on the sea-shore. This tree having fallen root and branch into the sea, they continued to worship it as long as any part of it remained visible.[||] The sacred tree of the Longobardi was the so-called blood-tree, and the ancient Germans worshiped chiefly the oak, though they had also great reverence for the alder:[¶] nor were the ancient Jews, Arabs[**] or Persians[††] without their fetich-trees. The goddess Ashera was originally worshiped under the form of a simple stock of wood.[‡‡] "The Diana of the isle of Eubœa was a piece of unhewed wood, the Thespian Juno of Cytheron the trunk of a tree, she of Samos a simple slab of wood, as was also the Delian Latona; the Carian Diana was a cylinder of wood, and the Pallas, and the Ceres at Athens were rough stakes, sine effigie rudis palus, et informe lignum." [§§]

As single trees, so also whole groves, with their green, umbrageous aisles, their mystic gloom, and the tuneful rustling of their leaves would

* Turner, p. 244.
† Ovid, Amor. III. 1, 1.
‡ Gerland, in Waitz, V. 2. 10.
§ Bosmann, II. 64, 323, III. 153; Des Marchais, II. 132.

* Tuckey, p. 366.
† Waitz, II. 523.
‡ Ib. 518.
§ Rytschkow, S. 161.
|| Charlevoix, p. 349.
¶ Grimm, D. M. S. 374.
** Merx, in Schenkel's Bibellex. Art. Aschera and Astarte.
†† Meiners, I. 152.
‡‡ Merx, ubi supr.
§§ De Brosses, p. 151.

make a most profound impression on the childlike fancy of the savage. The rustling of the leaves was regarded as the language of the trees : thus it was that the sacred oaks of Dodona spoke, and oracles were published founded on these words of the oaks. Athene, according to Apollodorus, fixed on the prow of the Argo a voiceful piece of wood from one of the Dodonian oaks (φωνῆεν φηγου τῆς Δωδωνίδος ξύλον), and the wooden ships of the Phœacians were possessed of souls (τιτυσκόμεναι φρεσὶ νῆες).*

Among the ancient Germans single trees as well as entire forests were held in the greatest reverence.† Such sacred groves were not to be entered by the profane : such sacred trees were not to be stripped of their leaves or branches, or to be hewed down. Compare sacrum nemus, nemus castum, in Tacitus, and Lucus erat longo numquam violatus ab ævo, in Lucan.‡ Amongst the sacred groves of German lands were the forest of the Semnones, the nemus of Nerthus, the Sclavic lucus Zutibure and the Prussian grove Romowe. Amongst the Esthonians it was held impious to break off a twig in a sacred grove, nor would they even pluck a strawberry within its shadow.§ Long after the introduction of Christianity the violation of trees was sternly punished in Germany.‖ Of the Esthonians at the present day we have this account : Only a few years ago, in the parish of Harjel, they *made offerings* (opferten) under certain trees on the nights of S. George's, S. John's and S. Michael's day . they killed a black hen. According to the superstitious belief of the Wends of Lausitz there are forests which annually demand a human sacrifice (as do many rivers) · and one man must annually yield his life.¶ For an account of the

* Odyss. VIII. 556.
† Cf. Grimm, D. M. 371 ff.
‡ Pharsal. III. 399.
§ "Ut umbra pertingit." Grimm, R. A. 57, 105.
‖ Grimm, Weisthümer, III. S. 309, 18, IV. 366, 15, 699.
¶ Grimm, D. M. *ub. supr.*

ecclesiastical prohibitions, vota ad. arbores facere aut ibi candelam sen. quodlibet munus deferre, arborem colere, votum persolvere, consult Grimm, D. M. Anhang. XXXIII. XXXIV.

6. *Animals as Fetiches.*

Christianity, that religion which sets the highest value upon the human individual, places a great abyss. between man and nature. She isolates man and places him infinitely above nature. Christianity therefore regards the animal as in every respect far inferior to man. The religions of India regard Nature as only the outward aspect of Brahma ; for them therefore the eternal Being is visible in the beast as well as in man. Consequently in the beast the Hindu recognizes a brother, of equal rights, and of like rank with himself. But the view which the savage takes of the animal world is different from both of these. He commonly regards the animal not simply as his equal, but as a superior being. Of the Negroes Waitz says : "In their view man has not his definitive place at the summit of Nature, and above the animals, but the latter appear to them as enigmatical beings whose nature is involved in obscurity and mystery, and whom they rank now as above themselves, again as beneath."* "The Indians," says the same author, "regard the animals as man's. ancestors and kindred and ascribe to them a human understanding and human principles of action, or even sometimes a higher intelligence and superhuman capacities. Those animals, however, which neither inspire them with fear nor display any notable sagacity they despise." † To understand why the savage views the animal creation thus, we need but know the nature of his intellect and the conditions of life in which he is placed.

As the understanding reaches only as far as its objects, it will always be

* Anthrop. II. 177.
† Anthrop. III. 192.

enlarged as the number of these increases. The greater a man's intelligence, the wider is the line of distinction between him and beings possessed of none at all, or of a less degree than himself. But so long as the number of his objects does not exceed that possessed by animals; so long as they are the same in kind as those possessed by the animal, and not more numerous, in other words so long as his *world* is that of the animal; just so long the intellectual condition of the lowest savage will not be distinguishable from that of the beast.

The will can be exerted only upon the objects exhibited to it in the understanding. Hence, so long as these objects are no higher than those of the animal, the will of the savage cannot have any higher aims than has the will of the beast.

As we have already seen, the savage has a very small number of objects. From the lack of objects of a higher nature, we have shown that his will must be concentrated on those which are purely material. Hence his only stimulus, his only great interest is to satisfy his hunger, his lust, or his desire of repose.

Thus as regards his intellectual status and the range of his desires, the savage, even where he has made some little progress, differs but little from the animal, while at a lower stage he scarcely differs at all. The world of the animal is his world also, and their interests are the same. Hence there is hardly any difference between the savage and a highly-organized animal. But as he differs so little from them, it is impossible for him to regard himself as something quite distinct from them. His pursuits and those of the animal are identical; their wants, their motives are the same; the animal is the counterpart of the man; therefore the savage regards the animal as his equal, as his kindred.

Hence, for the simple reason that the savage and the animal are *de facto* scarcely distinguishable, they would be apprehended as standing on an equality. And as the savage cannot attribute to the beings around him any internal properties save those of which he already has consciousness, he is forced, as we have seen, to form anthropopathic apprehensions of objects. The more closely these beings resemble man in their nature and habits, the sooner will he attribute to them the self-same motives which excite himself. In fact his conduct differs very little from theirs; not alone does he closely resemble them, he is in many respects perfectly identical with them. Hence, as he must have anthropopathic apprehension of a mountain, a river, or a tree, he cannot help regarding the animal as of his kindred. In the eastern part of South Africa Monteiro's ass was a novelty to the natives, and they at once commenced to ask the donkey what he thought about things, always regarding the ass's doings as human performances.[*]

But not only must the savage regard all, or at least some animals as his equals, he will even assign them a superior rank. Intellectual qualities he values little, as he knows but little about them; but on the contrary, like all men of uncultured minds, like boys, like the old giants in the heroic legend, he prizes bodily strength above everything else. The great chief who with a blow can split the skull of his antagonist; whose powerful voice can be heard at enormous distances, whose nails are like the claws of a bear, who lays hold of a man and tears him in twain, who when hot coals fall upon his body in sleep, is not awakened, but treats them as gnats; who every day devours an entire sheep, and drinks a skin of fermented and distilled milk without being drunk: such is the savage's ideal of true greatness. But nowhere does he find such bodily strength and agility, such fiery courage and uncurbed fury as he does in wild beasts, the lion, tiger, wolf, bear,

---

[*] Zeitschrift f. allg. Erdkunde, VI. 407.

elephant, etc. They are the realization of what he might be himself: they are the ideals, the prototypes whose names he delights to assume, and which he chooses as his Totems, and his guardian spirits. They indeed are the mighty ones of his country : his weapons are often insufficient to protect him against their attack ; he is at their mercy, and lives as it were by their favor. Then the colossal size of some of these beasts, or the majesty of their presence—the demon fascination of their gleaming eyes, must make on the savage a profounder impression than upon us, inasmuch as these are the very properties he is best acquainted with and which he values most highly.

Not only does this bodily strength inspire him with respect for the beast, as a being superior to himself; he attributes to him, furthermore, a higher degree of sagacity and circumspection. The unerring instinct of the animal : the cunning of the fox, the dog's acuteness of sense, the ingenuity of the beaver in constructing his house, of the bird in building its nest, of the bee in forming the comb : all this is in sharp contrast with the poverty and helplessness of man in the savage state. He knows nothing of the price the animals have to pay for the power they possess, nor reflects that they too do learn, and suffer anxiety and pain. Again the service rendered to him by several animals—as the ox, who with all his strengt his still so patient—disposes the savage to regard the beast as a being worthy of respect, and by no means as the pattern of stupidity.

This exposition of the relations between the savage and the brute which is based on the results of observation, is also confirmed on every side by observation. We find the best illustration of this in the Animal Legend (Thiersage), as it is found among our Germanic ancestors, "a form of composition which could have its origin only when men were in a very primitive state, and men and animals consorted together intimately and with a childlike ingenuousness."

Vilmar's remarks on this subject are apposite :* "The root of this legend" (Reynard the Fox), says he, "lies in the guileless natural simplicity of primitive man ; in the deep and kindly instincts of a sound and vigorous savage race. As they conceive a cordial and even passionate attachment for Nature in her varying phases ; exulting with her in the mildness of the spring time and in the genial heat of summer, sharing the melancholy of autumn, and in winter giving themselves up to the torpor which reigns all around : as they attribute to these different phases of Nature an individuality like their own, with like emotions, and develop these conceptions in the form of grand myths, in which the creatures of imagination are represented now as kindly and gracious, again as awful and majestic, as they appear respectively in Siegfried and Brunhild : so, very naturally, they form a very close and affectionate attachment for the brute creation, their nearer neighbors and their closer kindred. Nay, more, they admit them to intimate association with themselves, as though they were truly and essentia'ly, and not by adoption, or by imaginative fiction, members with themselves of one society. It is the pure, innocent delight which the savage takes in contemplating the brute creation—their lithe figure and flashing eye, their courage and ferocity, their cunning and agility ; it is his knowledge of their habits derived from the daily experiences of a life lived in common with them that gave rise to these fables of animals, to the animal-epic. But such life-experience can be obtained by man, only when he studies the animal with a calm and affectionate interest ; when he contemplates its inmost nature, its most recondite characteristics ; when he not alone shares himself the nature of the animal, but also in turn gives to the animal a share in his own human faculties of thought and of speech,

*Vilmar, Literaturgeschichte, I. 244 ff. 8 Aufl.

and attributes to the animal's actions the same importance, the same intelligent direction, which he claims for his own. This mutual commerce of Brute and Man is the absolute condition of the Thiersage. The brute of the legend is not a mere brute, of nature quite diverse from man's, and having no psychic communion with him: but no more is it a man disguised in the form of a brute. In the former case, the brute could never be the object of poesy, or at least would not furnish the true material of poesy, *action*. In the latter case, such legends would be only tedious allegory. The charm of the legend lies precisely in this dark background where the brute and the man have so much in common; and on this background we must not suffer the lights of our better informed understanding to fall, else the very essence of the legend vanishes."

There is no form of poetry, as Meiners thinks, more agreeable to the uncultured mind than the fable; and in point of fact fables are extremely numerous among savages. Their ultimate basis is the anthropopathic apprehension of the brute creation, the dark background of which Vilmar speaks.* Lessing supposes the object of the fable is to give palpable shape to a moral truth. Even the Hottentots have a large collection of animal-fables, with the recital of which they amuse one another. The Negroes, too, "when they come together to smoke tobacco, or to quaff their palm-wine, entertain one another by telling fables, and they dress up every passing occurrence in the garb of legend or fable. 'The Spider,' to give one example, 'the Spider would lay out a plantation, and set to work about it vigorously without delay. But he had not got the ground ready, when the seeding-time was gone by: and the same thing occurred year after year. The Termite who would build him a palace, having noticed this, called together his neighbors,

his slaves and his friends, to give him their aid; and lo! after a short time, the work was finished. Then said the Termite to the Spider : " If you had but done as I did, your plantation would have been laid out long ago." I once, in talking with a Negro named Quan, reproached his people with having killed off all the elephants for the sake of their ivory, and his answer was this: 'No, we have done no such thing. The elephants knew that the white man wanted the ivory, but they would not part with it without having something in return: so they went down to the coast, and sold their tusks for brandy. Having drunk the brandy, they were now left without anything—neither tusks nor brandy. So in their drunkenness they became desperate and all committed suicide, and that is why there are no longer elephants in Aquapin.' " *

" Man in his lowest stage of development considers himself and the brutes as almost alike, the difference between the two being, to his mind, rather external than internal and essential. The beast has a soul as well as man, and the soul of the beast is substantially the same as that of man. Men and animals belong to one race, and are identical with one another in sundry points." † How easy is the transition from man to animal, and *vice versa*, is shown in ancient German legends. "As in later times, after the grim legends of antiquity have been discredited, men become wolves and wolves are transformed into men, as we see in the belief in the Werewolf; so in primitive times men became dragons." ‡ The ancient ballads tell of Siegfrid's father and of his sister Signe, how they were transformed into wolves, and assumed all the savage instincts. This belief in "Marafilnas," the lycanthropi of the ancients, extends through Abyssinia, Senegambia and all eastern Negro lands as far as the Somali. Especially workers in

---

* *Cf.* Waitz, II 180.

* *Ib.* 343.
† Wuttke, I. 107.
‡ Vilmar, I. 121.

iron are supposed to transform themselves at night into beasts, and then
to feast on human flesh. In Fassokl
the Marafilnas are even organized
into secret guilds.* The Indians in
the interior of Oregon regard beavers
as human beings, metamorphosed by
the Great Spirit, in punishment of
their disobedience.† In Mexican
mythology, too, we find instances of
such transformations. Xapan was, for
adultery, changed into a black scorpion, and Tlahuitzin, the woman, into
a red scorpion; and Xaotl was changed into a grasshopper, for having over-
stepped the powers given to him by
the gods.‡ Lycaon was by Zeus transformed into a wolf. A number of
German myths speak of the mutual
transformations of men and serpents.§
The Centaurs and the Sirens show
also how readily man and beast coa-
lesce in Grecian mythology.

We have already seen from the instance cited in Chapter II. (the Are-
kunas) that there is nothing to prevent
the greatest familiarity between the
savage and the wild beast. The Malays of Malacca, and the Orangs consider the stronger animals as their own
equals—especially the shark, whom
they regard as a friend and a brother,
he being, like themselves, a pirate.
A similar view is taken of the tiger
and the crocodile, and this view prevails throughout many of the East

India, Philippine and South-Sea Islands.* In the East India isles it is
believed that sometimes women give
birth, not alone to boys and girls, but
also to crocodiles, and the latter are
never killed, but carefully placed in a
crocodile pond. Many of the natives
have their crocodile relatives, duly acknowledged, and these they never injure.† Hence the savage does not
hold it to be a disgrace to be descended from beasts; on the contrary,
they boast of such descent. The
Tlascalans used to say that the men
who escaped in the Deluge were transformed into apes, but that they by degrees recovered the use of reason and
speech.‡ Kadroma, a she-ape, wife of
the ape Cenresi, was the ancestress of
the whole population of Thibet. The
Thibetians are proud of this descent, and of their ape-like ugli-
ness of feature, which they trace to
their ape ancestors.§ Some of the
Orang-Benua trace their origin back
to white apes.‖ According to the
Aleutians¶ and the Chippeways** all
men are descended from the dog, and
hence the first men had canine paws.
Other N. American Indians say that
a woman that lived with a dog was
the mother of the human race.†† The
Delawares suppose themselves descended from the eagle;‡‡ the Tonka-
way trace their origin to the wolf, §§
others to the raven, ‖‖ the Osages to

* Waitz, II. 180, 504.
† Cox, Ross, The Columbia River, 3 ed.
Lond. 1832, I. 231; Dunn, Hist. of Oregon
Terr. Lond. 1844, p. 317.
‡ D. Francisco Saverio Clavigero, Hist.
antigua de Mejico, l. vi. p. 240: Entre otras
contaban que habiendo emprendido un hom-
bre llamado Japan hacer penitencia en un
monte, tentado por una mujer, cometio adul-
terio: por lo cual lo decapito immediatemente
Jaotl, a quien habian dado los dioses el encargo de velar la conducta de Japan. Este
fue transformado en escorpion negro. No
contento Jaotl con aquel castigo, perseguia
tambien a su mujer Tlahuitzin, la cual fue
transformada en escorpion rubio, y el mismo
Jaotl, por haber traspasado los limites de su
encargo, quedó convertido en langosta. A
la verguenza de aquel delito atribuyen la
propriedad del escorpion de huir de la luz y
de esconderse entre las piedras.
§ Grimm, D. M. 394 ff.

* J. Hawkesworth, Account of the voy.
undertaken for making Discoveries in the S.
Hemisphere by Capt. Byron Wallis, Carteret
and Cook, 1773. Lond. III. 758; Marsden,
Valentyn.
† Hawkesw. III. 756, 757.
‡ Clavigero, VI. p. 225. Cf. Garcia, Origen
de los Indios.
§ Klaproth, Tabl. hist. p. 131.
‖ Borie, in Tydschr. voor indische taal,
land en volkenkunde. Batavia, X. 415.
¶ Sarytschew. R. in Sibir. II. 164.
** Waitz, III. 191.
†† Hearne, Voyage from Fort Prince Wallis
to the North Sea (Germ. tr.), p. 281.
‡‡ Schoolcraft, V. 683.
§§ Wrangell. Statist. und ethnograph.
Nachrichten über die russ. Besitz. in Am.
(in Bär and Helmersen, Beitr. zur Kenntn.
des russ. Reichs. Petersh. 1839) 100, 111, 93;
Holmberg, Ethn. Skizzen üb. d. Völk. des
russ.
‖‖ Schoolcraft. IV. 305.

a serpent transformed into a man, and married to the daughter of the beaver;[*] the Kayuse, Nez Percés, Walla-Wallas, and some other tribes are descended, according to a tradition held by them all, from the various members of the beaver:[†] some S. American aborigines from a fish, others from the toad, still others from the rattlèsnake.[‡]

Conversely, several animals have a human origin. In Acra monkeys,—called "servants of the fetiches,"—are supposed to be men, whose creation miscarried; while among the Serracolets and on the Island of Madagascar they are supposed to be men who were metamorphosed on account of their sins.[§] The Manitu of the Iroquois, to reward a man who, though sore pressed by hunger, had abstained from human flesh, transformed him into a beaver, and such is the origin of the Beaver totem. A Missouri Indian was changed into a snake that had the power of speech.[||] Owing to this close relationship beasts understand the language of man, and *vice versa*. In Bornu this mutual understanding of languages ceased when a man betrayed a secret to a woman.[¶] In our legends and stories, too, animals speak, as did Diomed's steeds.

The souls of animals, and even of plants, enjoy the privilege of immortality.[**] The souls of men may pass into the bodies of animals, and animals' souls into men's bodies. Animals which root the bodies of dead men out of their graves thus make the souls of the deceased their own, devouring soul and body at once. This belief is oftentimes the foundation of the savage's reverence for animals, as is the case among the Kaffirs, who make an offering to the wild beasts of the bodies of the dead.[††]

To the larger beasts the savage often attributes a higher intelligence than he claims for himself. A very intelligent Indian seriously assured Parkman that he held the beaver and the white man to be the most ingenious of people.[*] Especially the white beaver, an animal which appears to exist only in fable, is represented as endowed with superhuman powers.[†] On the Senegal, in Kordofan and in Brazil, monkeys are possessed of a human understanding. It is believed by many savages that monkeys can speak, but refuse to do so, lest they should be forced to work.[‡] Dogs, too, can speak, and in primitive times did speak: but since the time when the descendants of the god Kutka sailed by them without replying to their inquiries, they have proudly refused to speak any more. It is only strangers that they bark at now, or rather it is only strangers to whom they now address the question, Who are you? Where are you going? So say the Kamtchatdales.[§] The Kaffirs say that the chameleon and the salamander are messengers sent on important errands to man by the god Umkulunkulu.[||] The Chippeways, like the Atnas, Kenai and Kolush,[¶] suppose the world was called into existence by a bird. In the beginning there was only a vast waste of water: above this was poised a monstrous bird, the beating of whose wings was as thunder, the flash of whose eye was as lightning. He swooped down and touched the sea, and at once the earth came to the surface and floated on the water.[**] Birds passed for beings gifted with extraordinary wisdom among the ancient Germans, Greeks and Romans.[††] The American In-

---

[*] Wilkes, IV. 467, *apud* Waitz, III. 345.
[†] Azara, Voy. II. 138.
[‡] Garcilasso, Commentar. reales, I. 18, 21.
[§] *Ib.* 178.
[||] M. v. Neuwied, II. 230.
[¶] Kölle, African Native Literature. Lond. 1854, p. 154.
[**] Steller, S. 269; Georgi, Beschr. S. 383.
[††] Waitz, II. 177.

[*] *Ib.* III. 193.
[†] Jones, Traditions of the N. Am. Ind., 2 ed. Lond. 1830, III. 69.
[‡] Raffenel, p. 90; Rüppel, R. in Nubien, Kordofan, etc. Frankf. 1829, S. 115; Bosmann, II. 243; Bowdich, p. 195.
[§] Steller, S. 280.
[||] Waitz, II. 410.
[¶] Waitz, III. 179.
[**] M. v. Neuwied, II. 221.
[††] *Cf.* Grimm, D. M. S. 388 ff.

dians credit the owl with greater intelligence than even the beaver or the rattlesnake, and treat him with the utmost reverence, call him "grandfather," and even incense him with tobacco-smoke — a solemn offering, with which oftentimes the morning sun is greeted. A legend represents the owl as one of the greatest benefactors of mankind, and he is considered to be the king or chief of the snakes.* In Mexican legend it was a dove that taught the dumb sons of Cojcoj, the Mexican Noah, to speak diverse tongues so that they could not understand one another.† On the mountain Kaf lives the monstrous bird Anka, endowed with reason and speech, known to the Persians under the name of Simorg, and in the Talmud called Jukneh. The books of the Zends tell of four sacred birds which are the guardians of the earth and of everything that lives thereon. Japanese mythology represents the bird Isi Tataki as the cause of the propagation of the human race; it was from him that the original divine pair got their knowledge of marriage rites. Chaldaic legend speaks of four worshipful beings, half man, half animal, which came out of the sea and made their appearance on the bank of the Euphrates near Babylon to give men instruction. The name of the first was Oannes, and he instructed them in those things which are pleasing to God, and gave to them religion, laws, science, culture; while it was the business of the other three to attend to the improvement of mankind by a repetition of the lessons given by the first. The Turks and the Arabs say that the cat meditates upon Mohammed's law, and that she will share with the faithful in the joys of Paradise, and they believe that the horse reads the Koran.*

From what has been already said not only will the fetichistic veneration of animals be placed in a clear light, but it will also appear that such veneration is necessarily incident to savage life. And it is the animal itself *in propria natura*, and without any reference to any divinity he may represent, that is worshiped. "The bear that is worshiped as a god is regarded as a true bear: the snake that is worshiped as a fetich is no mere passing theophania, but is ever a real snake."† It is not to be questioned that in the higher stages of development the worship of animals is connected with the *cultus* of spirits; and then the animals are considered as consecrated to the gods, and are on that ground worshiped: but that is beside our purpose.

The elephant is in Africa regarded as a superior being. The Kaffirs, out of respect to his understanding, will not eat his flesh. And yet they chase this animal, saying at the same time, "Do not kill us, great chief; do not trample on us, great chief."‡ In Dahomey he is the "great fetich" of the nation. Though the Dahomans are allowed to kill the animal, still they must perform a long purificatory ceremony after having slain one.§ In Siam the kings used once to appear seated on a white elephant, but that custom was abolished, for the elephant is as great a potentate as the king himself; and in him dwells a kingly soul. He has been even invested with imperial dignities.‖ The lion was worshiped in Arabia,¶ the tiger in New Calabar ** and in the East India islands. In Sumatra the natives give the tigers warning whenever Europeans set snares to catch

---

* Parkman, Hist. Conspir. Pontiac. Lond. 1851, II. 135; Jones, III. 69.
† Clavigero, Lib. VI. p. 225; .... tubieron muchos hijos, pero mudos, hasta que una paloma les communicó los idiomas desde las ramas de un arbol, pero tan diversos, que no podian entenderse entre si.

* Arvieux, Mém. mis en ordre par le P. Labat. Par. 1735, III. 223, 252.
† Wuttke, I. 82.
‡ Kay, Trav. and Researches in Kaffraria. Lond. 1833, p. 125, 138.
§ Forbes, p. 9; Kay, p. 341.
‖ Meiners, I. 221.
¶ *Ibid.* S. 192.
** Holman, I. 371: Köler. 61.

them: and we read of *Tiger-cities*, where the houses are thatched with women's hair. In Acra, too, where almost each village adores as its fetich some animal peculiar to itself, the hyena is regarded as sacred.* At the Cape of Good Hope they will not kill the leopard, even though the animal devour women and children. It is thought in Dahomey that those who are torn to pieces by leopards are peculiarly blest in the next life.† The principal object of worship of the West Africa negroes is the wolf. A soldier belonging to a Danish fort, who was not aware of the sacred character of these animals, killed one of them. The indignant natives demanded of the Fort Commandant a reparation of the offense; and he was compelled to yield to the demand, as the negroes threatened to quit the district if he refused to comply. If satisfaction were not made the murdered wolf would take a fearful revenge on them and their children. Accordingly the Commandant had the wolf's body wrapped in linen cloths, and provided gunpowder and brandy for the solemn rite of atonement. The natives having, during the grand obsequies, fired off the powder and drunk the brandy, the wolf was propitiated and avenged.‡ Some negroes worship goats, sheep and rams.§ In New Calabar the horse is worshiped, and in Wadai this animal is the subject of many wonderful stories, and of a multitude of superstitious beliefs.‖ Indeed the horse, as also the ox and the cow, have been regarded as sacred the world over. The religious views of many Indian tribes with regard to animal-fetiches are very curious. "The highest worship is paid to the Onkteri Gods who created the earth and man, and who instituted the medicine-dance. In form they resemble huge oxen: amongst them

the Spirit of Earth holds the pre-eminence, and has subject to him the serpents, lizards, frogs, the owl, the eagle, the spirits of the dead, etc. Another class of gods, sub-divided multifariously, is that of the Wakinyan, who are ever at war with the Onkteri, and who are principally destructive war-gods, though they possess also the creative power. To them the wild rice and a certain kind of grass owe their origin. In form they bear a fantastical resemblance to birds, and their home is on a lofty mountain in the west. The eastern gate of their dwelling is guarded by a butterfly, the western by a bear, the northern by the moose, the southern by the beaver," * etc. The worship of the beaver is diffused throughout almost the whole of America.†

Among birds it is the owl which is most frequently chosen for a fetich,‡ and even among our Teutonic ancestors this bird, as well as many others, was esteemed sacred.§ Many ancient Arab tribes regarded the eagle as their Great Fetich,‖ and by the Syrians the dove was worshiped.¶

In Africa, especially in Bonny; and in the E. Indian Islands, in Sumatra, Celebes, Butong, and the Philippines the crocodile is the principal object of worship.** In performing this worship, the natives go down to the haunts of the crocodile, to the sound of music vocal and instrumental, and throw food and tobacco to the animals. Nay, even in Celebes and in Butong tamed crocodiles are kept in the houses,†† probably because their presence is deemed lucky: and for this same reason, the Negro of Africa is glad when he finds these venerated animals dwelling near his hut without fear.‡‡ In Madagascar the cayman, the guardian deity of Little

---

* Bowdich, p. 362; Monrad, 33.
† Forbes, p. 35.
‡ Römer, S. 273 f.; Des Marchais, I. 297.
§ Bastian, 82, 208.
‖ Holman, Köler, ll. cc.

* Waitz, III. 190.
† *Ib.* III. 193.
‡ *Supra.* p. 77.
§ Grimm, D. M. 386–394.
‖ Meiners, I. 192.
¶ Xenoph. Anab. I. 4.
** Holman, Köler, ll. cc.
†† Hawkesworth, p. 757.
‡‡ Römer, 273 f.

Popo, is supposed to be an enchanted chieftain of old.* When the cayman takes any prey (so say the natives on the Senegal) he calls together his friends and kindred and counsels with them when the holiday is to be kept, for the distribution of the plunder. His most intimate friend is a bird, a kind of crane, which watches over him as he sleeps : and it is not permitted to kill this bird.†

In the E. India Islands,‡ as in Africa also,§ the shark is a mighty fetich along the sea-coast. Eels are worshiped in Cusaie and in the Marian Isles.‖ In the Carolines the God Mani is represented as a fish.¶ "At Eap there are kept in a pond of fresh water two fishes of extreme age, but yet only a span in length, which always stand in a right line, head to head, without moving. If any man touch them, and they are made to stand at right angles with each other, an earthquake is the result."** Xenophon states that the ancient Syrians paid worship to fishes ;†† and whoever ate of a sacred fish, his body was at once covered with ulcers, his bowels shriveled up, and his bones crumbled away.‡‡

"Mysterious in its whole nature ; amazingly agile though without limbs ; strong and formidable though simple in form ; of no great size and yet a match for the most powerful animals, owing to the instantaneousness of its attack ; gorgeous in its variegated coat ; silently and stealthily lying in wait for its victim, and then in an instant filling him with terror—the

Serpent is an object of reverence to the savage, and is by him regarded as a mighty being of a higher order." * In America, Africa and Europe serpents have been worshiped, oftentimes, indeed, as being possessed by the souls of the departed, but often also as actual fetiches. The reverence paid by American Indians to the rattlesnake was the means of saving the life of the Count von Zinzendorf (1742). The Cayugas, with whom he was staying, were about to put him to death, supposing that his presence was productive of ill-luck to them. The Count was seated one night on a bundle of sticks, writing by the light of a small fire. Unknown to him a rattlesnake lay alongside him. When the Indians who were to take his life approached and observed the snake, they withdrew, firmly convinced that the stranger was of divine origin.† In Europe the Lithuanians worshiped serpents, kept them in their houses and made offerings to them : yet possibly they may have supposed them possessed by the souls of their departed kinsmen. We find mention of snakeworship as practiced by the Longobardi, in the Vita Sancti Barbati in "Acta Sanctorum." ‡ Herodotus speaks of this worship among the Egyptians.§ The guardian of the Athenian Acropolis was a living serpent.‖ But Serpent-worship finds its highest development in Whida, in Africa.¶ The Egyptian Apis alone can compare for importance, power and sacredness with the marvelous serpent which once gave to the Negroes of Whida the victory over their enemies. This serpent, which never dies, is held so sacred that not even the king, but only the High-Priest, durst see him face to face. The sanctity of this one snake confers consecration and immunity upon all other snakes of the same species, which are naturally harmless ;

---

* Leguével, II. 223.
† Raffenel, p. 29, 208.
‡ Marsden, Hawkesworth, ll. cc.
§ Holman, Köler, ll. cc.
‖ Dumont d'Urville, Voy. de l'Astrolabe. Par. 1830, V. 121.
¶ Schirren, Die Wandersagen der Neuseeländer und der Maurimythus. Riga, 1856, S. 70.
** Gerland, ap. Waitz, V. 2, 137; Chamisso, Bemerk. auf einer Enldeckungsreise (1815-18). Weimar, 1821, S. 132.
†† Anab. I. 4: ἐπὶ τὸν Χάλον ποταμὸν πλήρη ἰχθύων μεγάλων καὶ πραέων, οὓς οἱ Σύροι θεοὺς ἐνόμιζον καὶ ἀδικεῖν οὐκ εἴων οὐδὲ τὰς περιστεράς.
‡‡ Meiners, I. 193.

---

* Wuttke, I. 82.
† Waitz, III. 192.
‡ Grimm, D. M. 395 ff.
§ II. 74.
‖ Herod. VIII. 41.
¶ Bosmann, 458 ff. ; Des Marchais, II. 153.

and it is a high crime to kill them. While Bosmann was in Whida, a swine killed one of these snakes, and in punishment not alone was the individual transgressor put to death, but a general persecution broke out against the whole tribe of swine. Indeed they would have been utterly exterminated had not the Serpent granted an amnesty. Each time the crown is put upon a new head, the queen-mother and the new king himself make a solemn pilgrimage to the temple of the serpent. In the court of this temple the faithful pronounce their prayers, and offer valuable gifts. In case there be no earthquakes or other great calamities, which would necessitate special offerings to appease the wrath of the deity, there is annually held a grand festival, when hecatombs are offered. Still the High-Priest may at any time demand, in the name of the serpent, offerings of valuables, herds, and even human victims; and he must be denied nothing. There is engaged in the service of the temple a numerous host of priests and priestesses. The snake's harem is well stocked with beautiful girls. Every year the priestesses, armed with clubs, go about the country, picking out and carrying away girls from 8 to 12 years of age, for the service of the god. These children are kindly treated and instructed in songs and dances in majorem gloriam of his Snakeship. In due time they are consecrated by tattooing on their bodies certain figures, especially those of serpents. The Negroes suppose it is the snake himself that marks his elect thus. Having received their training and consecration, which are paid for by the parents according to their means, the children return home; and when they attain their majority are espoused to the Serpent. The happy brides, tricked out in festival array, are brought by their parents to the temple. When night comes, they are let down by twos or threes into pits where, as the priestesses aver, the authorized proxies of the snake await them. Meanwhile the old priestesses sing and dance around the pits. On the morning after the bridal night the girls are sent back to their homes; there these chosen maids have never been known to give birth to serpents, but only to perfectly human infants. During the remainder of their lives they enjoy eminent privileges, as being the lawful wives of the god, and receive a portion of all the sacrifices and gifts offered to him. They are permitted to marry a human spouse, and then their power over their husbands is unlimited. Should the latter presume to set themselves in opposition to the will of their divine helpmeets, they run the risk of being assassinated by the priestesses and by the other spouses of the god.

Traces of animal-fetichism are to be found even in the more highly-developed forms of religion. The Israelitish worship of the Golden Calf, and of the golden calves set up by Jeroboam is the product of a rude intelligence, as yet unfitted for the purer worship of Jahve, which belongs to a higher state of intellectual development.[*] The raising up of the Brazen Serpent by Moses, the sight of which healed the people of Israel, would appear to be a relic of ancient serpent-fetichism. (See above, *Fernando Po*.) Of the worship of animals among the Egyptians Bastian says:[†] "At Heliopolis and at Thebes, good care was taken lest travelers should peep behind the curtain. But when the specious cloak of philosophy, by means of which the Egyptians imposed on their neighbors, is stripped off, but little is to be seen beyond γόητες πάντες. What we should despise as stupid fetichism in a Negro tribe, was admired as the profoundest wisdom in the world's metropolis. The close connection between the usages of the ancient Egyptians, and those of the other African races, is too evident to be overlooked."

As we have already seen, the savage does not view his fetich as a being so exalted that in no case he may

---

[*] *Cf.* Merx, Art. *Abgöttereei*, in Schenkel's Bibellexikon.
[†] San Salv. S. 300.

withhold from him obedience. His reverence for animals is all the more precarious, inasmuch as he is frequently brought into collision with them in the struggle for existence, as when hunger drives him to use their flesh for food, or when he is obliged to defend himself against the attacks of wild beasts. In such cases he kills the animal, how sacred soever it may be. The divine *nimbus*, however, which surrounds the animal is not thus dissipated, for the savage will pay due reverence to the body of the slaughtered beast, excusing his deed as best he may: having thus appeased the animal's soul, he contentedly feasts off its flesh, and clothes himself in its skin. "Hail, friend from the spirit-land," is the salutation with which the Indian greets the snake he meets; "we were unfortunate, and our friends yonder knew of it. The Great Spirit knew of it. Take this gift of tobacco (sprinkling tobacco dust on the snake's head); it will comfort you after your long journey." With these words he seizes the snake by the tail, passes his hand dexterously along the back, till he reaches the head, and then crushes the reptile to death. He strips off the skin, which he wears as a trophy.* "Be not angry with us," say the Indians to the bear they have killed, "for having slain you. You have understanding, and know that our children are hungry. They love you, and they want to eat your flesh. Is it not an honor for you to become food for the children of the great chief?" † Sometimes they appease the bear they have killed by placing in its mouth a tobacco-pipe, into the head of which they blow, filling the animal's throat with smoke, and meanwhile asking forgiveness. During a meal, of which the bear himself is the principal dish, they set up his head on an elevated place and chant songs of praise in his honor.‡ The Ostiaks attach the head of the

bear to a tree, and pay it divine honor; then they utter their laments over its carcass, in doleful tones, inquiring, "Who has deprived you of life?" and immediately themselves giving the answer, "The Russians! Who cut off your head? The ax of the Russians. Who has stripped you of your hide? Some Russian's knife."* The inhabitants of Northern Europe, from a feeling of reverence, never call the bear by his own name, but only "the old man in the coat of fur." † When the Madagascans kill a whale calf, they make their excuses to its dam, and entreat her to go away,‡ just as the Kaffirs do, after they have captured an elephant.§

As fetiches generally, in accordance with the principles already explained (Ch. III.), are regarded as the causes of phenomena, which in point of fact stand to them not at all in the relation of effects, so too those animals which are worshiped are by their devotees arranged in causal relation with phenomena, whenever the true cause cannot be found. Hence the Yakutes regarded the camel as the cause of the small-pox (p. 24). The Mexicans first became acquainted on the one hand with the horse, on the other with ships, when the Spaniards came to their shores. The report and the flash coming from the guns of the latter they took to be thunder and lightning. Who produced these phenomena? Not men; of that they were quite sure. The horse, however, was something entirely new to them, and therefore they regarded the horse as the producer of the thunder and lightning, and on this ground worshiped him as a god. "At his departure Cortez left with these friendly people one of his horses that had received an injury in the foot. The Indians conceived a sentiment of reverence

---

* Waitz, III. 192.
† Lettr. édif. N. E. VI. 174.
‡ Charlevoix, p. 117, 300.

* Isbrand, Voy. au Nord. VIII. 411.
† Georgi, Beschr. S. 14, 21.
‡ Owen, Narr. of a Voy. to explore the Shores of Africa, Arabia and Madagascar. Lond. 1833, I. 170.
§ Moodie, Ten years in S. Africa. Lond. 1835, II. 333.

for the beast, as being in some way connected with the mysterious power of the white man. After their visitors had taken their leave, they offered flowers to the horse, and prepared for him, it is said, many savory dishes of poultry, such as they were wont to prepare for the sick. The poor beast starved to death with such novel food. The terrified Indians set up his image in stone, in one of their teocallis, and worshiped it as a god. When, in 1618, two Franciscans came to this locality (which was then as little known to the Spaniards as before Cortez's visit) to preach the gospel there, one of the most notable things they found was this image of a horse, which was worshiped by the devout Indians as the god of thunder and lightning." [*]　Jacob Grimm cites numerous cases of animal-worship among the ancient Teutons. Thus, whoever kills the haus-otter (a small innoxious snake) will die within the year.[†]　The killing of a swallow (which is a sacred bird) causes rain to fall for four weeks.[‡]　The giant eagle Hraesvelgr, in Northern mythology, causes the winds by beating his wings on the outer verge of the earth.[§]　The dew of morning is the foam that falls to the earth from the mouth of Hrimfaxi, the black steed of the night.[‖]　Sköll and Hati, two gigantic wolves, are ever chasing the sun and the moon,[¶] and hence it is that the latter ever speed on—a thing they would not do, were it not that they feared being overtaken by the wolves. Eclipses of sun and moon occur when the wolves overtake their prey, and have commenced to gulp them down; but fortunately the victims have so far been always successful in making their escape. In Oriental fable the dragon takes the wolf's place. The serpent Jörmungandr, which lives in the sea, encloses the whole earth in his folds. When he drinks there is ebb : but when he ejects water, there is flow of tide. In the mythology of Japan and China, when the dragon Tat quits the sea to saunter through the air, we have the waterspout.

7. Men as Fetiches.

A fetich is an object perceptible by the senses, to which, anthropopathically apprehended, man attributes causal power, and which he worships. Hence objects the most widely diverse becomes fetiches. Hence too, man himself, if the conditions unite in him, will be a fetich. Both in Africa and in America identical views are taken of those individuals who possess any extraordinary deformity, whether of body or of mind—for instance, albinos, dwarfs, hunchbacks, fools, etc. In Bornoo albinos are objects of fear, as beings gifted with supernatural power; [*] in Senegambia, if they are slaves, they are given their freedom, are exempted from all labor, and are cheerfully supported at others' expense.[†]　In Congo the king keeps them in his palace, as "fetiches which give him influence over the Europeans."[‡]　They are held in such respect that they may take whatever they will ; and he who is deprived of his property by them, esteems himself honored. In Loango they are esteemed above the Gangas, and their hair is sold at a high price as a holy relic.[§]　Thus may a man become a fetich.

This fetichistic worship of man is a totally different thing from the respect which is paid to the man whose extraordinary power is due simply to the fact that he is the owner of certain mighty fetiches. This is the case with the ordinary fetich-priest, and with many kings, who by means of their fetiches may decree favorable or unfa-

---

[*] Prescott, Conq. Mex. II. 369.
[†] D. M. Anh. Aberglaube Nr. 143.
[‡] Ib. Nr. 378.
[§] D. M. S. 361.
D. M. S. 368.
[¶] D. M. S. 401.

[*] Kölle, p. 401.
[†] Raffenel, Nouv. Voy. dans le pays des Nègres. Par. 1856, I. 230.
[‡] Bastian, 34.
[§] Proyart, 172.

vorable weather, etc., as, for instance, when Ogautau and Möndull in the saga, by shaking their weather-bag (vedhrbelgr) cause wind and tempest; or when the Swedish king Eirikr, surnamed Weather-hat (vedhrhattr), caused the wind to blow from the point toward which he turned his hat.* But if such power was attributed to the individuals themselves, and not to their fetiches, then they themselves became fetiches. Thus the Chitome of Congo is regarded as a fetich, as also, probably, the king of Usambara, whose power is so unlimited, that one of his subjects, describing the actual relation between ruler and subject, said : " We are all the slaves of the Zumbe (king) and he is our Mulungu (god)." † The Tamol of the western Caroline Islands appears to belong to the same class as the Chitome.‡ The nobility in those islands have unlimited power over the people, but they themselves in turn are subject to a Tamol in each separate island, and he is absolute monarch. Whoever approaches him on business, must come with his head bowed down to the level of his knees. He takes his position in silence, and awaits the Tamol's order to speak. The potentate's words pass for those of a god, and his hands and feet are kissed as often as a petition is addressed to him. The idolatrous worship of the princes of Tonga, whose touch suffices to make any object holy, also appears to be fetichistic. But of a different kind was the honor which, for instance, the Mexicans paid to Cortez ; § the Sandwich Islanders to Captain Cook : ‖ the Kamtchatdales to the first Russian seen by them ;¶ the inhabitants of Cassegut to De Brue ;** the Gilbert Islanders to the Scotchman Wood ; †† the Oatafians to Captain

Hale.* In these cases the motive was different : these white men were considered gods. Hence they were viewed not from the fetichistic standpoint, but from that of polytheism, the origin of which we have already pointed out. On this account the Gilbert Islanders carried Wood about in their arms, and the Oatafians entertained Hale (whose ship, as they thought, had come down from heaven) with solemn dances, lest they should offend the deity ; and answered his questions in song. The white men were identified with deceased ancestors,† being supposed to be the latter either *in propriis personis* or in their ghosts. Accordingly, here we have no fetichistic worship.‡

CHAPTER VI.

THE HIGHEST GRADE OF FETICHISM.

1. *The New Object.*

ALL the objects which we have so far considered as fetiches, how much soever they may differ among themselves, have this in common, that they exist in man's immediate environment : that they are within his reach, and almost all tangible. They are all circumscribed by the limits of earth, and mostly confined to the very spot which is the savage's own habitat : he necessarily comes in contact with them, nor is there any need of special search to find them out. Furthermore, all the objects which the savage in the lowest stage of intellectual development considers use-

---

* Grimm, D. M. S. 368.
† Krapf, Reisen in O. Afrika (1837-55). Stuttg. 1858, I. 291, note.
‡ Gerland *ap.* Waitz, V. 2, 116.
§ Acosta, p. 204.
‖ Cook's Last Voyage, III.
¶ Müller, Sammlung russ. gesch. III. 19.
** Labat, Voy. V. 172.
†† Gerland, V. 141.

* Hale, Eth. and Philol. (U. S. Exp.) Phil. 1846, 151 seq.
† *Cf.* Gerland, V. 141.
† This fifth chapter makes no pretension to an exhaustive treatment of its topics. Its object is simply to indicate the principal points of view, from which the various objects of fetich worship are to be regarded, with reference to the matter in hand. To collect and describe all the forms of fetichism in use among the various races of men, will furnish matter for as many special investigations as there are peoples and religions.

ful or desirable, belong in like manner to the earth; as all his aspirations and all his interests are concerned with earthly things. For what interests has he? Those of a spiritual nature are unknown to him, and those which he does recognize have reference simply to his physical wellbeing; his bodily appetites are the only stimuli which excite his will, and engage his whole attention. But how is he to gratify these appetites? The sky with all its stars will not appease his hunger, nor has the firmament power to sate his lust. The gratification of these appetites is to be found only here below. It is the earth alone that can give him the objects of his desire, and he has no wish for the things lying beyond. For us these earthly objects are become also objects of higher, more spiritual interest, inasmuch as we have made them objects of knowledge; but they are not at all objects for the savage in this sense. He has no desire of knowledge for knowledge' sake: he desires things only so far as they can gratify his grosser passions. Whatsoever does not minister to these, is of no interest for him, is no object for him, does not arrest his attention; just as animals "in the state of freedom only have perfectly clear conceptions of the few things which are closely connected with their daily wants and with their daily life, but suffer everything else to pass by almost unnoticed."* A plant is an object for the savage only in so far as it may supply food: it has no value for him as a botanical specimen, and it is only as an article of food that it can interest him. These mere bodily interests of his are amply secured within the narrow earthly world with which he is acquainted. So long as he experiences none but simply physical interests, he rests content with his contracted world, and his mind remains confined within its narrow sphere. If therefore his world is to extend its limits, and his mind to take a broader

range, he must experience some higher interest. But now the will is never without its object, never stands by itself as *will* simply, but always as will *determined*, always as will directed towards an *object:* and it ever extends just as far as its objects. If therefore a higher will, a higher interest is to be awakened, a new object must necessarily be attained, by impelling toward which the energies of the will we give them a new direction and elevate them. But of what kind must this object be, in order to awaken a new and a higher interest?

To arouse such interest in the savage mind it must be adapted to the savage's modes of apprehension. If it had no aspect which the savage mind might grasp, it could excite in it no interest. Let us see the mode and the measure of the savage's mental grasp. Abstract ideas, spiritual conceptions, purely mental phenomena are to him unintelligible, and consequently uninteresting, indifferent. He apprehends only what is apprehensible through the senses, or what he can *see*. The new object, therefore, if it is to excite an interest in his mind must be one that is apprehensible through the senses.

But the new object must awaken in him a higher interest than any he has hitherto known, and to this end the interests which hitherto have stimulated him must in some degree be repressed. Now it is the new object which has to do this. Let us see what kind of objects will *fail* to displace the old interests, or in other words the bodily appetites of hunger and lust, and the natural emotions such as joy and anger, which have been hitherto supreme. The savage has so far recognized only these, and has prized only such objects as answer to them. So long as he comes in contact with such objects as these, so long will this class of interests be served and go on growing. The objects therefore which answer to these appetites and passions will never tend to check the growth of inferior interests. They are only to be repressed

---

* Waitz, I. 329.

by some object not answering to them, nor tending to enhance them, but which, *nevertheless*, can engage the savage's attention. If it can do this without at all gratifying his bodily appetites, the will of the savage will be thereby to a certain degree weaned of these appetites and turned in a new direction, *i.e.*, will have a new interest. Therefore the new object must not serve in any way for the gratification of sensuous desire; for whatsoever has that tendency belongs to the sphere of the lower interests, and so to the sphere of pure savagery. And conversely, everything that has hitherto been comprised within the sphere of the savage serves, in so far as his interests are centered in it, to gratify these sensuous desires, they being as yet his only interests. Hence every object which lies within his immediate sphere is liable at any time to become merely the object of these desires. If then the new object is to be of such a nature that it will not answer to these desires, it must be so remote from the savage's immediate sphere that these sensuous desires can never in it find their gratification: and it must ever stand on a plane high *above* these, never *beneath* them. Such grand objects as a mountain or the sea do not, it is true, serve to appease hunger or to gratify lust, but still they may in some manner be subordinated to the savage's will and desire: he can ascend the mountain, set his foot upon its summit, break fragments of rock from it, etc.; he can sail upon the sea, take water out of it, scourge it, etc. And so every object upon the earth may be brought into subjection to his power; and hence the new object must lie entirely beyond the limits of earth, and beyond the sphere of his sensuous desires. But now since it can in no way gratify these desires, and still must excite an interest in the savage's breast, how is it to attain its end? As we have seen, it must not be an object of sensuous gratification, nor yet an object for use or for consump-

tion. But if the savage cannot employ it for sensuous gratification, and yet is to make it an object of contemplation, his attitude towards it must be one of attention, gazing, observation. Hence the new object, which is to repress sensuous desire, must be of such a nature as to rivet the attention, and to draw upon itself the gaze of the savage. It must therefore be visible, and as has been already said, an object apprehensible by sense. Now what is that object of sense which alone can rivet his attention, and yet never be subordinated to man's use? Since it must not lie within the sphere of his sensuous desire, it must consequently lie without the earth: and yet it must be observable by the senses, and specially fitted to engage the attention—hence something noteworthy and wonderful which shall surpass all things else in splendor. But now if this object could be contemplated and its properties ascertained in a moment it could engage the attention of the savage only for a brief space, and then he would be again free to give himself up anew to merely sensuous gratification. The new object must therefore not alone surpass all others in magnitude and splendor, but it must also be so vast and stupendous, that man may find no end of contemplating it, that it shall lead him on to ever new contemplations, and so ever withdraw him from ministering to his sensuous appetites. If then there be found an object which irresistibly challenges his attention merely as an object of contemplation without in the least gratifying his lower passions, he has henceforth, in addition to his former sensuous interests, a new one which consists in observation, contemplation: and this new interest we call an intellectual one, as contrasted with the other, which is sensuous or materialistic.

Thus the savage could acquire an intellectual interest only through some object of sense lying without the sphere of his passions, and hence extra-terrestrial, which, however, was fitted to engage his attention by attracting his gaze: which should be possessed of preëminent sensuous splendor and be of such grand proportions that it might be contemplated forever and still ever invite to fresh contemplation. Now of all the objects in the universe there is but one which fulfills all these requirements, and that is the Firmament with its countless stars. The sky is the new object, being perceptible by the sense—the mightiest, grandest and most stupendous of all the objects of sense, with its blazing sun, its shining moon, its twinkling stars, its rosy blush at morn and eve, and the deep blue of its mighty arch. By the splendor of its ever-changing and sublime phenomena, it invites the savage to the contemplation of itself, without ministering to his lower nature. Thus this new object gives to his will a new direction, a new interest—that of contemplation, of thirst for knowledge: an intellectual interest.

We must go back in imagination to the time when man was without knowledge, when all was ignorance, when there was no school to give instruction, as instruction is given now. Then every step toward knowledge was an advance into the unknown land, and individual observation was the only schoolmaster. But observation was limited to those objects which Nature afforded: hence Nature was, after all, the true Teacher. Were it not that there was in the universe an object which irresistibly challenged attention, without ministering to man's lower passions, and which thus in some measure diminished the force of the latter, man could never have risen above his animal instincts, nor ever have conceived an intellectual interest. Hence wherever the savage has not yet made the heavens the object of his contemplation, we may be sure that his condition is that of extreme barbarism, which latter however diminishes, in proportion as his knowledge of the heavens advances. The firmament is the first object which awakens in him intellectual interest. It is only after he has with some interest contemplated this object, that his mind goes out to observe the universe, for knowledge' sake, and to study the other objects upon the earth, as objects of knowledge, which before were only objects of desire. This is perfectly consequent, for so soon as one thing is regarded with intellectual interest, all other things will be regarded from the like point of view, since they are all mutually related. Hence, of all the sciences worthy of the name, astronomy is the oldest and the first; and hence too do we find, even in the remotest historic times, and among the most ancient peoples, that the results of astronomy, such as the ascertainment of the year's length, and kindred facts, are more correctly apprehended than the results of any other science. The science of the heavens, so soon as there is any demand among savages for scientific knowledge, constitutes the first object of scientific instruction. I have said, *scientific* instruction, to distinguish it from religious, which no doubt precedes astronomical instruction: but this precedence of religious instruction is due simply to the fact that it is based upon a total ignorance of Nature, which of course is prior to knowledge. But the earliest scientific knowledge that man acquires is that of astronomy. Leaving out of view the instruction the savage gains as to the objects in daily use, even the rudest of savages oftentimes receives religious instruction, but never anything that can lay claim to the title of scientific education. If therefore we anywhere find scientific instruction given (and the first lessons will be always in astronomy) we may confidently assert that mental development has made considerable progress. This is verified in the case of the South-Sea Islanders in the Carolines. Canova, in describing the Caroline Islands, says, "In each district there are two places of public instruction, in the one of which the boys, and in the other the girls receive instruction in astronomy, as far as the natives' knowledge of that science goes. The master in giving his lessons uses a globe, on which the position of the principal stars is indicated with rude art." [*] Hence, too, astronomy is the first subject-matter of early scientific literature. The books of the Mexicans had on one page mythological figures, ritual directions, laws and the history of the country, while on the opposite page, out of all the objects of theoretical science, they set forth only those of astronomy and chronological calculations.[†] The "innumerable books" of the people of Yucatan, whose mental culture was about parallel with that of the Mexicans, give the constellations, chronological calculations, and the fauna and flora, and political history of the country.[‡] Science in antiquity developed similar phenomena in its beginnings, and the library of a German peasant consists of a hymn book and an almanac.

We will suppose the savage, then, beginning to contemplate the heavenly bodies with some interest. The phenomena which these produce, viz., light and heat, and all the effects of these latter, have so wide an influence, and so intimately concern man himself, and further, it is so patent that these heavenly bodies are in truth the efficient causes of the phenomena, that man establishes a relation between them and his own life, between them and all Nature. There can be nothing on earth mightier than they, their influence pervading all space: they are supreme, they can account for everything, they are for man Ultimate Causes. But these causes do not for him operate through mechanical laws: they are not for him inanimate bodies, being, like all other objects, apprehended by him anthropopathically. Hence they have life and will, even as man himself—and thus they become the supreme fetiches. But their energies are not restricted to the production of storms and tempests: man sees his own fate as depending upon their decrees. The changes which he observes taking place among them he interprets as tokens of their good-will or their enmity, their favor or their displeasure; and hence it is that the early contemplation of the heavens, as being coupled with anthropopathic apprehension, is necessarily fetichistic, and that astronomy makes its first appearance as astrology; hence, too, the latter precedes the former chronologically.

2. The Gradual Acquisition of Knowledge.

Time was when the heavenly bodies were not yet an object of contemplation. We do not say that then man did not notice, did not see the sun, moon and stars—even brute beasts have so much cognizance of the heavens: but the time was when man had no definite notion of the heavenly bodies, when he knew nothing either of the mode or of the regularity of their movements, or of their periods: in short, when his knowledge of them was limited to the general sensuous impression. Later he comes to see in the heavens an object made up of distinct parts. Between the point of departure, nescience, and this term, knowledge, lies the period of gradual acquisition, where, starting from small beginnings, the mind advances step by step to knowledge. Let us form a clear conception of the order in which the heavenly bodies would by degrees come to be known to man, and we shall at the same time understand the order in which they presented themselves to him as objects of fetichistic contemplation. When he begins to observe the sky with its various phenomena, his knowledge is limited to the sensuous impression. But in this case the observer is not one who has pushed his investigations deeply into other subjects, and now to this new investigation brings a disciplined mind which can keenly analyze the phenomena;

[*] Gerland *apud* Waitz, V. 2. 110.
[†] Waitz, IV. 171.
[‡] Waitz, IV. 311.

he is only an overgrown infant, with powers of thought all undeveloped. Such an observer will be chiefly guided by the impression left by the object on his senses. Hence that heavenly body which appears most striking to the eye, which exhibits the greatest number of varying phases, and which is easiest observed, will first attract and rivet his attention. Now such an object is not the Sun, but the Moon : and hence we find that, among savages, the latter is worshiped at a much earlier period than the former, and is considered of higher importance.* This fact, which to us who can more truly estimate the relative importance of the two luminaries, appears at first glance unaccountable, admits of a very easy explication, when we consider on the one hand the exterior, sensible aspects of the two, and on the other hand the intellectual status of the savage.

In the first place the savage has in the day-time little leisure for the contemplation of Nature in general, or of the Sun in particular : he must needs find his daily provision, and this care engrosses all his attention. For the more perfect the means and the implements, the machinery he employs, the sooner can he supply his bodily wants, and the more leisure he has for mental development. But the less developed he is, the clumsier are the means at his command for taking his prey, and the more time does he consume in gathering together his daily provision ; and hence a Tierra del Fuegian is his whole life long occupied with this one care, and this is his sole employment, viz., to gain his sustenance. As he neither sows nor plants, and as the desert region in which he lives yields him scarcely one natural product, he must needs be restricted to this one pursuit. If perchance he succeeds in finding a sufficiency for the present, the search has wearied him and he seeks repose in sleep : and when he awakes

the renewed cravings of hunger compel him again to resume his search. Thus, if he would support life, he must through the day keep his eyes steadily fixed on the earth. And then the Sun is no such object as would through the day very forcibly claim the attention of a man whose mind is void of thought, and whose only care is to still the cries of hunger. All nature is now bathed in light ; there are no dark shadows, no contrasts ; and contrast it is which enables an object to make a very deep impression. Day with its light is a very common occurrence—it is indeed a fact of *daily* experience. But suppose that the man directs his gaze toward the sun : beyond its daily traversing the heavens, no phases are observable which might readily impress the savage mind. The Sun changes not like the Moon : those changes which we observe in the place of its rising, from solstice to solstice, take place so gradually, and require so long a period, that only close observation can detect them at all ; and for this the savage has neither the will nor the perseverance. Hence the sun is an object rather of meditation than of contemplation ; and to study it requires a rather highly developed understanding. It is very different with the moon. At night the savage has finished his daily toil ; his wants are supplied : hence he is now at leisure. But, most important of all, the effect of contrast is here to be observed. The earth is wrapt in darkness ; the superstitious savage meanwhile shudders with fear, while every nerve and every sense is on the stretch. Then emerges from beneath the horizon the bright orb of the full Moon, round as a wheel, red as fire. Then how manifold are its apparitions, the like of which are never to be seen in the Sun, and which are specially fitted to call forth the astonishment of man, and to invite him to reflection. Now she is fiery red, in a moment pale and wan ; at one time a majestic full orb, at another wasted away, and resemb-

---

* *Cf.* Wuttke, I. 66.

ling a sickle. The dark spots upon her surface lead men to fancy that she has a human face, or give rise to other imaginations: oftentimes she is totally eclipsed. In short, several peculiar and directly visible phenomena are observed in the moon, which must attract the attention of man, and cause him thither to direct his gaze. He will also attempt to assign causes for these phenomena, and these attempts, how inept and anthropopathic soever they may be, still will at least have this effect, that they will connect notions together, i.e., will serve as the first steps in thinking. Thus then we need not be at all surprised if when a rude people first begin to contemplate and to worship as fetiches the heavenly bodies, the Moon has precedence of the Sun.*

But after the Moon has become an object of man's contemplation, it is not now the Sun which he next studies, but certain stars which, as they appear in the gloom of night, affect him more sensibly and offer for his contemplation properties stranger and more easily observable than does the Sun. There are five stars and constellations † which first attract the notice of man, and which we always find recognized by such savages as have even made a beginning in the study of astronomy. The first is Venus, which with its brilliant light attracts attention, particularly by appearing first of all the stars in the evening, and vanishing last of all in the morning—the Morning and the Evening Star, which at first passed for two distinct luminaries, and which Pythagoras was the first among the Greeks to recognize as one.‡ Next is the Ursa Major, the Great Bear, or the Wain, which never drops below the horizon in the northern hemisphere; together with his counterpart, the Ursa Minor, the Little Bear; both of these being noticeable from their pe-

culiar form. Then that chain of three brilliant stars, known to the Greeks as Orion, which the people in Upper Germany still call the Drei Mäder (Three Mowers), because they resemble three mowers standing one behind the other.* Finally, the space so thickly gemmed with stars, situate between the shoulders of Taurus, and of which chiefly seven (more exactly six) are easily discernible — the Seven Pleiades, which are distinguished as being in the center of the glorious system of the Milky Way, and which gain all the higher eminence from the fact that the space all around them, to the extent of six of their diameters, is relatively poor in stars; and from this, that for many regions of the South these stars never set. These five are the first to be recognized : they are *popular* stars the world over. It is toward these that Odysseus directed his eyes when, quitting Calypso's isle, he takes his homeward course over sea :

Αὐτὰρ ὁ πηδαλίῳ ἰθύνετο τεχνηέντως
Ἥμενος· οὐδέ οἱ ὕπνος ἐπὶ βλεφάροισιν ἔπιπτεν
Πληιάδος τ' ἐσορῶντι καὶ ὀψὲ δύοντα Βοώτην
Ἄρκτον θ', ἣν καὶ ἅμαξαν ἐπίκλησιν καλέουσιν,
Ἥ τ' αὐτοῦ στρέφεται καὶ τ' Ὠρίωνα δοκεύει,
Οἴη δ' ἄμμορός ἐστι λοετρῶν Ὠκεανοῖο.
                                    Od. V. 270 seqq.

These Hephæstos represented on Achilles' shield (Il. xviii. 487 seqq.). Of these it is said : "Canst thou check the sweet influence of Chima (Pleiades) or loose the band of Kesil (Orion)? Canst thou order Mazzaroth (Sirius) in his period ? or canst thou lead Aish (Arcturus) with his sons ?" (Tob. xxxviii. 31.) "Who made Arcturus and Orion and the Pleiades and the chambers of the South?" (Tob. ix. 9.) These were the favorite stars of the Ancient Germans, the Sclavs and the Finns.†

That the Moon was the first among the heavenly bodies to be distinctly studied by man, and that the stars and the Sun followed after, is clearly

---

* Cf. W. Whewell, Hist. Inductive Sciences, Vol. I.
† Cf. Grimm, D. M. S. 416.
‡ Whewell, Hist. Induct. Sciences, Vol. I. 106.

* Grimm, D. M. 417.
† D. M. 416.

evinced by the different modes of reckoning time at various periods and in various nations. The mode of reckoning by Moons is the primitive one. We meet with it in the earliest historic records of all civilized nations, and hence we also find it wherever a nation is in the lower stages of development. Here we meet with reckonings by Moons, and by the movements of certain stars: but never by the sun's periods. Nations in this stage of development are raised very considerably above the condition of the rudest barbarism. Last comes the reckoning by the Sun, and this indicates an intellectual status which leaves far behind it the barbarism of savage tribes.

Not to speak of the civilized nations of Europe and Asia, who in early historic times reckoned by moons, this mode of reckoning time is to this day followed throughout Africa[*] by most of the Negro tribes, as also in America, by the aborigines. The Indians of the latter continent generally reckon thus, and their months bear the names of various objects in Nature, especially animals and the products of the earth.[†] "Like most of the other tribes, the Dakota Indians reckon twelve months, five each for Summer and Winter, and one each for Spring and Autumn, and add an intercalary month every second year. According to Carver (216) and Heckewelder this intercalation of a so-called "lost month" without a name, occurred every 30th month: but according to Kohl (I. 167), every year. Schoolcraft (V. 419) says that the Algonquins reckon only eleven months, which are brothers, and take to wife, in succession, one woman, the Moon. The Algonquins do not appear to find any difficulty in the fact that between winter and winter there are now 12 now 13 months.[‡]

The next step in astronomy is to reckon time by the moon and the stars together, excluding the sun, except for noting the hours of the day; and this mode of reckoning is found among some of the more advanced of the American tribes. The Iroquois and the Ojibbeways had special names for a number of stars; and the latter defined with precision the hours of night by the rising and setting of these. The Osages, too, marked the progress of night by the stars, and recognized Venus, the three stars in Orion's belt, the Pleiades, and even the Polar Star and the apparent revolution of the neighboring stars around it.[*] But it is among the natives of the Marian and the Caroline Islands that we find this mode of reckoning time best developed. The Caroline islanders not alone define the periods of the night by the stars, but even divide the year into seasons according to the ascent of certain stars at fixed times; and into months, each having a fixed number of days, according to the moon's several phases. Not alone has each day, but also each division of the day, a distinct name.[†] "According to Freycinct (2. 105) the number of their months was ten, and of these, five (from June to November) constituted the season of winds and rains, and the other five the temperate season. But that writer himself doubts whether they had not two modes of reckoning the year, the one founded on climatic reasons, the other on lunations, and giving a greater number of months than the former." Among the natives of the Marian Islands there were two parties, one of them counting twelve, the other thirteen lunations to the year; and their disputes once even led to a war. The Caroline men, besides traversing the sea all round their own group of islands for business or pleasure, visit also, whether singly or in squadrons, the Marian Islands. In making this voyage they direct their course according to the starry heavens, which they divide into twelve regions. Cantova makes mention of these twelve

---

* Waitz, II. 224.
† Waitz, III. 224.
‡ Waitz, III. 224.

* Nuttall, Journal of Travels into the Arkansas Territory. Phila. 1821, 172 seqq.
† Gerland ap. Waitz, V. 286.

regions and of the twelve winds named by the Caroline men. But they had also another division of the heavens into twenty-four regions, which took their names from the stars which rose and set in them. They guide their course at sea by these regions, as also by the sun, stars and constellations, whose rising and setting they can observe, and to which they give special names."* Of the astronomical instruction in vogue amongst them we have already spoken.

The reckoning of time by the sun is therefore of more recent origin than the reckoning by the moon and stars. Among the Mexicans, who reckoned solar years, many regarded the planet Venus to be more ancient than the sun.† The discovery of the solar year presupposes an extended and laborious observation of the sun, and so a high degree of spiritual interest. Hence we might à priori assert (and experience will confirm the assertion) that wherever the solar year is accepted as a measure of time, culture has gone far beyond its barbarous stages. We may go farther (and here too experience will come to our support) and assert that the worship of the sun is only possible where the mind has reached a degree of development far higher than that required for the worship of the moon and stars. The nations which have brought the worship of the sun to its highest perfection are civilized—the Persians, for instance, the Phœnicians, Carthaginians, Mexicans and Peruvians.

3. The Worship of the Moon.

The first and lowest stage of the worship of the heavenly bodies is that where the Moon is worshiped and regarded as of more importance than the Sun.

The Kamtchatdales have not yet reached this stage, worshiping, according to Steller, neither Sun nor Moon.‡ The Payaguas, of S. America, on perceiving the New Moon beat the air with their fists, to give expression, as they say, to their gladness. Azara, who relates this fact, further says: "Ce qui a donné lieu à quelques personnes de croire qu'ils l'adoraient; mais le fait positif est, qu'ils ne rendent ni culte ni adoration à rien au monde et qu'ils n'ont aucune réligion."* This joy of the savage on beholding the luminous heavenly bodies leads him to contemplate them, and he soon begins to regard them as the causes of occurrences which in no wise depend upon them. The Botokuds think the moon is the cause of most of the phenomena of Nature.† In the Pelew Islands predictions are made from the appearance of the Moon.‡ Hence the Moon soon passes for a mighty fetich, and so is held in greater consideration than the Sun; and accordingly the Moon would be naturally regarded as a Man, the Sun as a Woman. Bleek says, with respect to the Hottentots, " In the lowest stage of culture to be met with among nations having sexual language, the worship of the heavenly bodies acts a very unimportant part, for the reason that the knowledge possessed by savages of the motions of these bodies is too slight to give a basis for reverential contemplation. And yet we find even here the rudiments of the mythologic (i.e., anthropopathic) conception. . . . For first the phases of the Moon will excite attention. Her gradual waxing and waning gives to the savage the notion of a Being which grows for a while, and then decays, and he readily personifies it. Hence it is not improbable that Moon-worship was the earliest phase of the worship of heavenly bodies. The Hottentots, as we are assured by Kolb, a competent witness, pay divine honor to the Moon. In their language ‖khap §

---

* *Ibid.* 85.
† Waitz, IV. 146.
‡ Steller, Kamtschatka, S. 281.

* Azara, II. 137.
† Pr. M. v. Neuwied, R. n. Brasil, II. 58 f.
‡ Hockin, Supplem. to the Account of the Pelew Islands. Lond. 1803, p. 15.
§ ‖ expresses the lateral clicking sound; Kh is a guttural consonant, and ˜ marks the nasal tone.

(Moon) is, as in ancient Teutonic, masculine, and the Sun feminine." The Namaquas, an offshoot of the Hottentots, regard the Sun as a lump of "clear fat," which seafarers attract to themselves by enchantment during the night, and then spurn after morning has come, and they have no further need of it. The Moon, on the other hand, they regard as a more important personage than even their own chief Spirit u-Tixo. He (the Moon) once commissioned the Hare to inform mankind that even as the Moon always recovers again his fullness after he has lost it, so they too may come to life again, after death. The hare mistook the message and told men that they must die away, even as the moon does. This was the origin of death. Old Namaquas never eat hare-flesh, probably because this animal is regarded as a divine messenger. The waning of the moon is due to his putting his hand up to his head when he has a headache.* The Mbocovies, neighbors of the Payaguas, take some of the stars for trees with luminous branches, and others for an ostrich pursued by dogs. (*Cf. supra*, Ch. III. § 3.) The Sun, they say, is a woman who once fell upon the Earth, and caused thereby great calamity: it was only with great difficulty that she was restored to her place. But the Moon is a man: and his eclipse is caused by a dog tearing out his bowels.† The Navajoes say that the Moon is a man riding on an ass: but that the Sun is set up in the heavens every morning by an old woman.‡ The Greenlanders say that Anningat, the Moon, is a man who is in pursuit of Mallina, the Sun, his sister, with whom he is in love.§ By the Lithuanians, Arabs ǁ and Hindus ¶ the Moon is also regard-

ed as a man. Our Teutonic ancestors had the same opinion : " Audio veteres Germanos Lunum quoque deum coluisse et appellasse Hermon, id est, dominum Lunum (Herr Mond)." (Gesner, *Mithridates*, Tur. 1555, p. 28.) Hulderic. Eyben (De titulo nobilis. Hemst. 1677, 4, p. 136) says : " Qua etiam ratione in vetere idololatrico luna non domina, *dominus* appellatur :

Bis gottwillkommen, neuer mon, holder herr,
Mach mir meines Geldes mehr.

And Eligius : nullus *dominos* solem aut lunam vocet. The Sun, too, they regarded as a woman : Vetulam novi, quæ credidit solem esse deam, vocans eam sanctam dominam. (Nicolaus de Gawe *ap.* Grimm.)* The Greeks had for the Moon the two appellations μήν, masculine, and σελήνη, feminine, and μήν is the more ancient name. The Romans likewise had the two words Lunus and Luna.† The citizens of Carræ believed that whoever regarded the Moon as a male deity, would be lord over women : whoever held him to be female, would be their slave.‡ With regard to the utterly barbarous aborigines of New California Bägert§ states that not alone are they without social organization, but that not even the trace of any religion is to be found among them. Picolo's account contradicts this, for he says that they worship the Moon.ǁ The Panches are by Gomara ¶ said to wor-

Indian mythology the Moon is a god, not a goddess."
* D. M. 400 ff.
† Macrob. III. c. 8. *Cf.* Meiners, I. 389.
‡ Spartian. in Vit. Anton. Carac. c. 7. Et quoniam Dei Luni fecimus mentionem, sciendum, doctissimis quibusque id memoriæ traditum atque ita nunc quoque a Carrenis præcipue haberi, ut qui lunam fœmineo nomine ac sexu putaverit nuncupandam, is addictus mulieribus semper inserviat : at vero qui marem deum esse crediderit, is dominetur uxori, neque ullas muliebres patiatur insidias. Unde quamvis Græci vel Aegyptii eo genere quo fœmineam hominem, etiam Lunam deam dicunt, mystice tamen deum dicunt.
§ Bägert, Nachricht. v. Californ. S. 168.
ǁ Ap. *Waitz*, IV. 250.
¶ Hist. gen. de las Indias, in Historiad. prim. de Ind. Madr. 1852, p. 202.

---

* Waitz, II. 342.
† Guevara, Hist. Paraguay, Rio de la Plata y Tucuman, I. 15. *Cf.* Waitz, III. 472.
‡ Davis, El Gringo, or New Mexico and her People. N. Y. 1857, p. 414.
§ Grimm, D. M. 400.
ǁ *Ibid.*
¶ Muir's Sanskrit Texts, vol. v. p. 76. " In

ship Sun and Moon, while Piedrahita * expressly affirms that they worship the Moon only. But these conflicting statements may perhaps be reconciled if we recollect that Piedrahita's account is of earlier date than Gomara's : thus Gomara's narrative would exhibit the progress to the worship of both Sun and Moon from simple Moon-worship. The difference between Bägert and Picolo admits of a similar explanation. With regard to the Kaffirs, too, we have accounts on the one hand asserting that they do not regard Sun or Moon as objects of worship, though they hold them to be animate beings ; and on the other hand accounts affirming explicitly that they hold festival and conduct religious dances at the time of the New Moon.† The Maravi celebrate the return of the New Moon.‡ Traces of the old German moon-worship, in addition to those already mentioned, are found in the following passage from Nicolaus de Gawe's work *de Superstitionibus :* " Insuper hodie inveniuntur homines tam layci quam clerici, literati quam illiterati, et quod plus dolendum est, valde magni, qui cum *nouilunium primo viderint flexis genibus adorant: vel deposito capucio vel pileo inclinato capite honorant* alloquendo et suscipiendo. Ymmo eciam plures ieiunant ipso die novilunii, sive sit dies dominica in qua secundum ordinacionem ecclesiæ non est ieiunandum propter resurrectionis leticiam siue quacunque alia die, eciamsi esset dies dominice nativitatis. Quæ omnia habent speciem ydolatrie, ab ydolatris relicte." §

The Moon being an animated thing and regarded with such veneration, it cannot surprise us to find the liveliest sympathy excited in her favor, especially whenever she appeared in danger of perishing, *i. e.,* when she is eclipsed. We have already seen that several tribes of savages account for this phenomenon by attributing it to the attack of a wolf on the Moon. Hence they hasten to render her assistance by making a fearful noise, with a view to frighten the monster away.* " Nullus, si quando luna obscuratur, vociferare præsumat," says Eligius in a sermon. " Vince Luna," was the cry of the Romans, prompted by a similar belief : and we meet with the same usage in other nations, for instance, among the Christians of Abyssinia.† The Mbocovies, as we have seen, supposed that a dog was tearing out the entrails of the Man-Moon. Similar beliefs are entertained by American Indians, and this circumstance will explain their custom of beating their dogs, during an eclipse of the Moon, as the Hurons did, according to Charlevoix, and also the Peruvians. The Potowatomies, who are Sun-worshipers and who regard the moon as a maleficent deity, as compared with the Sun, suppose that in the Moon there dwells an old woman who weaves a basket, on the completion of which the world will come to an end : but the basket is always torn in pieces by a dog, before it is finished. Whenever the woman struggles with the dog there is a lunar eclipse.‡ Many of the South Sea Islanders explain this phenomenon differently,§ accounting for it in accordance with the dogmas of Soul-worship, which appears to overmaster their fetichism, and to force it into the background. According to them the Moon is the food of departed spirits, and by feasting off it, they make it smaller ; just as the Dakota Indians say that the waning of the Moon is caused by the gnawing of a number of little mice (Mice-souls ?). But it ever waxes again. When therefore the Moon is eclipsed, these islanders

* Ilist. de las conq. del nuevo reyno de Granada, I. parte. Amberes, 1688, V. 1.
† Waitz, II. 411 f.
‡ Monteiro in the Ztschr. f. Allg. Erdkunde, VI. 260 ff. Ausland, 1858, p. 260; Waitz, II. 419.
§ Grimm, D. M. Anhang. S. XLIV.

* Cf. Grimm, D. M. 401.
† Waitz, II. 503.
‡ De Smet, Missions de l'Oregon et Voyages aux Montagnes rocheuses (1845). Gand. 1848, p. 298.
§ Turner, p. 529 seqq.

are alarmed, lest the souls should go without sustenance. To prevent so great a calamity they make a great offering of cocoa-nuts. On the island of Eap * it is a wizard that causes the Moon to wane, by his enchantments.

We need not be surprised if we find a well-developed worship of spirits among people who pay no worship to the stars. The conception and worship of ghosts and spirits belong to the lowest grades of human development, and are parallel with those phases of fetichism which have all their objects upon the earth itself. More recent than either of these is Star-worship; and to the highest grade of this, which is the climax of fetichism, answers polytheism, the climax of spirit-worship. Where the two intersect, monotheism results. But of course we can only state these points here as theses susceptible of proof.

4. The Worship of the Stars.

The Hottentots, who are Moon-worshipers, and who take the Sun to be a lump of fat, have names for several stars, yet do not worship them.† The ancient religion of the Moxos differed for each village. They worshiped severally the Sun, the Moon and the Stars, as well as spirits and fetiches of every description. Their principal objects of worship were the evil spirit Choquigua and the jaguar: yet they kept a festival at the time of the New Moon, and Carasco is inclined to consider Star-worship as their primitive religion.‡ The Abipones of S. America worshiped as fetiches the Pleiades, which for them never set. They regarded this constellation as the founder of their race, and gave to it the same name which they gave to their conjuring doctors, Keebet.§ The Pawnee Indians used to offer human sacrifice annually to the "great star" which they worshiped, viz., Venus; and the same planet

had a chapel dedicated in its honor among the Mexicans, who held it to be more ancient than the Sun. The last sacrifice offered to the "Great Star" by the Pawnees was offered in 1837 or 1838. Then a Sioux girl was the victim, and she, after having been carefully tended and well fed, without any intimation of her fate being given her, was bound fast upon a funeral pile and shot to death with arrows. Whilst yet she lived, they carved pieces of flesh off her body, and suffered her blood to flow over the young shoots of corn.*

5. The Transition to Sun-Worship.

Wherever the Moon and the Stars are objects of worship, the Sun's claims to adoration will soon be recognized, and then the Sun and the Moon will at first receive equal veneration, to the prejudice of the stars, which will hold but a subordinate position. But when once attention has been directed to the Sun, it will quickly be seen that, as compared with the Moon, he is the superior Being, and then their mutual relations will be reversed, the Sun coming prominently into the foreground. Hence in the worship of Sun and Moon, we recognize two stages: in the one these two luminaries jointly receive equal worship; in the other they are both worshiped indeed, but still the Sun far outranks the Moon, and the religious halo surrounding the latter is as pale as her beams. For all these stages we can find representatives, and of the latter it is to be observed that their intellectual advancement will correspond with the progress they have made in the worship of the heavenly bodies.

The Comanche Indians † worship the Sun and Moon ex æquo. They call the Sun the God of Day, the Moon the God of Night, and the Earth, the Common Mother of all.

---

* Gerland apud Waitz, V. 2, 147.
† Campbell, First voyage.
‡ Waitz, III. 538.
§ Dobrizhofer, II, 80, 87 seqq. 317.

* De Smet; J. Irving, Indian sketches. Lond. 1835; Schoolcraft, IV. 50, V. 77.
† Waitz, IV. 213, ff.

In their view the Sun and the Moon are both *men:* they stand on terms of equality, not of subordination, which latter would not be the case were they regarded as Man and Woman. The savage considers woman to be immeasurably the inferior of man, and in the earlier stages of the worship of Sun and Moon the latter would be male, the former female. In that stage which the Comanches have reached they are both male: and it is only later that the Sun is held to be a man, the Moon a woman. As for the intellectual culture of these savages, it may be estimated from the following circumstances. On journeys they direct their course by the Polar Star. They do not follow agriculture, living solely by the chase. Their clothing is of tanned deer-skin. Their weapons are bows and arrows, the lasso and the shield; and now muskets. Each individual is allowed unrestricted freedom of action, but yet offenses are punished by decree of a council summoned annually by the chief. Debauchery is common, and polygamy prevails amongst them. They have no word meaning *virgin,* and it is simple politeness to offer to the stranger a female companion.

On the stage next above this, both Sun and Moon are also worshiped, but the Sun has precedence of the Moon, the latter being female, the former male. The Muzos say the Sun is their Father, the Moon their Mother. The natives of Cumana, one of the Caribees, used to worship Sun and Moon as man and wife.* The Sun goes on increasing in importance: thus the Potowatomies † hold the Moon to be an evil female deity (*supra*, p. 93); the Sun-worshiping Winnebagoes ‡ do not believe that the Moon has any power over mankind; while the Osages regard the Sun as the Great Spirit, ruling over Moon and Earth.* Here we reach that stage in the worship of the heavenly bodies, where the Sun assumes the unchallenged pre-eminence.

6. *The Worship of the Sun.*

Almost all the tribes of American Indians worship the Sun as the Supreme Deity. In North America, according to Waitz (III. 180) this is true as regards all the tribes as far west as the Crows and the Blackfeet, and as far north as the Ottawas. In Florida the worship of the Sun reigned, and it extended thence to the Apache country. Sun-worship, however, reached its highest stage of development in Middle and South America, among the Mexicans and the Peruvians.

The Indians of Florida prayed to the Sun, whom they held to be a man, for victory in battle, and sang hymns of praise in his honor.† The chief offering made to the Sun by the Indians is tobacco-smoke from the pipe, and thus smoking is among them a religious rite. The Hurons, Mandans, Menitarees and other tribes held the tobacco-pipe, whose high importance as the pipe of peace is well known, to be the gift of the Sun: and they, as well as many tribes lying further south, offer this incense to the Sun, to the four cardinal points of the heavens, and to Mother Earth.‡ The chiefs of the Hudson's Bay Indians used to direct three puffs of smoke toward the rising Sun, and greet him with a reverential salutation.§ In the Council, the pipe is always passed around, following thus the Sun's course, as they say.‖ In Virginia, the aborigines used to crouch at sunrise and sunset, and direct their

---

* Gomara, 208; Herrera, Descripcion de las Indias occidentales. Madrid, 1730, III. 4. 10 seq.
† Keating, I. 216.
‡ Schoolcraft, IV. 240.

* Morse, Rep. to Sec. of War, on Ind. Affairs. New Haven, 1822, Appendix, 229.
† Landonnière, Histoire notable de la Floride (1562–67). Par. 1853, 8, 99; Herrera, VII. 1, 15, 2, 6; Buschmann *ap.* Abhandl. d. Akad. d. Wiss. zu Berl. 1854, S. 300.
‡ Lafitau, II. 134 seqq.; Lettr. édif. I. 763; Nuttall, 274; Keating, I. 408 *et alibi.*
§ De la Potherie, I. 121, 131, II. 106.
‖ Perrin du Lac, I. 179.

eyes and their hands toward that luminary.* The Osages † each morning pronounce a prayer to the Sun, and in the chants of the Algonquin prophets ‡ the Sun is honored as supreme Deity. The Potowatomics § used occasionally to get upon the roofs of their huts at the rising of the Sun and on bended knees make an offering to him of maize gruel. The Spokans call themselves "Sons of the Sun." We can estimate the intellectual status of these Indians from the grade of religious development which they have reached; and the notable researches made by Waitz show that the former is on the whole considerably higher than has been commonly supposed. The nearer we approach to Mexico, the higher is the development of Sun-worship, and the higher the intellectual status of the aborigines. Even the natives of the lower Colorado country,‖ who were Sun-worshipers, did not practice polygamy, jealously watched over the chastity of the young women previous to marriage, and were of mild manners, though warlike. The Pueblos,¶ dwelling in the N. E. part of New Mexico, whose chief god is the Sun, are very industrious farmers with well-constructed implements of husbandry; weave woolen and cotton fabrics; are well clothed, and build houses of stone and adobes, three or four stories in height. As well in geographical position as in culture and worship the Mexicans had for neighbors the Natchez of Louisiana, together with the kindred people of Texas, whose principal tribe was that of the Assinais.** Waitz

says that among these is to be found "the truest and most definite expression of Sun-worship, in conjunction with a theocratic form of government." The Natchez lived under an absolute monarchy, and the royal family, descendants of the Sun, stood high above the common people, like the family of the Incas of Peru.

American Sun-worship found its highest development among the Mexicans and Peruvians. These races at the period of their coming in contact with Europeans were no longer savages, but civilized nations in the strict sense of the word, and capable of still further native development. This civilization would have produced the fairest fruit had it not been ruthlessly interrupted by the fanatic zeal of a Cortez and a Pizarro, and later purposely, persistently and violently stamped out by the barbarities of Christian tyrants.

Although polytheism was fully developed among the Mexicans,* still the Sun was their Supreme Deity, especially among the Toltecs, who were the authors of all Mexican culture. It has occasioned surprise to many to find polytheism and Sun-worship co-existent, as in the religion of Mexico. One explanation accounts for this by supposing that this religion had its origin among several diverse nations who coalesced into one, each importing its own religious ideas. But this supposition cannot be established on historical grounds, nor is it at all necessary. We have already more than once remarked that the worship of spirits and the worship of material objects are developed simultaneously and side-by-side. The one *never* arises alone, and unaccompanied by the other. The development of spirit-worship advances *pari passu* with that of matter-worship. Wherever the latter as-

* Strachey, Hist. of Trav. into Virginia Britannia. Lond. 1849, p. 93.
† Nuttall, 95.
‡ Schoolcraft, I. 399.
§ Journal étranger, 1762, Mai p. 7, *ap.* Waitz, III. 182.
‖ Castañeda, Relation du Voy. de Cibola (1540), éd. Ternaux. Par. 1838, p. 299 seqq.; Herrera, VI. 9, 14.
¶ Rivera, Diario y Derrotero de la Visita general de los Presidios de N. España. Guatemala, 1736; Villa-Señor, Teatro Americano, Descr. gen. de los Reynos y Provinc. de la N. España. Mex. 1746. *Cf.* Waitz, IV. 227.
** Waitz, III. 219 ff.

* *Cf.* Prescott, Conq. Mex. I.; Waitz, IV. S. 1-180; Wuttke, Gesch. d. Heidenth. S. 251-299; D. Fr. Saverio Clavigero, Hist. Antig. de Megico, sacada de los mejores historiadores españoles y de los manuscritos y de las pinturas indias, etc. Londres, 1826.

sumes the form of Sun-worship, the former becomes a complex polytheism : hence we find in the religion of Mexico not two incongruous elements, but rather the regular combination of two lines of objects of worship which constitute the inception of religious development in the mind of man. We have no need, therefore, of supposing that the Mexican religion came from different peoples : its two phases are rather the genuine products of the Mexican understanding itself.

The Sun's preëminence over the other gods is shown in the Mexican myth which traced the origin of the Sun, as also in the fact that the Mexicans called themselves "the Sun's children." This myth is given in full by Clavigero,[*] but we need here refer only to that portion which speaks of the heroes or demigods (heroes o semidioses), who, prior to the appearance of the Sun, ruled over men, and opposed that god when he began to run his course ; but seeing that they could not make head against him, such of them as had not already been slain by the Sun made away with themselves, leaving him sole master. Quetzalcoatl, a sort of Mexican Christ,[†] is said to have been created by the breath of Tonacateotl, the Sun.[‡] Whereas offerings were made to the other gods only four times a day, in the morning, at noon, in the evening and at midnight, there were nine daily offerings to the sun, four by day and five through the night, of copal or other fragrant gum, such as chapopotli [§] (called by Clavigero betun judaico, asphaltum). They offered also quails to the Sun at his rising, and solemnly greeted his appearance with music.[‖] That their conception of the Sun was anthropopathic though a most exalted one

we see from all their myths. At the solemn naming of the new-born infant, when ceremonies were used having a strange resemblance to those accompanying the baptismal rite in Christian churches—as, for instance, their sprinkling the babe with water and then entreating the deity "that he would cause these holy drops of water to wash away the sin which became the infant's heritage before the creation of the world, to the end that the babe might be born anew "[*]—the mother thus addressed the Sun and the Earth : "Thou Sun, Father of all that live, and thou Earth, our Mother, take ye this child and guard it as your son."[†] They often employed this solemn form of asseveration, "By the life of the Sun and of our Lady, the Earth."

The Mexicans, who thus paid supreme honor to the Sun, and made him the object of constant observation, gained an astonishing degree of accuracy in their knowledge of his course. All who have studied the matter are agreed [‡] that the Mexicans, who used sun-dials, calculated the length of the solar year with the utmost possible exactitude. First, their year consisted of 18 months having 20 days each—360 days. To the last month they added 5 days, which they called *nemontemi*, unemployed, as they did nothing on those days but pay visits.[§] "But what is most wonderful in their reckonings, and what will appear scarce credible to those who are unacquainted with Mexican antiquities, is this," says Clavigero,[‖] "that the difference of some hours between the civil and the solar years was noted by them, and that they resorted to intercalation to equalize them. There was, however,

---

* Lib. VI. p. 228, Apoteosis del Sol y de la Luna.

† Cf. Waitz, IV. 141 f.

‡ Kingsborough, Antiq. of Mex. Lond., 1831, V. 135, 184.

§ Clavigero, VI. 251 : Al sol incensaban nueve veces, cuatro de dia y cinco de noche.

Ib., p. 260.

* *Vide* Prescott, I.

† Clavigero, p. 290 : Tú, sol, decia la partera, padre de todos los vivientes, y tú, tierra, nuestra madre, acoged á este niño y protegedlo como á hijo vuestro.

‡ Cf. Prescott, I. ; Waitz, IV. 174.

§ Gama, Descripcion Historica y Cronologica de los Dos Piedras. Mejico, 1832, II. 111 seqq.

‖ Libro. VI. p. 269.

between their mode of intercalation and that of Julius Cæsar which is adopted for the Roman Calendar, this difference, that instead of intercalating one day every fourth year, they added 13 days every fifty-second year. "They waited," says Prescott, "till the expiration of 52 years, when they interposed 13 days, or rather 12 days and a half, this being the number that had fallen in arrear. Had they inserted 13, it would have been too much, since the annual excess over 365 is about 11 minutes less than 6 hours. But as their calendar, at the time of the Conquest, was found to correspond with the European (making allowance for the subsequent Gregorian reform), they would seem to have adopted the shorter period of 12 days and a half, which brought them within an almost inappreciable fraction, to the exact length of the solar year, as established by the most accurate observations. (*Cf.* La Place ; *Exposition*, p. 350.) Indeed, the intercalation of 25 days in every 104 years, shows a nicer adjustment of civil to solar time than is presented by any European calendar; since more than 5 centuries must elapse, before the loss of an entire day.* Such was the astonishing precision displayed by the Aztecs, or, perhaps, by their more polished Toltec predecessors, in these computations, so difficult as to have baffled, till a comparatively recent period, the most enlightened nations of Christendom ! "

In addition to their solar year they had also a sacerdotal, or, so to speak, an ecclesiastical year of 20 times 13 days, and this year was called the Metzlapohualli (Lunar Reckoning), as distinguished from the civil year Tonalpohualli (Solar Reckoning).† This religious computation of time, which served to regulate the festivals,

as also the circumstance that one word, Metzli, served to express both *month* and *moon*, are evidences of an earlier computation by Moons. which in fact Echevarria asserts to have been their more ancient mode of reckoning.*

But even as the Moon lost importance for computing time, so too did her worship decline. She came to be regarded as the wife of the Sun, as the Stars were his sisters.† As for her eclipses, the true cause of which they very probably recognized,‡ they were not regarded with the same emotions as by savages.§ Amid the countless temples and chapels of Mexico two were specially famous, the great temple of the Sun, and the smaller temple of the Moon at Teotihuacan, and around each of these stood a cluster of minor temples, probably dedicated to the worship of the Stars. ‖ The planet Venus had a temple called Ilhuicatitlan.¶ The Stars were objects especially of astrological observation, and were consulted with regard to the most trifling domestic affairs as well as the weightiest concerns of the State ;** even the kings were attentive observers of the stars, and one of them, Nezahualcoiotl, built for his own use an observatory.

The Mexican State was a carefully articulated organism, down even to its minutest subdivisions. The affairs of the army, the revenues, the courts of justice, the police, etc., were thoroughly organized. The king, vicegerent of God on earth, was possessed of powers limited only by divine authority and the prescriptions of religion. The prayers addressed by him to the deity, to obtain strength and light for the discharge of his important duties, sound like some of David's Psalms.

---

* Gama, parte 1, p. 23. El corto exceso de 4 hor. 38 min. 40 seg., que hay de mas de los 25 dias en el periodo de 104 años, no puede componer un dia entero, hasta que pasen mas de cinco de estos periodos máximos ó 538 años.

† *Cf.* Waitz. IV. 174.

* De Echevarria y Veitia, Hist. del Origen de las Gentes que poblaron la N. España (Ap. Kingsborough, VIII.) I. 4.

† *Cf.* Waitz, IV. 154.

‡ Humboldt, Vues des Cordillères, 282; Prescott, I.

§ Kingsborough, V. 156.

‖ Clavigero, I. 247 seq.

¶ Clavigero, p. 244.

** *Ibid.* 1. 209 seqq. 271, 291, etc.

No Jewish prophet could use more impressive language than this, addressed to a Mexican King : * "Graciously and meekly receive all who come to you in anguish and distress; neither speak nor act from passion. Calmly and patiently listen to the complaints and reports that are brought to you. Silence not the speaker, for you are God's image, and his representative : he dwells in you, using you as the organ (flute) through which he speaks ; and he hears through your ears. Punish no man without cause, for the right of inflicting punishment, which you hold, is of God :—it is as it were the talons and the teeth of God, to execute justice. Be just, and let who will be offended ; for such is God's decree. Be it your care that in the tribunals all things be done according to order, and without precipitancy, and nothing in passion. Let it never enter your heart, to say, I am Master, and will do as I please ; for that would tend to destroy your power, lower you in men's esteem, and impair your royal majesty. Suffer not your power and dignity to be to you the occasion of pride and arrogance, but let them rather remind you of the lowliness from which you have been raised, without any merit of yours. Be not given to sleep, nor to indolence and sensuality, nor to reveling. Squander not the sweat and the toil of your subjects. The favor which God has shown you, abuse not for profane and senseless purposes. Our Lord and King! God has his eye upon the rulers of States, and when they commit a fault, he laughs in scorn, but is silent : for he is God, and does what he will, and derides whom he will : for he holds us ·in his hand, tosses us from side to side, laughing at us when we totter and fall."

The material progress of the Mexican nation may be judged by the number and size of the cities. The city of Mexico had from fifty to sixty thousand families, or *houses*, as some

authors suppose ; Tezcuco was of equal magnitude ; Tzimpantzinco had 20,000 ; Cholula, Huexocinco and Tepeaca, each 40,000 ; Xochimilco 80,000 ; According to Cortez himself Tlascala was in every respect a more opulent place than Granada in Spain. These cities all possessed buildings of considerable magnificence, and there were besides a number of smaller cities.*

The earnestness of their moral sentiments is evinced by the rigid discipline enforced as well in their domestic education as in that of their schools and seminaries, and by the exhortations, the prayers and the proverbs which were learned by rote. " Nothing," says Padre Acosta, "astonished me more or appeared to me more praiseworthy and notable, than the system followed by the Mexicans in the education of their children." " In truth it were difficult to find a nation," adds Clavigero, " that bestows more diligent care than they upon a matter which so nearly concerns the well-being of the state. Doubtless," he continues, "they disfigured their teaching with superstitions ; but still the zeal they showed for education might well put to shame many a father of a family in Europe : and many of the instructions which they gave to the pupils would make profitable reading for our own young people." †

As a specimen of these I give the exhortation addressed by a Mexican to his son, which is admitted to be genuine by all the critics : ‡ " My son, you came forth out of your mother's

---

* Sahagun, *ap.* Waitz, IV. 68.

* *Cf.* Waitz, IV. 93.
† Clavigero, I. 299.
‡ I translate it from Clavigero's work (*ubi supra*). He says it came to his hands from those of Motolinia, Olmos and Sahagun, missionaries in Mexico, perfect masters of the language, and zealous students of Mexican manners, etc. Besides this address of the father to his son, Clavigero gives a similar address of the mother to her daughter, to be found in Prescott (Append. II.), and which is even a more charming composition than the address given in the text. (See the latter also in Waitz, IV. 125, who takes it from Sahagun, Hist. de N. España, VI. 18.)

womb as the chick from the egg, and as you grow you are like the chick preparing for your flight over the earth, nor is it given us to know how long Heaven will insure to us the jewel which we possess in you. However that may be, be it your care to lead a correct life, praying unceasingly to God for his support. It was he that created you, and he is your owner. He is your Father, and loves you more than I. Turn your thoughts God-ward, and let your aspirations rise to him by day and by night. Honor and greet those who are older than yourself, and never give them tokens of contempt. Be not deaf for the poor and the unfortunate, but rather make haste to console them with kindly words. Pay respect to all men, especially your parents, to whom you owe obedience, reverence and dutiful service. Have a care never to follow the examples of those wayward boys, who are like wild beasts void of reason, and who do not respect those who have given them their being, nor heed their admonitions, nor submit to correction: for whoso walks his own ways will come to a disastrous end, dying in blank despair: he will either be hurled down a precipice, or will fall under the claws of wild beasts. Make not merry, my son, over the aged, nor over those who have any bodily defect. Mock not those who happen to make a misstep, nor reproach them therewith; on the contrary be humble, and fear lest what offends you in others become your own. Go not whither you are not invited, nor meddle in affairs which are none of yours. In all that you say, and in all that you do, be it your study to show your good breeding. When you converse with any one, do not annoy him with your hands (mit den Händen belästigen) nor be too voluble: do not interrupt or disturb others with your remarks. If perchance you hear a man speaking foolishly, and it is not your business to correct him, hold your peace: but if it is your business, then consider first what you will say, and speak not arrogantly, that your corrections may avail the more. When any man addresses you, listen to him attentively and with proper demeanor, neither shuffling your feet, nor munching your mantle, nor spitting out, nor jumping up every moment if you are seated: for such conduct shows levity and bad breeding. When you are seated at table, eat not ravenously, nor betray signs of displeasure, if any dish fails to please you. If any one comes in while you are at table share with him what you have, and when one sits at your board, fix not your gaze upon him. When you go out, keep your eyes directed forward lest you hustle against those you meet. When any one approaches you, walking on the same path, give place a little that he may have room to pass. Never walk in advance of your superiors, except when necessity requires that you should, or they command it. When you eat in company with them, serve them with whatever they wish, and so you will gain their favor. If a man make you a gift, receive it with tokens of gratitude: if the gift is of great value, be not vain of it: if it is trifling, do not despise it, nor grow angry, nor anger the man who does you a friendly act. If you are rich, be not supercilious toward the poor and the needy: for the gods who refused riches to others in order to bestow them on you, disgusted at your arrogance, may strip you of them, and give them to others. Live by the fruits of your labor, and then your bread will taste sweet. Hitherto, my son, I have supported you with the sweat of my brow and I have discharged all the duties of a father; I have given you the necessaries of life, without wronging any man. Do you the same. Never tell a lie, for lying is a grievous sin. Whenever you recount to another what you yourself have heard, then tell the simple truth without adding anything. Speak not evil of any man. Conceal the misconduct of others, unless it be your duty to mend it. Avoid gossiping, sow not the seeds of discord. If you are the bearer of a message to any one, and he grows angry, and he vituperates the sender of the message, do not take back that reply, but strive rather to deprive it of its harshness, and if possible say not a word of what you have heard so that there may not be dissensions and disagreements, which you could only regret. Tarry not in the market-place longer than is needful, for such places afford frequent temptations to debauchery. If an office is tendered you, regard the offer as made with a view to test you: therefore do not accept at once, even though you know you are more capable than others; but excuse yourself, until they oblige you to accept: thus you will be all the more esteemed. Keep your passions in check, else the gods will be angered with you and cover you with disgrace. Repress your sensual desires, my son, for you are still young; and patiently await the time when the maid, whom the gods have chosen for your wife, shall have reached the required age. Leave such concerns to the care of the gods; they will do what is best for you. When the time comes for you to marry take no step without your parents' consent, else you will meet with an evil end. Steal not, rob not, if you would not disgrace your parents: it is your duty rather to reflect honor upon them and to show that they brought you up properly. That is all, my son; I have discharged my duty as father. It was my purpose to confirm you in good dispositions by this instruction. Do not despise my words: for your happiness through life depends upon your fidelity."

Prescott gives a number of Mexican proverbs,* which, according to him, may compare with any found in the moral codes of antiquity. He discovers in the following admonition "a most striking resemblance to Holy Writ": " Regard not curiously the walk and demeanor of the great, nor of women, especially married wo-

men, for the old proverb says: Whoso regards a woman with curiosity, commits adultery with his eyes." * Monogamy was the rule amongst the Mexicans, and in this respect they came up to that moral standard of marriage with which we are familiar. Nor was the idea they had of their gods unworthy of their moral code, and Clavigero, who compares Grecian and Roman Mythology with that of Mexico, thus expresses himself : "There is not to be found anywhere in Mexican Mythology a trace of those immoralities with which other nations have disgraced their gods. The Mexicans paid homage to virtue rather than to vice, in the objects of their religious veneration : in Huitzilapochli they honored valor; in Centeotl and others, benevolence; in Quetzalcoatl, chastity, justice and prudence. Though their gods were of both sexes, still they did not marry them to one another, nor did they attribute to them that love of obscenity with which the Greeks and Romans credited their gods. They represented them as averse to all kind of vicious indulgence and hence their worship was intended merely to appease the wrath of the gods, excited by the sins of mankind, and to secure their protection by repentance and religious service." It is no wonder if so enlightened a religious system as this surprised the Christian priests; and the latter would no doubt have preferred to find it of a lower type. The language of Mexico, rich in metaphysical and moral expressions, opposed no obstacle to the teaching of the Christian Doctrine, and Clavigero gives specimens of the writings of 84 European and Creole authors "who treated of Christian Doctrine and morals in the languages of Anahuac," as also a list of 49 Autores de Gramaticas y

---

* Sahagun, VI. 22. Tampoco mires con curiosidad el gesto y disposicion de la gente principal, mayormente de las mugeres, y sobre todo de las casadas, porque dice el refran, que él que curiosamente mira à la muger adultera con la vista.

Diccionarios de las lenguas de Anahuac.*

King Nezahualcoiotl endeavored to do away with the human sacrifices which were so frequent in Mexico, but without success, and the attempt only served to show him how difficult it is to convince the people of the falsity of ancient religious notions which have taken root in their affections. We may justly reproach the Mexicans with their religious fanaticism as displayed in these sacrifices: but we must not charge them with inhuman cruelty. In fact no action is *per se* either good or evil, but owes its moral quality to the motive which prompts it: and the same is to be said of human sacrifice. The Mexicans offered to the gods the most precious goods they possessed, *viz.*, themselves, human beings. No animal could suffice, and man alone was the becoming victim to atone for sin. And is not the profoundest teaching of Christianity based on that last and greatest human sacrifice? Hence the motive which led them to offer human victims was the profound earnestness of their religious convictions. Besides, as the Mexicans sacrificed only condemned criminals and prisoners of war, Montezuma could with some show of reason excuse this custom, as he did, by saying to Cortez: "We have the right, as you also have, of slaying our foes in battle. Where, then, is the injustice if we sacrifice in honor of our gods men already doomed to death?"†

That we should find remnants of the lower grades of fetichism in company with the worship of the Sun and of Gods, was to be expected. The Mexicans appear to have been largely given to Animal-fetichism. It included the frog, the God of fishery, as also the butterfly and other insects.‡ A grave containing the bones of some unknown animal, was found in 1790,

and in it was also discovered the famous Calendar-Stone.*

Oajaca, Chiapas, Yucatan, Guatemala and Nicaragua † stand on the same level with Mexico, as regards religion and culture. The Peruvians, who were the equals of the Mexicans in intellectual and material advancement, surpassed them perhaps in moral culture.‡

Although the Peruvians, no less than the Mexicans, worshiped a multitude of gods § they too held the Sun to be supreme, none of the other gods coming near him in sanctity or eminence, except perhaps Pachacamac. Previous to the Inca period the Peruvians were by no means such savages as they are represented to have been by Garcilasso, who attributes to them all kinds of fetichism, and who asserts that Sun-worship was introduced by the Incas. On the contrary, the Sun was worshiped in Peru, before the time of the Incas, having been introduced by the Aymaras, "the predecessors and teachers of the Inca-Peruvians."‖ But the Incas, to whose family Garcilasso belonged, had an interest in ascribing to themselves the honor of having been the founders of the State and of the religion of Peru. The story which they told in confirmation of their claim is characteristic.¶ "The Sun, our Father, seeing the pitiable condition of mankind, was moved to compassion and sent to them from heaven two of his children, a son and a daughter, to teach them how to do him honor, and pay him divine worship. These two children of the Sun were further charged to give laws to men, and to direct them how to live like rational creatures, to acquire culture, to dwell in houses, to inhabit cities, till the soil, cultivate plants, save the harvest, breed cattle, enjoy

---

* Clavigero, II. 394.
† Clavigero, Tom. II. Append. VIII.
‡ Riétos Antiguos, Sacrificios e Idolatrias de los Ind. de la N. Esp. p. un frayle menor (1541) (ap. Kingsborough, IX.) 21; Gomara, 444.

* Gama, I. 12.
† *Cf.* Waitz, IV. 312.
‡ Prescott, Conq. of Peru, I. Book 1; Wuttke, Gesch. d. II. I. S. 303-336; Waitz, IV. 378-477; Garcilasso de la Vega, Hist. Gen. del Peru. Cordova, 1617.
§ *Cf.* Waitz, IV. 452 seqq.
‖ Waitz, IV. 447.
¶ Garcilasso, I. c. XV. XVI.

the benefits derived from all these sources, prepare the products of the soil for food : in a word, their mission was to teach the people how to live like men, rather than like wild beasts. It having pleased the Sun, our Father, to give his children such commands as these, he let them down upon the earth in the neighborhood of Lake Titicaca, bidding them to go whithersoever they would. They were however instructed to drive into the earth a golden staff wherever they thought of establishing their residence in any particular spot : if the staff on the first blow sank into the earth, it was the will of the Sun, our Father, that they should settle there. On coming to the spot where Cuzco was afterwards founded, the sign which had been foretold was given to them. The savages soon began to flock around them, gazing with wonder on the pair, who were arrayed in the precious apparel of the Sun, and who, no less by their speech than by the majesty of their countenance, gave evidence that they were the children of the Sun. Then the Inca instructed the men in all needful arts, such as house-building and agriculture ; while his sister and spouse gave instruction to the women in all kinds of feminine work, such as needlework, and the weaving of cotton and woolen cloth, the making of garments, etc. Furthermore, they both taught the natives the worship of the Sun, their Father."

Thus the Sun was worshiped, and we have now to ascertain in what light they regarded this object of religious veneration. Man can attribute to any object only those notions which he already possesses. The higher then his development, in an intellectual and in a moral sense, the nobler will be the conception he has of the object which he takes for his supreme ideal. The Peruvian will regard the Sun as combining all those virtues and properties which he has himself.

They were an industrious and an ingenious people. Agriculture formed the basis of the commonwealth, and was pursued with the greatest dili-

gence and skill. No spot of ground was untilled, maize and potatoes being the chief products of the soil.* Even the stony sides of the mountains were turned into blooming gardens, by means of terracing, artificial irrigation and the use of guano as manure. They produced excellent cotton and woolen fabrics, and their metal manufactures, in gold, silver, copper and tin (they had no iron) bore the stamp of skilful workmanship. Every part of the country was connected with Cuzco, the capital, by means of excellent highways, some paved, others macadamized,† having well-constructed bridges, a service of posts and a sort of telegraphic system. The latter enabled them to send dispatches a distance of 900 miles in three or four hours.‡ Cuzco had a population of 200,000 souls, exclusive of an equal number dwelling in its suburbs. The other cities were smaller, and yet had a considerable population.§ By means of a division of the population into decads the most exemplary order was maintained.‖ The entire population formed one family, the Inca being its head. All labored and earned for the good of all. The state, not the individual, was an owner of property. Hence none were rich, but also none were poor. The contrast between proprietors and non-proprietors was done away, and all enjoyed prosperity. There were neither beggars nor drones.¶ The citizen's obligation to labor was correlative with that of the state, which owned his labor and its total product, to reward him for his toil. Under the guardian rule of the Incas, whose duties were prescribed to them by the Sun their Father, and who but rarely, as history attests, failed to exercise a paternal care for the commonwealth, the people lived in peace and happiness. Each conquered nation were

---

* Prescott, I.
† Waitz, IV. 429.
‡ Garcilasso, VI. c. 7; Wuttke, I. 334.
§ Cf. Waitz, IV. 424.
‖ Prescott, I.
¶ Ib. I.

immediately allowed to share the rights and privileges of their conquerors. Indeed, it was the desire to extend civilization that led them to undertake wars of conquest.*

It is evident that such a constitution of the empire must have had many defects, and that it hindered individual development, as well as favored the abuse of power by a tyrannical Inca. It was for the interest of the Incas to keep the people in subjection, and hence they cut them off too jealously from all intellectual culture, the possession of which they reserved for themselves alone.

A state organized on such principle cannot subsist without a morality quite free from selfishness, that root of all evil. Their family-life was chaste and pure; their women were not chattels, as among savages, but persons who, as represented in the virgins of the Sun, held a high position in the ceremonies of religion. Intellectual culture, in the sense of erudition, was restricted to the Inca caste; still the education of the people was a function of the state. The picture-writing of the Mexicans was here replaced by that curious contrivance, the quipu,† which was employed by many scholars, and also, but in a less degree, by the people generally. Garcilasso speaks of maps of the whole country and of particular districts and of charts of cities. The learned class did not, as in Mexico, belong exclusively to the priesthood, and they were classed as astrologers, physicians, botanists, poets, designers, painters, etc.‡ The Quechua, like the Mexican language, contained a number of very abstract terms, such as *spirit, thought, eternal*, etc., which will enable us to form some notion of the degree of mental development attained by this people.§

As to the Peruvian mode of reckoning time we have not the same accurate information as we have with regard to that of the Mexicans. Humboldt * says that the year was made up of 12 lunar months, giving a total of 354d. 8h. 48m.; and according to Rivero and Tschudi,† 11 intercalary days were added at the end of each year, but according to Herrera ‡ there were 12 intercalary days, one being added at the end of each month. In the face of these statements Desjardins § maintains that the Peruvian computation was more exact than the Mexican, and Montesinos ‖ speaks of very precise intercalations, and of cycles of 10, of 100 and 1000 years. But Waitz has strong doubts as to these statements.

Prescott ranks the Peruvians above the Mexicans for skillful workmanship in house-building, tillage, and the construction of roads and canals. Their inferiority to the Mexicans in intellectual culture—for instance, in astronomy—he strives to explain by showing that the Mexicans owed their intellectual advancement, not to their own native qualities, but to that mysterious Toltec stock, which the eye of history fails to discern, and which Prescott supposes to have been equaled by the Peruvians in all other departments of culture.¶

Among a people, who have reached so high a degree of moral and intellectual development, the ideal object of worship must exhibit these moral characteristics in the highest degree. And such is here the case, for the Peruvians regarded the Sun "on the one hand, according to his position in Nature, as the great Power of the universe which upholds all things (a mere heavenly body); but on the other hand (anthropopathically) as a spiritual power, having mind and will. Not that there was supposed to be any spiritual object whose symbol

---

* *Ib.* I.
† *Cf.* Waitz, IV. 470.
‡ *Ib.* 473.
§ *Ib.*

* Vues des Cordillères, 129.
† Riv. y Tschudi, Antig. Peruanas. Viena, 1851, p. 127.
‡ Herrera, V. 4, 5.
§ Desj. Le Pérou avant la Conq. Espagn. Par. 1858, p. 122.
‖ *Ap.* Waitz, IV. 474.
¶ Prescott, Peru, I.

was the Sun (*i.e.*, the object of worship was not a spirit inhabiting the Sun); but the bright luminary itself (in his own proper form and shape) was truly and really the deity, though not as a simple, soulless sphere, but as a divine and animated body, imparting to all things around him light and life." * When once a monk expounded the Christian doctrine to the Inca Atahuallpa, and asked him to renounce his faith, the eyes of the prince flashed fire, and he exclaimed: " I will never change my faith. Your God was, as you say, put to death by the men he himself had created. But my God," said he, pointing to the Sun which was then setting in full splendor behind the mountains, " my God lives in the heavens, and looks down upon his children." † When the Sun sent his children down upon the earth he thus addressed them : " My children, when you have subjected these people to our obedience, it must be your study to hold them by the laws of reason, of piety, of mercy and of justice, doing for them all that a father is wont to do for the children whom he has begotten and whom he tenderly loves. Herein you will follow my example, for, as you know, I never cease to do good to all mortals. I illumine them with my light, to the end they may see and go about their affairs : when they are cold, I warm them ; I make their fields and their meadows productive, bring forth fruit on their trees, increase their herds and send them rain and fair weather as need may be. Further, I journey around the world daily, to see what the earth needs, and to restore all things to order, for the comfort of its inhabitants. Therefore it is my will that ye follow my example, as most dear children, whom I send on earth for the welfare and the instruction of these poor men, who live like beasts. Hence I give you the title of kings, and I desire that your kingdom be extended over all the nations whom ye shall instruct in right principles and good morals, especially by your example and mild rule." * Through reverence for the Sun, even the Inca durst not look upon its face.†

The offerings made to the Sun consisted, besides the morning prayer, at his rising, of a libation (as among the Persians); then of fruits, herbs, flowers. and animals, llamas especially.‡ Garcilasso expressly denies that they offered human sacrifices, and often mentions the laws which forbade the sacrifice of captives : still other accounts render it tolerably certain that on high festivals they sacrificed a child or a beautiful maiden.

Where Sun-worship is so highly developed, the worship of the other heavenly bodies holds a very subordinate position. They worshiped the Moon as the Sun's sister and spouse, and the stars (among which Venus and the Pleiades were specially observed) § were considered as their suite.‖ The most famous temple in Peru was that of the Sun, at Cuzco, which, on account of its fabulously rich endowments, was called Coricancha—Place of Gold;¶ and the temple next in renown was that of Pachacamac, also at Cuzco. The Temple of the Sun included a chapel plated all over with silver, and dedicated to the Moon, as also three other chapels, richly plated with gold and silver, and sacred to the Stars, to Thunder and Lightning, and to the Rainbow.

With the Peruvians we may class, from the religious point of view, first the Araucanians,** who dwell to the south, in Chile, and who reckoned a solar year of 12 months, each month having 30 days, and five days being intercalated through the year. They were able to determine the time of

---

* Wuttke, I. 306 seq.
† Prescott, I. 3.

* Garcilasso. I. lib. I. c. XV.
† *Ib.* IX. c. X.
‡ *Ib.* II. c. VIII.
§ *Cf.* Waitz, IV. 475.
‖ Prescott, I.
¶ *Ib.*
** *Cf.* Waitz, III. 515 ff.

the solstices from the length of shadows. Then came a very advanced people, of higher culture than the Araucanians, viz., the Chibchas,* and their kinsmen, living in New Granada, a country whose antiquities bespeak for its inhabitants a relatively high degree of culture in very early times. Among the Chibchas the Sun held the same important position as among the Peruvians. There is no evidence to show that they imported from Peru their religion and their intellectual culture, but rather everything tends to prove that their development was of native growth.

7. The Worship of the Heavens.

In the view taken of the heavens by all men on the basis of the external appearances, the heavenly bodies pass for bright points fixed in the blue vault of the sky, rather than for spheres free-poised in infinite space. Sun, moon and stars are only parts of the celestial vault. Hence, howsoever they may differ from one another, still essentially they are of equal value, being all celestial. The supremacy therefore does not belong to this or to that one body, but to the entire firmament. It is therefore really no new standpoint, but rather the sum of the data already obtained, if now the religious consciousness considers no longer the sun, the moon, or the stars, but the sum-total of them all, the celestial vault, the sky itself, as the supreme fetich, the supreme god. And here too, as in all the objects of fetich-worship, it is the vault of heaven, as such, anthropopathically apprehended, and not any god supposed to be symbolized by it, that receives religious honors. But this worship of the entire heavens does by no means interfere with the worship of the individual heavenly bodies, but rather, on the contrary, favors it. Sun, moon and stars may each receive its peculiar worship and sacrifice ; but no one of them has the absolute ascendency.

* Ib. IV. 532 ff.

That the people who stand on this stage of fetichism are, from a mental and moral point of view, very advanced, follows from what has been already said. As representatives of this stage we might cite the Persians, as described by Herodotus ; also the Chinese.

"To erect statues of the gods, altars and temples," says Herodotus, "is not the custom of the Persians, and indeed they reproach those who do so with folly, and this, as it appears to me, for the reason that they do not believe, as do the Greeks, that the gods are anthropomorphic. On the contrary, they are wont to sacrifice to Zeus on the summits of high mountains, and to invoke the entire celestial vault as Zeus. They also sacrifice to the sun and the moon : to the earth, to fire and to the winds. . . . . The Persians have no holocausts, no libations, no meat-offering, no flutes, no garlands, no barley cakes : but whoever would sacrifice to one of these gods puts a crown of myrtle around his tiara, conducts the animal to some place free from pollution, and there prays to the god to whom he is about to make the offering. Still he prays not for himself alone, but prays rather that it may be well with all Persians and with the king. Then the animal is slain, cut up, seethed, and afterward spread upon the green sweet grass ; the Magi then chaunt a song of consecration, standing by the side of the one who makes the offering, and the latter finally takes the flesh home, to make such use of it as he may wish. . . . . The Persians believe that the gods desire only the soul of the beast as a sacrifice, disdaining the flesh ; hence they do not burn the flesh, lest they should pollute the fire, which is sacred to the gods : nay, even one durst not even blow on the fire, to quicken it, for that is an offense that is punished with death. As they make offerings to fire, so too do they to water, betaking themselves to some lake, or river, or fountain, and digging a trench in the vicinity, lest the blood should defile the water. There they slay the victim, and spread the pieces on sprigs of bay or myrtle; the magi, who are present, make libations of oil, milk or honey, and chaunt a sacred song; and the sacrificant takes away the flesh of the victim." This conception of sacrifice, where only the soul of the victim is accepted by the gods, (*gods* as defined by Herodotus himself) shows that the Persians no longer viewed their gods from the gross materialistic point of view, and subordinated the material to the spiritual. Their praying for all Persians and not for themselves individually is evidence that they stood high above the egotism of the savage, who cares only for himself.

As objects of religious contemplation, the sky is regarded as the Father, the Earth the Mother of all things by the Chinese, the religious views of the masses being but little affected by the more philosophical and abstract speculations of their later teachers.* Yang, the Sky, is procreative, strong, masculine; Yu, the Earth, is conceptive, weakly, feminine.† All things are the products of these two. "So soon as Yu and Yang unite, an actual existence results, and this is the work of Heaven and Earth."‡ That this Sky-worship is most intimately connected with Sun-worship, nay, even that it derives its origin from Sun-worship, appears to be beyond question. The Y-King, for instance, says that Yang makes his most perfect apparition in the Sun.§ The movement of Yang, again says the Y-King, is in a circle, being accelerated from the beginning of spring until the solstice, and then retarded. He consists of an extremely subtle matter, invisible to our eyes, but yet most real, and has a fixed and never ceasing circular motion; and his form is spherical,

whereas that of the earth is angular, and therefore less capable of motion.*

In the Spring and Summer, when the quickening power of the heavens is greatest, Yang bears sway, but in Autumn and Winter, when the quiescent earth predominates, Yu assumes rule. Yang is lord of the day, culminating at noon, and then gradually yielding to Yu, who rules the night.† All these functions of Yang belong more properly to the Sun than to the Sky.

"Wherever," says Wuttke,‡ "in accordance with our habits of thought, we expect to find mention of God in Chinese writings, it is always the Sky that we find named, sometimes Sky and Earth, but more commonly the Sky alone. And the Sky which is meant is the visible heavens, whose apparent revolution around the earth is held to be the cause of all life and movement. Sun, Moon and Stars are set in this blue Sky, which is the manifestation of deity." Uninfluenced by the nice distinctions which the philosophers of China have made as to the essence of the Heavens the popular mind takes the anthropopathic view, which, however, as was to have been expected of a people so advanced in moral culture as the Chinese, attributes to the Sky only the noblest and sublimest characteristics. They give to the Heavens the name Shang-to, "Sublime Ruler, Supreme Lord." § He is almighty and omnipresent. His all-embracing love is shown in the saying: "The Sublime Ruler of the Universe is to be feared and reverenced: he hates none. Who durst say that He hates any man?"‖ His justice is not to be bribed, and is as immutable as his celestial movement: great is his wrath against the unjust; ¶ from

---

* *Cf.* Wuttke, Gesch. des H. Bd. II. S. 1–208; Bluntschli, Altasiatische Gottes-u. Weltideen S. 135–164; le Chou-King par Confucius, trad. par P. Gaubil, revu par M. de Guignes. Par. 1770, p. 88–150.
† Y-King, ex Interpr. Regis. Ed. Mohl, 1834, I. p. 165–169, II. p. 381.
‡ *Ib.* II. 547.
§ *Ib.* II. 406.

* *Ib.* II. 385 seq.; I. 203.
† *Ib.* I. 196, 214; Tschu-hi, übersetzt von Neumann, in Illgen's Zeitschr. 1837, Bd. I. 56, 74, 82.
‡ II. S. 25.
§ Chou-King, p. 13, Note 7; Y-King, II. p. 216.
‖ Confucii Chi-King, s. Liber Carminum, ex Lat. P. Lacharme Interpr. Ed. Jul. Mohl. Stuttg. 1830, II. 4, S.
¶ *Ib.* II. 4, 8; II. 5, 1.

his omniscence naught is hidden.[*] And these things are all predicative of the blue vault above our heads, v.g. "O blue Sky, look down with scorn upon the proud, and have pity on the unfortunate," is a Chinese prayer.[†] The Sky so considered is man's moral prototype, which he must reproduce in his own life. "His four properties set forth the ideal of a prince: he is so great, that he encompasses all things; so mighty that he creates all things; so orderly that he adapts all things to their ends; so persistent that he never stands still, never ceases to be."[‡] The Sky is the supreme lord. He requires of man perfect righteousness and sinlessness. Being omniscient he knows when a man is guilty of sin. His wrath is enkindled against all injustice, and he manifests it on occasion by celestial phenomena and by the convulsions of Nature, which are thus brought into relations with the moral life of man. Eclipses of Sun and Moon, earthquakes, thunder and lightning and the other grave phenomena of Nature are warnings sent from Heaven to man.[§] Crops fail on account of the sins of the people or of their rulers. "When virtue reigns," says Kitse in the 12th century B.C., "the rain falls betimes; when the sovereign rules justly, there is fair weather, etc.; when sin reigns, the rain falls incessantly, or else there is a drought," etc.[‖] The guilty are oftentimes punished directly by the Heavens. An emperor of the second dynasty having defiantly shot arrows at the sky, and erected idols was slain by the lightning.[¶] For the space of three days did the Heavens envelop the earth in dark clouds, because another emperor had committed a crime.[*] We might cite a multitude of similar instances;[†] but as our purpose here is only to define the position of China with regard to religious development, we refrain from any further illustration of this point.

However just the claim of the sky to the undivided worship of man, and howsoever strictly philosophico-religious speculation may show it to be the one object that deserves to be worshiped, still the popular mind will not renounce its own nature as a fecund principle, and so it fashions for itself notions of spirits and gods on purely empiric grounds. Hence in China, besides sky-worship there is a complex system of spirit-worship and polytheism.[‡] In addition to the Ancestral Spirits, which are the principal objects of veneration, there are the Celestial Spirits, which dwell in the heavenly bodies, in the Sun, the Moon, the Stars, the Earth; on mountains, in rivers; in the thunder and in the winds. There are the guardian Spirits of families, of houses, of communities, of cities, of provinces, of agriculture, etc., and we find mention of these even in remote times: yet they rank so far beneath the Sky that by an ancient law it was forbidden to make offerings to them such as were made to the Sky, and it was allowed only to make them gifts of food, and to show them a limited amount of reverence.[§]

In Africa, too, among the more advanced nations, we find traces of a growing Sun and Sky worship. In Dahomey, a country ruled with barbarous rigor, but yet possessing a well-organized monarchical government, the Sun is held to be the highest of all beings but yet is not worshiped.[‖] The Duallas call the Sun and the Great Spirit by one name.[¶]

[*] Histoire Générale de la Chine, trad. du Kong-Kien-Kang-Mon par de Mailla, publ. par Grosier. Par. 1777, I. p. 92, 111.
[†] Chi-King, II. 5, 6.
[‡] Wuttke, II. 26.
[§] Chou-King, p. 13, 54, 87, 96, 99, 142, 160, 347; Chi-King, p. 291, II. 5, 6, 8; De Mailla, I. 78.
[‖] Chou-King, p. 172.
[¶] De Mailla, I. 227.

[*] Chou-King, p. 91.
[†] Cf. Wuttke, II. 55 ff.
[‡] Ib. II. 36 ff.
[§] De Mailla, Hist. gén. I. 33.
[‖] Omboni, Viaggi nell' Africa Occidentale. Milano, 1845, p. 309.
[¶] Allen and Thomson, Narr. of the Exped. to the R. Niger in 1841. Lond. 1848, II. 199, 395 note.

In Acra Römer discovered a sort of worship paid to the Sun.* The Negroes of the Gold Coast, at least their devotees and fetichmen, call Njongmo (the Sky), which is omnipresent and *ab ævo*, the Supreme God, and the Maker of the world.† "You may every day see," said a fetichman, "how the rain and sunshine sent by him cause the grass and grain and trees to grow: he must therefore be the Creator." Every morning they go down to the stream, wash themselves, dash a handful of water or sand on their heads, and with eyes turned to the sky, utter this prayer: "O God, give me this day rice and yams, gold and *agries :* give me slaves, wealth and health, and grant that I be quick and swift." The same belief, substantially, prevails in Akwapim, the Supreme Deity being the firmament, and the Earth, the Universal Mother, holding the second rank, while in the third rank stands Bosumbra, the head Fetich. Before embarking in any new enterprise the people of Akwapim offer a libation to these three, saying: "Creator, come, drink; Earth, come, drink; Bosumbra, come, drink." ‡

CHAPTER VII.

THE AIM OF FETICHISM.

HAVING traced the development of religious ideas from their earliest origin to their more advanced stages, we would now gather the results of our analyses in order to show the ulterior aim to which the system is directed.

1. *Retrospect.*

The understanding has cognizance only of its own conceptions, and these conceptions are its objects. Hence its range is limited to the conceptions and objects it has, and hence too it

grows as the number of its objects is increased. If we would appreciate a man's intellectual status, we must know what are his conceptions, his *objects.* In his lowest condition man has but few objects : but as these are multiplied the more, the more does he advance in every respect.

It is a law of our mind that we shall range our conceptions in the order of cause and effect. But we can so range such conceptions as we possess. *Cause,* as being the efficient, the productive principle we can conceive of only as something possessed of power, of special efficiency. Accordingly that object or that conception will pass for causal and efficient, which appears to be the stronger, the more excellent. We have seen how, as the number of objects was greater or less, their values differed proportionally, and how the mind with few objects must set as high a value on trifles (as viewed from a higher standpoint) as a superior understanding sets upon its more important objects : for a relatively trifling object assumes importance when its surroundings are more trifling still than itself. Hence we have seen that because he has but few objects, and a very narrow *world,* the fetichist takes to be causal an object which for him is momentous, though insignificant for us. We have seen that as he increases the number of his conceptions, the number of assignable causes is increased in proportion ; and then we considered the various objects regarded as fetiches : stocks, stones, mountains, plants, etc. All these lay in man's own sphere, and he was attached to them by bodily interest. A new and spiritual interest could be awakened only by an entirely new object, and this he found in the heavenly bodies, by the worship of which man stepped beyond simply material interests and entered a spiritual sphere.

In proportion as the spiritual interest increases the more is the will detached from the simply corporeal. Animal passions are repressed in proportion as objects of spiritual interest

* Römer, S. 84.
† Waitz, II. 170.
‡ *Ibidem.*

attract the will to themselves. But in order to devote himself to spiritual interests man had need of repose, tranquillity and bodily security. The higher this spiritual interest rises, the more is fierce and destructive egotism repressed. Life is more tranquil, more orderly. Man builds up commonwealths, and his thoughts are now no longer concerned about himself alone, but about the commonwealth also. But in proportion as he abandons egotism, the more does he acknowledge moral control. In the higher stages of the worship of heavenly bodies we therefore found a high degree of development, not only intellectually but also morally. For morality being will-stimulus, or will-direction, and the will being elevated only by gaining higher and ever higher objects, therefore morality is elevated in proportion to the elevation of the objects.

2. *The New Problem.*

Sky-worship, including Star and Sun-worship, is the highest grade of fetichism, not only because its objects are the most exalted, but also because it contains the nucleus of something altogether new. So far, man has been tracing causes from object to object, and in the pursuit of the final cause at length passed from earth to sky. But even there his final cause was found to belong to the order of sensuous things. His eyes discern his efficient causes ; he *sees* them producing all phenomena, all objects. But the law of the mind is that he shall still search for a cause, and when once the mind has begun to question, it will never cease to question. What is the cause of A? it asks : and the answer is, B. But further it will ask, What then of B? and an answer it must have. Now so far it has taken the Stars, the Sun, the Sky for its ultimate cause : but the greater man's reverence for this cause, and the more he contemplates it, the more he learns as to its true nature. Soon all manner of thoughts will spring up, and he

will observe contradictions between its actual, empirical phenomena and his own conception thereof, and of the mode in which it must operate. How is this? he will inquire. And when such and such effects are produced by the Sun, the question will come up,. But what produced the Sun itself, with its phenomena? And in fact wherever this worship of heavenly bodies attains its highest stage, as among the Mexicans, Peruvians and Persians, this question did actually arise. The Persians not alone put this question, but they found the answer to it, and the result was a new religion, that of Zoroaster. But the Mexicans and the Peruvians had their development interrupted by the fanaticism of a Cortez and a Pizarro, and hence they could not reach a solution of the problem, though it was explicitly stated by some eminent minds among them, and the nation was in a fair way soon to enter on a new religious epoch.

But let us see how the problem must be solved by a people in their stage of development. As long as the objects of sense afforded the grounds for considering them as causes, so long did man ascend the series. But when the last link in that chain is reached, the senses fail ; and the eye cannot penetrate beyond the blue vault of the heavens. Hence when he comes to inquire as to the cause of the sky itself, he cannot assign any sensible object, there being none that is greater than this. If therefore he would still pursue his search after a cause, he must needs go beyond the domain of sense, and assign causes not apprehensible to the senses, prætersensual or super-sensual. But now he could not assign anything super-sensual as a cause, if he had no conception of the "super-sensual." But his gods and spirits have furnished him with such a notion, and he has often held them to be the causes of sundry phenomena in the world of sense. All his conceptions are empirical, and his conception of gods also had an empirical origin. It is not our business here to account for the idea of gods and spirits: it suffices if we know that it exists. When therefore an ultimate cause is to be assigned for the ultimate of sensible causes, it will be a God. But just as when he looked for the ultimate Cause among sensible objects, that passed for ultimate which was unique, supreme, and above all things else in power and dominion: so too must this God be unique, supreme, exclusive. Here then is the point where, by the crossing of the two series of conceptions (referred to already at p. 26)—viz.: on the one hand sensible objects, and on the other spirits or gods, both in their highest state of development (Sun and Sky-worship, and Polytheism)—Monotheism is evolved. The proofs of this proposition are not in place in an essay on fetichism: it will be sufficient if we show from history that the *question* we have spoken of does actually arise where man has reached the highest stage of fetichism, and that it is answered precisely as we have said.

Of the famous Inca, Tupac Jupanqui,* Garcilasso states that "he was wont to say: Many hold that the sun is endowed with life, and that he is the creator of all things. But whoever creates a thing must be present when he creates it: but now sundry ,things are produced in the absence of the Sun: therefore the Sun is not the creator of all things. Furthermore, his never tiring is proof that he is not a living thing. If he had life, he would weary even as we: and were he free, he would visit other regions of heaven besides those in which his daily course now lies. He is, as it were, an object that is restricted in its movements, and which ever describes the self-same course; or like the arrow which flies in the direction in which it is shot, and which cannot choose its own course." Another Inca was once, upon the feast of Raymi, attentively contemplating the Sun.

A priest having twice reminded him that the reverence due to that luminary forbade such conduct, the monarch replied: "I will put you two questions. I am your king and lord. Would any of you venture to order me to rise from my throne and set out on a long journey? And would any of my vassals be so bold as to refuse obedience, were I to command him forthwith to hasten off to Chile?" The priest having answered both questions in the negative, the monarch thus continued: "My word for it, there must be over the Sun, our Father, a master greater and mightier still, who requires him to perform his daily course: for were the Sun himself the Supreme Lord, he would not pursue forever the same daily path: he would rest when it pleased him, even though he had no need of rest."*

One of the most eminent of the Mexican kings, "an intellectual hero of the New World," was Nezahualcoyotl. "His enlightened mind, and the love he had for his subjects, largely contributed to make his court famous, and it was ever after regarded as the home of the arts and the center of refined culture. At Tezcuco, his capital, the Mexican language was spoken with the greatest purity and correctness; and there were always to be found the best artists, and a vast assemblage of poets, orators and historians. Not alone the Mexicans themselves, but many other nations received laws from Tezcuco, and hence we might say that Nezahualcoyotl was the Solon, and his capital the Athens of Anahuac."† Well-versed in the poetry of his native land, the king was himself a poet of some distinction, and as late as the 16th century sixty hymns composed by him in honor of the Creator of the heavens were held in high esteem even by the Spaniards. "But nothing possessed so deep an interest for Nezahualcoyotl as the study of Nature. He acquired a considerable

* Garcilasso, VIII. 8.

* Acosta, Balboa, 59; *apud* Waitz, IV. 449.
† Clavigero, I. p. 175 seq.

amount of astronomical knowledge
from the numerous observations which
he directed to be made of the courses
of the stars. He also devoted much
time to the study of botany and zoology, and those specimens which, as
requiring a different climate, could
not live at the capital, he had painted
in the natural size on the walls of his
palace. *He studied attentively the
causes of the phenomena of Nature, and
this study led him to recognize the worth-
lessness of idolatry.* He told his
sons, in confidence, that whilst they
paid exterior reverence to the idols,
in deference to public sentiment,
they should in their hearts abhor this
contemptible worship of inanimate
things. As for himself, he acknowledged no god save the Creator of the
Heavens, but he did not forbid idolatry, much as he wished to do so, lest
any man should charge him with setting himself in opposition to the teachings of his forefathers. He prohibited
human sacrifices, but succeeded only
so far as to limit them to the offering
of prisoners of war." * To his " Unseen God," "the Unknown God, the
Cause of Causes," † he dedicated a

tower of nine stories, with roof pain ed
blue, and studded with golden stars.*
At stated hours certain officials appointed for the purpose struck a son-
orous metallic plate in the tower, at
which signal the king knelt and re-
cited a prayer. From the ornamenta-
tion of this tower, as well as from his
poems,† it is plain that, as Prescott
says, " he combined star-worship with
worship of the Almighty ; " or rather,
by combining star-worship with Polytheism, he reached Monotheism.
This is clear from what Ijtliljochitl
says of him, viz., that although he
"invoked the Almighty, by whose
grace we live, and who hath in himself all things," still he also " acknowledged the sun to be his father and the
earth his mother."‡

---

* Clavigero, I. p. 175 seq.
† "Al Dios no conocido, Causa de las

Causas." M. S. de Ijtliljochitl apud Prescott, I. 155.
* " Su boveda estaba pintada de azul."
Clavigero, I. 176.
† " Let us strive heavenward, for there all
is everlasting and incorruptible." Aspiremos
ál cielo, que allí todo es eterno y nada se cor-
rompe. " The horrors of the grave are but
the Sun's cradle ; and the sombre shadows
only brilliant lights for the stars." El horror
del sepulcro es lisongera cuña para el, y las
funestas sombras brillantes luces para los as-
tros.
‡ *Apud* Prescott, I.

The Humboldt Library of Science

Is the only publication of its kind, the only one containing *popular scientific works at low prices.* For the most part it contains only *works of acknowledged excellence,* by authors of the first rank in the world of science.
In this series are well represented the writings of

DARWIN,	HUXLEY,	SPENCER,	TYNDALL,	PROCTOR,
CLIFFORD,	CLODD,	BAGEHOT,	BAIN,	BATES,
WALLACE,	TRENCH,	ROMANES,	GRANT ALLEN,	GEIKIE,
HINTON,	SULLY,	FLAMMARION,	PICTON,	WILLIAMS,
	BALFOUR STEWART,		WILSON,	

And other leaders of thought in our time. The books are Complete and Unabridged
Editions, in Neat Paper Covers.

Price, FIFTEEN Cents a Number.   *Double Numbers, THIRTY Cents.*

No. 1. **Light Science for Leisure Hours.** A series of familiar essays on astronomical and other natural phenomena. By Richard A. Proctor, F.R.A.S.

No. 2. **Forms of Water** in Clouds and Rivers, Ice and Glaciers (*19 illustrations*). By John Tyndall, F.R.S.

No. 3. **Physics and Politics.** An application of the principles of Natural Science to Political Society. By Walter Bagehot, author of "The English Constitution."

No. 4. **Man's Place in Nature,** (*with numerous illustrations*). By Thomas H. Huxley, F.R.S.

No. 5. **Education,** Intellectual, Moral, and Physical. By Herbert Spencer.

No. 6. **Town Geology.** With Appendix on Coral and Coral Reefs. By Rev. Chas. Kingsley.

No. 7. **The Conservation of Energy,** (*with numerous illustrations*). By Balfour Stewart, LL.D.

No. 8. **The Study of Languages,** brought back to its true principles. By C. Marcel.

No. 9. **The Data of Ethics.** By Herbert Spencer.

No. 10. **The Theory of Sound in its Relation to Music,** (*numerous illustrations*). By Prof. Pietro Blaserna.

No. 11. { **The Naturalist on the River Amazon.** A record of 11 years of travel. By Henry Walton Bates,
No. 12. { F.L.S. (Double number. *Not sold separately*).

No. 13. **Mind and Body.** The theories of their relation. By Alex. Bain, LL.D.

No. 14. **The Wonders of the Heavens,** (*thirty-two illustrations*). By Camille Flammarion.

No. 15. **Longevity.** The means of prolonging life after middle age. By John Gardner, M.D.

No. 16. **On the Origin of Species.** By Thomas H. Huxley, F.R.S.

No. 17. **Progress: Its Law and Cause.** With other disquisitions. By Herbert Spencer.

No. 18. **Lessons in Electricity,** (*sixty illustrations*). By John Tyndall, F.R.S.

No. 19. **Familiar Essays on Scientific Subjects.** By Richard A. Proctor.

No. 20. **The Romance of Astronomy.** By R. Kalley Miller, M.A.

No. 21. **The Physical Basis of Life,** with other essays. By Thomas H. Huxley, F.R.S.

No. 22. **Seeing and Thinking.** By William Kingdon Clifford, F.R.S.

No. 23. **Scientific Sophisms.** A review of current theories concerning Atoms, Apes and Men. By Samuel Wainwright, D.D.

No. 24. **Popular Scientific Lectures,** (*illustrated*). By Prof. H. Helmholtz.

No. 25. **The Origin of Nations.** By Prof. Geo. Rawlinson, Oxford University.

No. 26. **The Evolutionist at Large.** By Grant Allen.

No. 27. **The History of Landholding in England.** By Joseph Fisher, F.R.H.S.

No. 28. **Fashion in Deformity,** as illustrated in the customs of Barbarous and Civilized Races, (*numerous illustrations*). By William Henry Flower, F.R.S.

No. 29. **Facts and Fictions of Zoology,** (*numerous illustrations*). By Andrew Wilson, Ph. D.

No. 30. **The Study of Words.** Part I. By Richard Chenevix Trench.

No. 31. **The Study of Words.** Part II.

No. 32. **Hereditary Traits and Other Essays.** By Richard A. Proctor.

No. 33. **Vignettes from Nature.** By Grant Allen.

No. 34. **The Philosophy of Style.** By Herbert Spencer.

No. 35. **Oriental Religions.** By John Caird, Pres. Univ. Glasgow, and Others.

No. 36. **Lectures on Evolution.** (*Illustrated*). By Prof. T. H. Huxley.

No. 37. **Six Lectures on Light.** (*Illustrated*). By Prof. Tyndall.

No. 38. **Geological Sketches.** Part I. By Archibald Geikie, F.R.S.

No. 39. **Geological Sketches.** Part II.

No. 40. **The Evidence of Organic Evolution.** By George J. Romanes, F.R.S.

No. 41. **Current Discussion in Science.** By W. M. Williams, F.C.S.

No. 42. **History of the Science of Politics.** By Frederick Pollock.

No. 43. **Darwin and Humboldt.** By Prof. Huxley, Prof. Agassiz, and others.

No. 44. **The Dawn of History.** Part I. By G. F. Keary, of the British Museum.

No. 45. **The Dawn of History.** Part II.

No. 46. **The Diseases of Memory.** By Th. Ribot. Translated from the French by J. Fitzgerald, M.A.

No. 47. **The Childhood of Religion.** By Edward Clodd, F.R.A.S.

No. 48. **Life in Nature.** (*Illustrated*). By James Hinton.

No. 49. **The Sun:** its Constitution, its Phenomena, its Condition. By Judge Nathan T. Carr.

No. 50. **Money and the Mechanism of Exchange.** By Prof. W. Stanley Jevons, F.R.S. Part I.

No. 51. **Money and the Mechanism of Exchange.** Part II.

No. 52. **The Diseases of the Will.** By Th. Ribot. Translated from the French by J. Fitzgerald, M.A.

No. 53. **Animal Automatism,** and other Essays. By Prof. T. H. Huxley, F.R.S.

No. 54. **The Birth and Growth of Myth.** By Edward Clodd, F.R.A.S.

No. 55. **The Scientific Basis of Morals,** and other Essays. By William Kingdon Clifford, F.R.S.

No. 56. **Illusions.** By James Sully. Part I.

No. 57. **Illusions.** Part II.

No. 58. **The Origin of Species.** By Charles Darwin. Part I. (Double number).

No. 59. **The Origin of Species.** Part II. (Double Number).

No. 60. **The Childhood of the World.** By Edward Clodd, F.R.A.S.

No. 61. **Miscellaneous Essays.** By Richard A. Proctor.

No. 62. **The Religions of the Ancient World.** By Prof. Geo. Rawlinson, Univ. of Oxford. (Double number).

No. 63. **Progressive Morality.** By Thomas Fowler, LL.D., President of Corpus Christi Coll., Oxford.

No. 64. **The Distribution of Animals and Plants.** By A. Russell Wallace and W. T. Thistleton Dyer.

No. 65. **Conditions of Mental Development, and other Essays.** By William Kingdon Clifford.

No. 66. **Technical Education, and other Essays.** By Thomas H. Huxley, F.R.S.

No. 67. **The Black Death.** An account of the Great Pestilence of the 14th Century. By J. F. C. Hecker, M.D.

No. 68. **Three Essays.** By Herbert Spencer.

No. 69. **Fetichism:** A Contribution to Anthropology and the History of Religion. By Fritz Schultze, Ph. D. (Double number).

No. 70. **Essays Speculative and Practical.** By Herbert Spencer.

No. 71. **Anthropology.** By Daniel Wilson, Ph. D. With Appendix on Archæology. By E. B. Tylor, F.R.S.

No. 72. **The Dancing Mania of the Middle Ages.** By J. F. C. Hecker, M.D.

No. 73. **Evolution in History, Language and Science.** Four addresses delivered at the London Crystal Palace School of Art, Science and Literature.

No. 74. No. 75. No. 76. No. 77. **The Descent of Man,** and Selection in Relation to Sex. (*Numerous Illustrations*). By Charles Darwin. *Nos.* 74, 75, 76 *are single Nos.;* No. 77 *is a double No.*

No. 78. **Historical Sketch of the Distribution of Land in England.** By William Lloyd Birbeck, M.A.

No. 79. **Scientific Aspect of some Familiar Things.** By W. M. Williams.

No. 80. **Charles Darwin.** His Life and Work. By Grant Allen. (Double Number).

No. 81. **The Mystery of Matter, and the Philosophy of Ignorance.** Two Essays by J. Allanson Picton.

No. 82. **Illusions of the Senses,** and other Essays. By Richard A. Proctor.

No. 83. **Profit-Sharing Between Capital and Labor.** Six Essays. By Sedley Taylor, M.A.

No. 84. **Studies of Animated Nature.** Four Essays on Natural History. By W. S. Dallas, F.L.S., and Others.

No. 85. **The Essential Nature of Religion.** By J. Allanson Picton.

No. 86. **The Unseen Universe,** and the Philosophy of the Pure Sciences. By Prof. Wm. Kingdon Clifford, F.R.S.

No. 87. **The Morphine Habit.** By Dr. B. Ball, of the Paris Faculty of Medicine.

No 88   Science and Crime and other Essays. By Andrew Wilson, F.R.S.E.

No. 89   The Genesis of Science. By Herbert Spencer.

No 90.   Notes on Earthquakes: with Fourteen Miscellaneous Essays. By Richard A. Proctor.

No 91.   The Rise of Universities. By S. S. Laurie, LL.D. (Double number).

No 92.   The Formation of Vegetable Mould through the Action of Earth Worms. By Charles Darwin, LL.D., F.R.S. (Double number).

No. 93.   Scientific Methods of Capital Punishment. By J. Mount Bleyer, M.D.

No. 94.   The Factors of Organic Evolution. By Herbert Spencer.

No 95.   The Diseases of Personality. By Th. Ribot Translated from the French by J. Fitzgerald, M.A.

No. 96   A Half-Century of Science. By Thomas H. Huxley, and Grant Allen.

No. 97.   The Pleasures of Life. By Sir John Lubbock.

No. 98.   Cosmic Emotion: Also the Teachings of Science. By William Kingdon Clifford.

No. 99.   Nature Studies. By Prof. F. R. Eaton Lowe; Dr. Robert Brown, F.L.S; Geo G. Chisholm, F.R.G.S.; and James Dallas, F.L.S.

No. 100.   Science and Poetry. with other Essays. By Andrew Wilson, F.R.S.E.

No. 101.   Æsthetics; Dreams and Association of Ideas. By James Sully and Geo. Croom Robertson.

No. 102.   Ultimate Finance; A True Theory of Co-operation. By William Nelson Black.

No. 103.   The Coming Slavery: The Sins of Legislators; The Great Political Superstition. By Herbert Spencer.

No. 104.   Tropical Africa. By Henry Drummond, F.R.S.

No. 105.   Freedom in Science and Teaching. By Ernst Haeckel, of the University of Jena. With a prefatory Note by Prof. Huxley.

No. 106.   Force and Energy. A Theory of Dynamics. By Grant Allen.

No. 107.   Ultimate Finance. A True Theory of Wealth. By William Nelson Black.

No. 108.   English, Past and Present. By Richard Chenevix Trench. Part I. (Double number).

No. 109.   English, Past and Present. Part II.

No. 110.   The Story of Creation. A Plain Account of Evolution. By Edward Clodd. (Double number).

No. 111.   The Pleasures of Life. Part II. By Sir John Lubbock.

No. 112.   Psychology of Attention. By Th. Ribot Translated from the French by J. Fitzgerald, M.A.

No. 113.   Hypnotism. Its History and Development. By Fredrik Björnström, M.D., Head Physician of the Stockholm Hospital, Professor of Psychiatry. Late Royal Swedish Medical Councillor. Authorized Translation from the Second Swedish Edition by Baron Nils Posse, M.G., Director of the Boston School of Gymnastics. (Double number).

No. 114.   Christianity and Agnosticism. A Controversy. Consisting of papers contributed to The Nineteenth Century by Henry Wace, D.D., Prof. Thos. H. Huxley, The Bishop of Petersborough, W. H. Mallock, Mrs. Humphrey Ward. (Double number).

No. 115.   Darwinism: An Exposition of the Theory of Natural Selection, with some of its Applications. By Alfred Russel Wallace, LL.D., F.L.S., etc. Illustrated. Part I. (Double number).

No. 116.   Darwinism. Illustrated. Part II. (Double number).

No. 117.   Modern Science and Modern Thought. By S. Laing. Illustrated. (Double number).

No. 118.   Modern Science and Modern Thought. Part II.

No. 119.   The Electric Light and The Storing of Electrical Energy. Illustrated. Gerald Molloy, D.D., D.Sc.

No. 120.   The Modern Theory of Heat and The Sun as a Storehouse of Energy. Illustrated. Gerald Molloy, D.D., D.Sc.

No. 121.   Utilitarianism. By John Stuart Mill.

No. 122.   Upon the Origin of Alpine and Italian Lakes and upon Glacial Erosion. Maps and Illustrations. By Ramsey, Ball, Murchison, Studer, Favre, Whymper and Spencer. Part I. (Double number).

No. 123.   Upon the Origin of Alpine and Italian Lakes, Etc., Etc. Part II.

No. 124.   The Quintessence of Socialism. By Prof. A. Schäffle.

No. 125.   Darwinism and Politics. By David G. Ritchie, M.A. Administrative Nihilism. By Thomas Huxley, F.R.S.

No. 126.   Physiognomy and Expression. By P. Mantegazza. Illustrated. Part I. (Double number).

No. 127.   Physiognomy and Expression. Part II. (Double number).

No. 128.   The Industrial Revolution. By Arnold Toynbee, Tutor of Balliol College, Oxford. With a short memoir by B. Jowett. Part I. (Double number).

No. 129.   The Industrial Revolution. Part II. (Double number).

No. 130.   The Origin of the Aryans. By Dr Isaac Taylor. Illustrated. Part I. (Double number).

No. 131. **The Origin of the Aryans.** Part II. (Double number).

No. 132. **The Evolution of Sex.** By Prof. P. Geddes and J. Arthur Thomson. Illustrated. Part I (Double number).

No. 133. **The Evolution of Sex.** Part II. (Double number)

No. 134. **The Law of Private Right.** By George H Smith. (Double number).

No. 135. **Capital.** A Critical Analysis of Capitalist Production. By Karl Marx. Part I (Double number)

No. 136. **Capital.** Part II (Double number).

No. 137. **Capital.** Part III (Double number).

No. 138. **Capital.** Part IV (Double number).

No. 139. **Lightning.** Thunder and Lightning Conductors Illustrated. By Gerald Molloy, D D., D Sc.

No. 140. **What is Music?** With an appendix on How the Geometrical Lines have their Counterparts in Music. By Isaac L. Rice.

No. 141. **Are the Effects of Use and Disuse Inherited?** By William Platt Ball.

No. 142. **A Vindication of the Rights of Woman.** By Mary Wollstonecraft. With an Introduction by Mrs Henry Fawcet. Part I. (Double number).

No. 143. **A Vindication of the Rights of Woman.** Part II. (Double number).

No. 144. **Civilization; Its Cause and Cure.** By Edward Carpenter

No. 145. **Body and Mind.** By William Kingdon Clifford.

No. 146. **Social Diseases and Worse Remedies.** By Thomas H Huxley, F.R.S.

No. 147. **The Soul of Man under Socialism.** By Oscar Wilde.

No. 148. **Electricity, the Science of the Nineteenth Century.** By E. C. Caillard. (Illustrated) Part I. (Double number).

No 149. **Electricity.** Part II.

No. 150. **Degeneration; A Chapter in Darwinism.** Illustrated. By E. Ray Dankester, M.A., LL.D., F.R.S.

No. 151. **Mental Suggestion.** By Dr. J. Ochorowicz. Part I. (Double number).

No. 152. **Mental Suggestion.** Part II. (Double number.)

No. 153. **Mental Suggestion.** Part III. (Double number.)

No. 157. **Mental Suggestion.** Part IV. (Double number.)

No. 159. **Modern Science; The Science of the Future.** By Edward Carpenter.

No. 160. **Studies in Pessimism.** By Schopenhauer.

No. 161. **Flowers, Fruits and Leaves.** Illustrated. By Sir John Lubbock, F.R.S. (Double number).

No. 163. **Glimpses of Nature.** Illustrated. By Dr. Andrew Wilson, F.R.S.E. Part I. (Double number).

No. 165. **Glimpses of Nature.** Part II.

No. 166. **Problems of the Future.** By Samuel Lang. Part I.

No. 167. **Problems of the Future.** Part II. (Double number).

No. 168. **Problems of the Future.** Part III. (Double number).

No. 169. **The Moral Teachings of Science.** By Arabella B. Buckley.

No. 170. **The Wisdom of Life.** By Schopenhauer. (Double number).

No. 171. **The Mystery of Pain.** By James Hinton.

No. 172. **What is Property?** An inquiry into the Principle of Right and of Government. By P. J. Proudhon. (Four double numbers, $1.20).

No. 176. **The History and Scope of Zoology.** By E. Ray Lankester.

No. 177. **Evolution and Ethics.** By Prof. T. H. Huxley.

A NEW SERIES.

The Social Science Library

OF THE BEST AUTHORS.

PUBLISHED MONTHLY AT POPULAR PRICES.

Paper Cover, 25 cents each; Cloth, extra, 75 cents each.

NOW READY.

No. 1. **Six Centuries of Work and Wages.** By James E. Thorold Rogers, M.P. Abridged, with charts and summary. By W. D. P. Bliss. Introduction by Prof. R. T. Ely.

No. 2. **The Socialism of John Stuart Mill.** The only collection of Mill's Writings on Socialism.

No. 3. **The Socialism and Unsocialism of Thomas Carlyle.** A collection of Carlyle's social writings; together with Joseph Mazzini's famous essay protesting against Carlyle's views. Vol. I.

No. 4. **The Socialism and Unsocialism of Thomas Carlyle.** Vol. II.

No. 5. **William Morris, Poet, Artist, Socialist.** A selection from his writings together with a sketch of the man. Edited by Francis Watts Lee.

No. 6. **The Fabian Essays.** American Edition, with Introduction and Notes by H. G. Wilshire.

No. 7. **The Economics of Herbert Spencer.** By W. C. Owen.

No. 8. **The Communism of John Ruskin.**

No. 9. **Horace Greeley and other Pioneers of American Socialism.** By Charles Sotheran.

Special Number, 35 cents, in Paper Cover.

The Humboldt Library Series.

The volumes of this series are printed on a superior quality of paper, and bound in extra cloth. They are from fifty to seventy-five per cent. cheaper than any other edition of the same books.

STANDARD WORKS BY VARIOUS AUTHORS.

A Vindication of the Rights of Woman With Strictures on Political and Moral Subjects. By Mary Wollstonecraft. New Edition, with an introduction by Mrs. Henry Fawcett. Cloth $1.00

Electricity: the Science of the Nineteenth Century. A Sketch for General Readers. By E. M. Caillard, author of "The Invisible Powers of Nature." With Illustrations. Cloth . . . . 75 cts

Mental Suggestion. By J. Ochorowicz. Sometime Professor Extraordinarius of Psychology and Nature-Philosophy in the University of Lemberg. With a Preface by Chas. Richet. Translated from the French by J. Fitzgerald, M.A. Cloth $2.00

Flowers, Fruits, and Leaves. By Sir John Lubbock, F.R.S, D.C.L., LL.D. With Ninety-five Illustrations. Cloth . . . . 75 cts

Glimpses of Nature. By Andrew Wilson, F.R.S.E., F.L.S. With Thirty-five Illustrations. Cloth . . . . 75 cts

Problems of the Future, and Essays. By Samuel Laing, author of "Modern Science and Modern Thought," etc. Cloth . . . $1.25

The Naturalist on the River Amazon. A Record of Adventures, Habits of Animals, Sketches of Brazilian and Indian Life, and Aspects of Nature under the Equator, during Eleven Years of Travel. By Henry Walter Bates, F.L.S., Assistant Secretary of the Royal Geographical Society of England. New Edition. Large Type. Illustrated. Cloth $1.00

The Religions of the Ancient World: including Egypt, Assyria and Babylonia, Persia, India, Phœnicia, Etruria, Greece, Rome. By George Rawlinson, M.A., Camden Professor of Ancient History, Oxford, and Canon of Canterbury. Author of "The Origin of Nations," "The Five Great Monarchies," Etc. Cloth . . . . 75 cts

The Rise and Early Constitution of Universities, with a Survey of Mediæval Education. By S. S. Laurie, LL.D., Professor of the Institutes and History of Education in the University of Edinburgh. Cloth . . 75 cts

Fetichism. A Contribution to Anthropology and the History of Religion. By Fritz Schultze, Ph.D Translated from the German by J. Fitzgerald, M.A. Cloth . . . . . 75 cts

Money and the Mechanism of Exchange. By W. Stanley Jevons, M.A., F.R.S., Professor of Logic and Political Economy in the Owens College, Manchester, England. Cloth . . . . 75 cts

On the Study of Words. By Richard Chenevix Trench, D.D., Archbishop of Dublin. Cloth . . . . 75 cts

The Dawn of History. An Introduction to Prehistoric Study. Edited by C. F. Keary, M.A., of the British Museum. Cloth . . 75 cts

Geological Sketches at Home and Abroad. By Archibald Geikie, LL.D., F.R.S., Director-General of the Geological Surveys of Great Britain and Ireland. Cloth . . . . 75 cts

Illusions: A Psychological Study. By James Sully, author of "Sensation and Intuition,' "Pessimism," etc. Cloth . . . 75 cts

The Pleasures of Life. Part I and Part II. By Sir John Lubbock, Bart. Two Parts in One. Cloth . . . . 75 cts.

English, Past and Present. Part I. and Part II. By Richard Chenevix Trench, D.D., Archbishop of Dublin. Two Parts in One. Cloth . . . . 75 cts

Hypnotism: Its History and Present Development. By Fredrik Björnström, M.D., Head Physician of the Stockholm Hospital, Professor of Psychiatry, late Royal Swedish Medical Councillor. Cloth . . 75 cts

The Story of Creation. A Plain Account of Evolution. By Edward Clodd, F.R.A.S. With over eighty illustrations . . . . 75 cts

Christianity and Agnosticism. A controversy, consisting of papers by Henry Wace, D.D., Prebendary of St. Paul's Cathedral; Principal of King's College, London. Professor Thomas H. Huxley.—W. C. Magee, D.D., Bishop of Petersborough.—W. H. Mallock, Mrs. Humphrey Ward. Cloth . . 75 cts

Darwinism: An Exposition of the Theory of Natural Selection, with some of its applications. By Alfred Russel Wallace, LL.D., F.L.S. With portrait of the author, colored map, and numerous illustrations. Cloth $1.25

The ablest living Darwinian writer.—*Cincinnati Commercial Gazette.*

The most important contribution to the study of the origin of species and the evolution of man which has been published since Darwin's death. —*New York Sun.*

There is no better book than this in which to look for an intelligent, complete, and fair presentation of both sides of the discussion on evolution.—*New York Herald.*

Modern Science and Modern Thought. A Clear and Concise View of the Principal Results of Modern Science, and of the Revolution which they have effected in Modern Thought. With a Supplemental Chapter on Gladstone's "Dawn of Creation" and "Proem to Genesis," and on Drummond "Natural Law in the Spiritual World." By S. Laing. Cloth . . . . 75 cts

Upon the Origin of Alpine and Italian Lakes; and Upon Glacial Erosion. By A. C. Ramsay, F.R.S., Etc.; John Ball, M.R.I.A., F.L.S., Etc.; Sir Roderick I. Murchison, F.R.S., D.C.L., Etc.; Prof. B. Studer, of Berne; Prof. A. Favre, of Geneva; and Edward Whymper With an Introduction, and Notes upon the American Lakes, by Prof. J. W. Spencer, Ph.D., F G.S., State Geologist of Georgia. Cloth . . . . 75 cts

Physiognomy and Expression. By Paolo Mantegazza, Senator; Director of the National Museum of Anthropology, Florence ; President of the Italian Society of Anthropology With Illustrations. Cloth $1.00

The Industrial Revolution of the Eighteenth Century in England. Popular Addresses, Notes, and other Fragments. By the late Arnold Toynbee. Tutor of Balliol College, Oxford. Together with a short memoir by B. Jowett, Master of Balliol College, Oxford. Cloth $1.00

The Origin of the Aryans. An Account of the Prehistoric Ethnology and Civilization of Europe. By Isaac Taylor, M.A., Litt. D., Hon. LL.D. Illustrated. Cloth $1.00

The Law of Private Right. By George H. Smith, author of "Elements of Right, and of the Law," and of Essays on "The Certainty of the Law, and the Uncertainty of Judicial Decisions," "The True Method of Legal Education," Etc., Etc. Cloth . . 75 cts

The Evolution of Sex. By Prof. Patrick Geddes and J. Arthur Thomson. With 104 Illustrations. Cloth $1.00

Such a work as this, written by Prof. Geddes who has contributed many articles on the same and kindred subjects to the Encyclopædia Britannica, and by Mr. J. Arthur Thomson, is not for the specialist, though the specialist may find it good reading, nor for the reader of light literature, though the latter would do well to grapple with it. Those who have followed Darwin, Wallace, Huxley and Haeckel in their various publications, and have heard of the later arguments against heredity brought forward by Prof. Weissman, will not be likely to put it down unread. . . . The authors have some extremely interesting ideas to state, particularly with regard to the great questions of sex and environment in their relation to the growth of life on earth. . . . They are to be congratulated on the scholarly and clear way in which they have handled a difficult and delicate subject.—*Times.*

Capital: A Critical Analysis of Capitalistic Production. By Karl Marx. Translated from the third German edition by Samuel Moore and Edward Aveling, edited by Frederick Engels. *The only American Edition.* Carefully Revised. Cloth, $1.75

The great merit of Marx, therefore, lies in the work he has done as a scientific inquirer into the economic movement of modern times, as the philosophic historian of the capitalistic era.— *Encyclopædia Brittanica.*

So great a position has not been won by any work on Economic Science since the appearance of *The Wealth of Nations.* . . . . All these circumstances invest, therefore, the teachings of this particularly acute thinker with an interest such as cannot be claimed by any other thinker of the present day.—*The Athenæum.*

What is Property? An Inquiry into the Principle of Right and of Government. By P. J. Proudhon. Cloth $2.00

The Philosophy of Misery. A System of Economical Contradictions. By P. J Proudhon. Cloth $2.00

Works by Professor Huxley.

Evidence as to Man's Place in Nature. With numerous illustrations

AND

On the Origin of Species; or, the Causes of the Phenomena of Organic Nature. Two books in one volume. Cloth . . . 75 cts

---

The Physical Basis of Life. With other Essays

AND

Lectures on Evolution. With an Appendix on the Study of Biology. Two books in one volume. Cloth . . . . 75 cts